THE LIBRARY
ST. M...
ST. M...

W9-BZF-655

HITLER AND HIS ADMIRALS

Anthony Martienssen *is Editor of* "Fuehrer Conferences on Naval Affairs"

HITLER
AND HIS ADMIRALS

BY
ANTHONY MARTIENSSEN

New York
E. P. DUTTON & CO., INC.
1949

Copyright, 1949, by Anthony Martienssen

All rights reserved. Printed in the U. S. A.

FIRST EDITION

NO PART *of this book may be reproduced in any form without permission in writing from the publisher, except by a reviewer who wishes to quote brief passages in connection with a review written for inclusion in magazine or newspaper or radio broadcast.*

CONTENTS

PART I

PREPARATIONS FOR WAR
1933–September 1939

PART II

ATTACK
September 1939–October 1942

PART III

DEFENCE
October 1942–July 1944

PART IV

DEFEAT
July 1944–May 1945

LIST OF ILLUSTRATIONS

These plates will be found in one section between pages 116 *and* 117

MAPS

SOURCES

PRINCIPAL DOCUMENTARY SOURCES.

MARKED IN
TEXT

Fuehrer Conferences on Naval Affairs (issued by the
Admiralty) . . . . (1)

Documentary evidence produced at Nuremberg Trials—
general . . . . (2)

Evidence of Raeder . . . . (3)

Evidence of Doenitz . . . . (4)

Statements of German Admirals at the end of the war
(issued by the Admiralty):

   Weichold—*War in the Mediterranean* . . (5)

   Assmann—*Aspects of the War at Sea* . . (6)

   Documents relating to the resignation of Grand-
Admiral Raeder . . . . . . (7)

Documents relating to war in the Air (issued by Air
Ministry) . . . . (8)

Files of the *Frankfürter Zeitung* . . . . . (9)

INTRODUCTION

DURING the final stages of the Second World War, enemy State documents were captured on a scale which was unique in history. Beginning with a more or less accidental haul of papers in Paris, specially organized Intelligence units tracked down one German hiding-place after another, until, with few exceptions, they had recovered most of the German archives.

The largest and most important haul of documents was made at *Schloss Tambach*, near Coburg, where some 60,000 files of the German naval archives, together with the historians guarding them, were captured. These documents contained practically all the signals, ships' logs, diaries, memoranda, etc., relating to the German Navy from 1868 until the date of their capture—April 1945. When they came to be examined, four sets of papers stood out in importance: the minutes of Hitler's conferences with the Commander-in-Chief of the Navy; the War Diaries of the Naval Staff; operational orders covering every major activity, military and political, in which the Navy had been concerned; and the personal files of Raeder who had been Commander-in-Chief from 1928 until January 1943.

These four sets of papers made it possible to reconstruct an accurate and detailed account of the higher direction of the German Navy. Together with the numerous other political and military papers which were unearthed, they also made possible a comprehensive history of Nazi Germany at war.

The first attempt to piece together this history was made at the Nuremberg Trials at the end of 1945. In criminal trials, however, the specific act is more important than the general background into which that act fits; so, at Nuremberg, the evidence revealed a series of individual crimes rather than a connected history of Nazi activities. Such reconstruction as there was of background events, was necessarily sketchy.

The second attempt—the second, that is, based on original

documents rather than on the post-war interrogation of senior German officers—was made by myself on behalf of the Admiralty in a series of books known as the *Fuehrer Conferences on Naval Affairs*. The series was designed primarily to present a selection of the most important of the Tambach documents, but I also tried then to build up round the framework of the documents a general account of the German political and naval events.

In this present book I have combined the evidence given at Nuremberg with the material contained in the *Fuehrer Conferences on Naval Affairs*. It is impossible to cover every aspect of the war in one volume, and I have confined myself to the history, naval and political, which is, I think, a most revealing side of Nazi Germany.

In one sense this book is an experiment in historical writing. It is unusual to be able to attempt a history based on State documents within only three years of the events described. Normally at least fifty years elapse before such documents are made available to the public, and it was only the extraordinary confusion prevailing in Germany at the end of the war that has made this attempt possible. I am convinced that the historian, provided his sources are sufficiently complete, cannot be too close to his history. Impartiality is an attitude of mind, and the only advantage the historian gains from being remote is the possible extension of his knowledge by the discovery of new facts. It is because all the important facts about Nazi Germany are virtually complete that such a history as this can be written now. Half a century later much of the atmosphere and many of the factors that influenced men will have been forgotten.

I must warn the reader that, as this history deals mainly with strategy and diplomacy, there are only a few examples of individual Nazi crimes. It should be borne in mind that the Nazis imprisoned, murdered and tortured—at a conservative estimate—twelve million people.

It is also inevitable that Hitler should emerge from these pages as a talented and very able man. He was the sole ruler of a powerful, modern nation for twelve years, and obviously he could not have been a fool; but lest there are some who think that cleverness is the sole criterion of greatness, I should like to quote from Hitler's sixteenth-century tutor, Nicolo Machiavelli: " Yet it cannot be called talent to slay fellow-citizens, to deceive friends, to be without faith, without mercy, without religion. . . . His barbarous cruelty and inhumanity with infinite wickednesses do not permit him to be celebrated among the most excellent men. What he achieved cannot be attributed either to fortune or to genius."

ANTHONY MARTIENSSEN.

ACKNOWLEDGMENTS

I should like to thank Commander G. Saunders, R.N., and his staff at the Admiralty for the invaluable assistance that they gave me while editing the *Fuehrer Conferences*—translating, ferreting and advising, in spite of their own heavy programme of work. I only hope they enjoyed the partnership which produced the *Fuehrer Conferences* as much as I did.

I should also like to thank Miss Beryl Maishment for her cheerful patience with my somewhat unwieldy manuscript.

I must thank, too, the Admiralty for permission to publish the documents and photographs quoted in this book.

Above all, I thank my wife who, in spite of the constant demands of our children and the rigours of present-day housekeeping, yet found time to read and correct the manuscript. In all gratitude this book is dedicated to her.

PART I

PREPARATIONS FOR WAR

1933–September 1939

Chapter I

PERSONALITIES

ON 1 October 1946 Grand-Admiral Erich Raeder of the German Navy was sentenced by the International Military Tribunal at Nuremberg to imprisonment for life. The sentence came as something of a surprise, as many found it difficult to believe that one who appeared to be so much the professional seaman should have been so involved in the crimes of Nazi Germany as to merit such a punishment. Yet it was so. Observers at his trial reported that no story of naval affairs ever smacked less of ships and the sea, and although they did not perhaps realize how closely international politics are connected with naval strength and sea power, Raeder's share in Hitler's deliberations was abnormal. Raeder, like many naval officers before him, was also a politician, and as such shared with the other leaders of Nazi Germany the guilt of crimes against peace and humanity. His successor, Karl Doenitz, was even more closely linked with the German Supreme Command—so close indeed that he eventually became Fuehrer himself.

This story of Hitler, Raeder, and Doenitz is thus not only the story of the German Navy, but also the story of the inner war councils of Nazi Germany. The dominance of the overwhelming personality of Hitler lends it a cohesion, a unity, which is generally absent from other periods of history. The events narrated here unfold themselves with dramatic continuity, exhibiting the development, the triumph, and the fall of a potent, evil power. Unlike the account given at Nuremberg this book does contain much about ships and the sea, because it was at sea that Germany was weakest and therefore most revealing. But in spite of the emphasis on naval affairs, the drama is essentially one of personalities.

1

The principal and most complex personality was Adolf Hitler. Few things demonstrate his character and power more clearly than his control over the German Navy. He once told Raeder: "On land I am a hero, but at sea I am a coward." [6] And yet, instead of arousing Raeder's contempt, this remark evoked his respect. It was a subtle respect, compounded partly of admiration for a strong man admitting to a solitary weakness, and partly of the realization that it increased his (Raeder's) own power. It was also a respect which was deliberately engendered. Raeder was essential to Hitler, and Hitler was prepared to pander to him. It was through Raeder that Hitler obtained control of the Navy, and from the start he had set out to win him to loyalty and obedience.

His task had not been difficult. The restrictions of the Treaty of Versailles and of the pacifist Weimar Republic had chafed the Officer Corps, of which Raeder was a stalwart member, almost beyond endurance. They had thus been ripe for Hitler's ideas. The Nazi Party had promised them encouragement and inspiration, and when Hitler seized power in 1933 there was not much doubt in the minds of Germany's military leaders that Germany had at last found a man capable of leading her in the traditional paths of military discipline and glory. Raeder, with the rest, had applauded Hitler's political victories. He had regarded Hitler as a miracle—a leader risen from the people who nevertheless understood and even encouraged the old Prussian concepts of blind obedience and iron command.

Raeder met Hitler for the first time a week or so after the *coup d'état*. It was at a special dinner given by the Chief of the Defence Ministry, General Freiherr von Hammerstein, to Hitler and a gathering of the Generals and Admirals of the Wehrmacht. [3] In an after-dinner speech Hitler introduced himself and gave an account of his activities and his intentions. He stressed the fact that he himself would now assume full control of Home and Foreign policy, and that the Armed Forces would not be used for internal political purposes: on the contrary they were to work in complete freedom on military expansion for the protection of the Reich against its enemies.

But for Raeder Hitler had a special word. [3] At a later conference he took Raeder on one side and assured him that the Navy would not be neglected. He discussed complicated questions of naval construction and showed a surprising knowledge of technical details, explaining that he had studied the subject as a necessary preparation for his role as Fuehrer. He showed a great interest in what Raeder had already done to revive the German Navy. He discussed naval personalities with him and freely admitted his ignorance of naval strategy. Raeder, much the older man, was flattered and overwhelmed. The High Command had, prior to Hitler's accession, shown every indication of putting the Navy at the bottom of the list of priorities, and now here was the Reich Chancellor himself only too anxious to encourage and foster the Navy. Raeder's loyalty was assured. It appeared to him that here for the first time was a ruler of Germany who appreciated the importance of sea power.

Hitler sealed Raeder's loyalty, and the loyalty of the rest of the Officer Corps, by persuading the old President, Hindenburg, to appoint him his successor. With Hindenburg's support his authority was guaranteed, and, when Hindenburg died in August 1934, the generals and admirals willingly and freely transferred their oath of allegiance to Hitler, thus binding themselves to him by the most rigid moral bond they knew.

Hitler's tactics with Raeder, however, were not all flattery and appeasement. He knew his man well, and did not hesitate to show that he intended to command, realising that Raeder, with his background of discipline and obedience, would respect a firm control. He treated Raeder as a technical adviser, and although he allowed Raeder's advice to transcend purely naval matters, he reserved for himself the right of decision. On the other hand, Raeder had complete freedom in the administration of the Navy and in the planning and execution of operational schemes within the framework of Hitler's general strategy. It was only later that Hitler assumed the powers of an absolute dictator, but even then he still occasionally deferred to the opinion of his admirals.

As a dictator Hitler did not differ much from the other dictators the world has known. He shared with them the arrogance of power and the constant fear of assassination. In an address to his Commanders-in-Chief at the Obersalzberg ten days before the outbreak of war, he boasted: " There will probably never again be a man with more authority than I have." [2] He added: " My existence is therefore a factor of great value. But, I can be eliminated at any time by a criminal or an idiot."

Grand-Admiral Erich Raeder was a naval officer of the old school. He had received his training and naval education during the heyday of the Kaiser's High Seas Fleet, and he carried with him throughout his career the stamp of the Prussian traditions in which he had been moulded. As a Commander-in-Chief he was unique in that he had never commanded a ship at sea, although he had had much sea experience, both as a junior executive officer and, during the First World War, as Chief of Staff to Admiral von Hipper's cruiser squadron.

Raeder's principal weakness was his mistaken conviction that he had an exceptional flair for domestic politics. He prided himself on his political sense with the result that his career was chequered with escapades which have done much to discredit his real ability as a naval strategist. In 1922 he became an ardent follower of Kapp, and during the Kapp Putsch [9] strongly recommended his superiors to throw in what remained of the German Navy for Kapp's support. Kapp reigned in Berlin for five days, and Raeder was suspended from his duties for two years.

Other minor political episodes followed, but his loyalty to the German Navy and his marked competence as a staff officer kept him in favour with the German Navy Office until he was eventually appointed Commander-in-Chief on 1 October 1928—during the rule of the Weimar Republic.

On the day before his appointment he once again nearly ended his career by an ill-timed political gesture. In spite of the pacifist protestations of Weimar and the necessity for the Germany of that period to maintain friendly relations with England and France, Raeder shocked the Western world by publicly toasting the ex-Kaiser at a Yacht Club dinner given in honour of his new appointment. [9] The reactions and publicity inside Germany were considerable. The *Frankfürter Zeitung* led a press campaign against him and strongly hinted that his appointment was not in the best interests of the peace-loving Weimar Republic. The Liberal Press followed the *Frankfürter Zeitung*'s lead and the old scandals against Raeder were revived. With unusual skill Raeder extricated himself from the compromising situation in which he had become involved, and, after a large press conference, succeeded in getting himself reported as " no enemy of the Republic," thus securing his tenure of office.

Apart from his weakness for politics, Raeder was peculiarly suited to his high position. As Chief of Staff to von Hipper he had shown a phenomenal grasp of naval strategy, and his book on cruiser warfare, written during his " retirement " in 1922, was a standard work on the subject. In foreign affairs, unlike his adventures in domestic politics, Raeder's judgment was sure and matter of fact. He appreciated and developed the principle of wedding foreign policy to naval strength, realizing that the mobility of naval forces, combined with their ability to exert continuous pressure in any given area, constitute a factor which can make or mar a foreign policy, especially a policy based on power. It was this cardinal principle of Raeder's that gave his work the diplomatic flavour which was so noticeable during his evidence at Nuremberg.

Raeder possessed the duller attributes of a good organizer, and he was also a planner of considerable foresight. He believed in maintaining the old traditions of strict obedience, and he kept a tight control over every branch of the Navy, welding it into a hard, efficient force, capable of executing his plans. As an individual he combined a stern and forbidding manner with a genuine feeling of friendliness for his fellow officers, but although he won their respect, he never succeeded in winning their warm, human regard.

Raeder's feelings towards Hitler have already been partly described. His attitude to other Nazis and to the Party was totally different. He hated Goering, and at Nuremberg he gave this portrait of his fellow Commander-in-Chief:

> " The personality of Goering had a disastrous influence on the fate of the German Reich. Unimaginable vanity and unrestrained ambition were two of his principal characteristics; he had a craving for cheap popularity and effect, and was distinguished for dishonesty, ignorance and selfishness. He ignored the interests of State and people, and was both avaricious and extravagant—an effeminate and unsoldierly character."

Raeder also resented and feared Goering's influence with Hitler. In 1938, after General von Blomberg had been forcibly retired from the High Command, Raeder refused Hitler's offer of the post of Supreme Commander as he knew that the post was Goering's chief ambition and he doubted his ability to withstand the fat Reichsmarschall's ceaseless intrigues. In a further comment during the Nuremberg trials, Raeder wrote:

" The situation can well be judged from the fact that when
I laid down my Command my last words to the Fuehrer were:
' Please protect the Navy and my successor from Goering ! '
—words which he perfectly well understood."

With the Nazi Party in general, Raeder maintained an aloof,
but cautious attitude. Probably as a result of his own political
escapades, he strictly enforced an order that naval personnel
were to take no part in politics. This did not in any way affect
their faith in Hitler or their adherence to Nazi principles—it
was not so intended—but it did serve to separate the Navy from
the ordinary Nazi authorities. (Doenitz later relaxed this order
when he succeeded Raeder, and earned from his old commander
the scornful nickname of " Hitler-Youth Doenitz." [3])
On the question of Nazi crimes and the treatment of Jews his
attitude was more complex. Raeder's own son-in-law was partly
Jewish, but, as he said: " Increased caution enabled me to circum-
navigate all dangers from this quarter." Nevertheless the son-
in-law was obliged to live abroad. Raeder has also asserted [3]
that he frequently applied for the retention in the Navy of Jewish
officers who were of special value, and that he personally inter-
vened on the behalf of Jewish families of his acquaintance,
achieving some alleviation of their circumstances. Even so he
maintained that, until three months before the end of the war,
he had no knowledge of the horrors of Belsen, Dachau, or
Buchenwald. It is difficult to assess how much truth there is in
these statements, but it is highly improbable that Raeder could
have been ignorant of what was common knowledge even before
the war. It is more likely that, like so many other Germans,
custom staled his conscience, causing him to consider the Nazi
atrocities as little more than the ordinary dirt normally associated
with politics in Germany.

Such was the character of Erich Raeder, Commander-in-Chief
of the German Navy. Hitler promoted him to Grand-Admiral,
the highest rank open to him, on 1 April 1939, and from then
until his resignation at the end of January 1943 he was second
only to Goering as Hitler's principal adviser for the prosecution
of the war.

Raeder's successor, Admiral Karl Doenitz, did not, during the
pre-war years, create a very strong impression. The key to his

character is contained in the motif of a paper he once wrote on midget submarines: " Cunning is the strength of the weak," [4] and throughout his career he obtained his ends by subtlety rather than by the open, direct methods of his senior. His later close bond with Hitler was fundamentally due to this characteristic. A U-boat officer in the First World War and later a cruiser captain, Doenitz was promoted to Flag rank and appointed Commodore of Submarines in 1935. He was an ardent follower of the Nazis, though not a member of the party, and a fanatical believer in Hitler. His relations with Raeder were poor—in Raeder's words: " I did not like Doenitz's rather conceited and tactless manner " [3]—but, as a young and ambitious man, he contrived to win the popular support of the junior officers of the Navy, and his selection for the post of U-boat Admiral was particularly apt. He devoted himself to the U-boat branch, the development of which he promoted with exceptional skill and imagination, but he remained ignorant of the wider aspects of naval administration and strategy. His subtlety was accompanied by a narrow outlook which prevented him from acquiring the extensive knowledge essential to the administrator and strategist, but this ignorance did not deter him in the last years of the war from undertaking many duties beyond his ability and outside the scope of his intelligence.

Unlike Raeder, his relations with the Nazi leaders were cordial, and he enjoyed their confidence to an extent never attained by his predecessor. Above all, he won the firm regard of Goering with whom he joked and talked in a manner which Raeder would have found degrading, but which ensured him the support of the man who for a long time was the most powerful figure in Hitler's court.

In the years before the war, however, Doenitz remained in the background. He was regarded only as a member of the Naval Staff, and few realized his overweening ambition or foresaw that he would eventually become the last Fuehrer of the Third German Reich.

The organization within which these men played their dramatic parts was designed by Hitler after the dismissal of von Blomberg from the War Ministry in 1938. Hitler himself then took over the position of Supreme Commander of the Armed Forces and reorganized the entire system of the higher levels of command. [2]

He separated the three Services from the War Ministry, which virtually ceased to exist, and placed them in independent headquarters under their respective Commanders-in-Chief. Instead of the old High Command, he created a new and smaller organization with the title of the Supreme Command of the Armed Forces (Oberkommando der Wehrmacht—the OKW) which was made responsible for giving effect to his orders and for co-ordinating the activities of the Army, Air Force, and Navy.

The Supreme Command was headed by General Keitel, who was known as the Chief of the Armed Forces (Chef der Wehrmacht). He had no real power, however, and his principal duty was merely to draft Hitler's orders. He seldom voiced an opinion, and he was regarded with contempt by most of the senior officers. Of very different calibre was General Jodl, who directed a special planning staff within the Supreme Command, and who was responsible for working out the broad outlines of major operations. He understood the principles of inter-service co-operation more clearly than most, and his cold intelligence fitted him well for his duties. Theoretically, Jodl was subordinate to Keitel, but in practice he served as an equal, and both generals worked together as Hitler's private staff officers.

The three Commanders-in-Chief, Goering (Air Force), Raeder (Navy), and von Brauchitsch (Army), were senior to Keitel and Jodl, and, depending on their personal relations with Hitler, more or less directed their own operations within the framework laid down by the Supreme Command. Each Commander-in-Chief had the right of direct access to Hitler and periodically discussed with him future plans and the progress of current operations. These 'Fuehrer Conferences' were the nearest approach to a Council of War in Nazi Germany—they were the only occasions on which Hitler did not do all the talking—but they never attained the status of a genuine council as the three Commanders-in-Chief were seldom allowed to report together. The conferences were essentially reports by the Commander-in-Chief concerned to Hitler; and although the reports were frequently advisory as well as descriptive, it depended on Hitler whether a free discussion followed or not. The other officers present, usually Keitel, Jodl, and minor staff officers of the Supreme Command, were there simply to note decisions reached, or to provide information on specific points raised at the conference.

Hitler's normal method of working was to sound his commanders and staff officers individually on any particular problem before coming to a decision himself.[3] Once he had issued a ' directive ' he seldom changed his mind, but in the preceding discussion period he was not always dictatorial, and his commanders did from time to time cause him to alter his views.[1] They even succeeded on a few occasions in getting him to accept original suggestions of their own, but in general he, himself, was the source of the plans and stratagems of the Supreme Command—and the architect of this tragedy, the ' Gale of the World ', which uprooted whole nations and murdered twelve million people.

Chapter II

THE PRE-WAR DEVELOPMENT OF THE GERMAN NAVY

UNDER the Weimar Republic, Field-Marshal von Blomberg and General von Fritsch had already begun to rebuild the Wehrmacht.[2]

It is probable that at this early stage the military leaders of Germany were genuinely preparing only a defensive force. The hostility of France and the growth of Soviet Russia were to them sufficient justification for rearmament, and the planning of the General Staff was directed at first merely towards the security of Germany's frontiers. When, under the fanatical inspiration of the Nazi regime, they did come to consider aggression, they continued to plan in the name of ' defence '—the proposition being that the expansion of a country's power beyond its frontiers was a surer defence against attack than the static defence of the frontiers themselves.

They had carefully studied the records of the First World War with the object of avoiding the mistakes of their predecessors, and in endless debates the Officer Corps had considered innumerable theories of warfare. New methods of fighting had been tried out in secret exercises, and new weapons had been planned and ordered.

But in spite of this reforming zeal, the German High Command had failed to learn the outstanding lesson of the First World War—the decisive importance of sea power, even to a continental nation. They did not, in the beginning, envisage war against England, the only country whose sea power they respected, and they did not consider that naval forces would be required as a defence against France or Russia.

Raeder had refused to tolerate the land-minded attitude of the High Command, and, pointing out to von Blomberg the expansion of the French Navy, had won from him a small allocation of the funds which had been dedicated to defence. With these funds Raeder had laid the foundations of a small, balanced fleet. He had initiated designs for the ' pocket ' battleships, had secretly placed orders for U-boats in foreign dockyards (Spain, Finland, and Holland), [2] and had encouraged scientific research in naval weapons, particularly torpedoes and mines. (This last brought him the honorary degree of Doctor from a German university. [9])

It was not until Hitler seized power, however, that Raeder saw any chance of expanding the German Navy to a size comparable with that of other world powers. Hitler had so far mastered the elementary principles of power politics that one of his first steps in improving Germany's position was, of his own accord, to endeavour to increase the size of the German Navy.

Under the Versailles Treaty the German Navy was limited to 15,000 men and a very small number of ships. Hitler decided to overcome this restriction, not by openly repudiating the whole Treaty of Versailles, which would reveal his intentions before he was ready, but by coming to an agreement with the strongest naval power, England. The German Fleet was to be limited to a proportion of the British Fleet. [3] This proportion would be worked out so as not to be a serious threat against England, but so as to enable Germany to hold her own against France or Russia.

Early in 1935, Hitler put his suggestions to Raeder, who enthusiastically agreed. Hitler said that he hoped that such an agreement would win England permanently to a peace policy. [3] Raeder was sceptical, but nevertheless the proposed expansion was very desirable and it was calculated that, with her limited shipbuilding capacity, Germany could undertake the construction of about a third of the number of ships in the British Fleet. [1]

Diplomatic negotiations with England were begun, and on 18 June 1935, the London Treaty was signed between Great

Britain and Germany.   The treaty limited the German Navy to
35 per cent. of the British surface fleet, and later agreements
allowed the Germans to extend U-boat building to 100 per cent.
of the British submarine fleet.

The London Treaty tacitly freed Germany from some of the
restrictions of Versailles and allowed her to proceed with the
development of naval power, which, though apparently harmless
at the time, laid the foundations of one of the most serious threats
in history against Great Britain.   The London Treaty was in
fact the first act of appeasement from which Hitler rose to attempt
the domination of the world.

Raeder's immediate problem was, what sort of a fleet should
Germany build ?   In 1935 he had understood from Hitler that it
was his intention to maintain peace with England, Italy and
Japan, and that the potential enemies of Germany were France
and Russia.[1]   This meant that Germany could risk fighting a
fleet action—an impossibility against the overwhelming superiority
of the British—and that therefore a balanced fleet would be more
important than ships intended for individual actions.   Equal
priority was thus given to the building of all types of warships,
and the attention of the small number of designers and marine
engineers was directed over a wide field, ranging from U-boats to
aircraft carriers.

But the political considerations which governed German naval
rearmament altered as various countries began to show their
reactions to Hitler's government.   To the hostility of France was
added the growing hostility of England.

Field-Marshal von Blomberg, who attended the coronation
celebrations in London, reported to Hitler how the Queen Mother
had taken him by the hand and entreated him to see that a situation like that of 1914 should never occur again.[3]   But after von
Ribbentrop had replaced von Neurath as Ambassador to the
Court of St. James', Anglo-German relations rapidly deteriorated.

Then, on 4 November 1937, Hitler informed his Commanders-
in-Chief of his real intentions for Germany.   He expounded the
theories of ' Lebensraum ' and of ' Weltpolitik ' as the reason
for creating ' Greater Germany '.   He presupposed the use of
force, and for the first time named England as a ' hateful enemy '.
The British Empire was to be the eventual target for the
Wehrmacht, and it was only a question of deciding how and

when. In the meantime Germany was to consolidate her position in Europe. Austria, Czechoslovakia, the Sudetenland and Poland were to be incorporated in the German Reich. Then France and the Lowlands were to be neutralized, and finally the British Empire was to be conquered. Russia was not mentioned.*

Hitler's altered plans and the changed international situation were all important to the German Navy. War with England had become now a near-certainty. And such a war meant first and last a naval war. England was wholly dependent on her sea communications and, being so vulnerable herself, knew better than most how to impose the full force of a naval blockade. The British Fleet was then the most powerful fleet in the world, and, if Germany was to survive a war with England, superhuman efforts would have to be made to build a fleet capable of meeting the British.

Time was badly needed, and Hitler promised that there would be no war with England until 1944 or 1945.[2, 3]

But at Munich, in September 1938, Raeder was deeply impressed by the English attitude, believing that the inadequate state of her air defences was the only reason which had kept England from war. He was still assured by Hitler that the original promise to delay war until at least 1944 held good, but he began at once to put the German Navy on a war footing.[1] A plan was drawn up to increase naval rearmament as much as possible.

Known as the ' Z ' plan,[1] it was based on the top capacity of German shipbuilding yards and on the type of warfare to be waged. U-boats and battleships predominated. The idea of the ' balanced fleet ' was postponed, for Raeder had decided that though there was no time to equal the British Fleet, there was time to build a number of independent units which would be strong enough to wage a successful war against Britain's long sea communications.

Raeder's conception of naval war against England was to aim at avoiding major Fleet actions, and to concentrate on attacks against British merchant shipping. U-boats and fast powerful surface ships acting independently or with aircraft carriers were envisaged as the best means of carrying out this policy. The development of a Naval Air Arm was strongly opposed by Goering, who believed implicitly that his land-based

* Nuremberg Trials. Evidence of Hoszbach, Hitler's quondam military adjutant.

Luftwaffe would be more than a match for any ship, and that he could afford neither the men nor the aircraft for the Navy. The High Command were also 'land-minded', and resented Raeder's demands for material and manpower. Nevertheless Hitler supported Raeder's plans, and encouraged the building of a surface fleet as well as the development of the U-boats.

In February 1939 the 'Z' plan was as follows:

6	Battleships	.	.	By the end of 1944
8 {	4 Heavy cruisers	.	.	" " 1943
	4 " "	.	.	" " 1945
17 {	4 Light cruisers	.	.	" " 1944
	13 " "	.	.	" " 1948
4 {	2 Aircraft carriers	.	.	" " 1941
	2 " "	.	.	" " 1947
221 {	126 U-boats (all types)	.	.	" " 1943
	95 " "	.	.	" " 1947

(Destroyers, etc., not included.)

To these figures should be added the ships which had already been built:

3 Pocket battleships (*Deutschland, Scheer, Graf Spee*).
2 Battleships (*Gneisenau* and *Scharnhorst*).
2   "   completing (*Bismarck* and *Tirpitz*).
7 Cruisers (*Hipper, Bluecher, Nuernberg, Leipzig, Koeln, Karlsruhe, Koenigsberg*).
1 Cruiser completing (*Prinz Eugen*).
46 U-boats.
          (Destroyers, etc., again not included.)

The completed fleet would therefore eventually have been in 1948:

13 Battleships ;
33 Cruisers ;
4 Aircraft carriers ;
267 U-boats ;
and a large number of destroyers, auxiliaries, etc.

But, by the spring of 1939, the completion of the annexation of Czechoslovakia and the issue of preliminary orders for the invasion of Poland made it clear to Raeder and the Naval Staff that war with England must now take place much earlier than the previous forecasts of 1944–45. Raeder stressed the lack of naval preparations to Hitler, but Hitler pointed out that the rearmament of England and the other democracies was proceeding at such a pace that if he did not strike soon Germany would be outstripped. [1]

The imminence of war meant a complete revision of the 'Z' plan, and Raeder was forced to postpone all long-term shipbuilding plans. Instead he had to build and build quickly a fleet which would be capable of dealing sharp hit-and-run blows against British sea communications, but which would be unsuitable either for major fleet actions or for normal defensive duties.

A priority list was drawn up:

1. U-boats and battleships.
2. Heavy cruisers.
3. Aircraft carriers.
4. Light reconnaissance cruisers.
5. Destroyers and torpedo boats.
6. Minesweepers.
7. Auxiliaries.
8. Supply ships.

By 1 September 1939 the German Fleet consisted of:

2 Battleships (*Scharnhorst* and *Gneisenau*).
2   "   nearing completion (*Bismarck* and *Tirpitz*).
3 Pocket battleships (*Deutschland, Scheer, Graf Spee*).
3 Heavy cruisers (*Hipper, Bluecher* and *Prinz Eugen*).
5 Light cruisers (*Koenigsberg, Nuernberg, Leipzig, Koeln, Karlsruhe*).
57 U-boats.
There was also a fair number of destroyers, motor torpedo boats, minesweepers, and auxiliary vessels.
26 Merchant vessels were to be converted to armed merchant cruisers.

Training Flotilla:

2 Old Battleships (*Schlesien, Schleswig-Holstein*).
1 Cruiser (*Emden*).

Such was the development of the German Navy under the Nazi régime up to the beginning of the Second World War. The officers and men of the German Navy had been carefully trained. The old traditions had been leavened with a Nazi outlook, but Raeder and the older officers had succeeded in producing a loyal and efficient body of seamen. Raeder, himself, maintained strict control over every branch of the Navy, but at the same time he chose able men as his immediate assistants. Admiral Schniewind, his Chief of Staff, had a brilliant flair for planning the type of naval operations best suited to the German Fleet; Admiral Doenitz had developed imaginative theories for U-boat warfare; and the Fleet Commanders, Admirals Luetjens, Ciliax and Carls, were all tried and experienced officers. It remained to be seen how Hitler, as Supreme Commander of the Armed Forces, would use the compact, but powerful weapon that Raeder had created.

Chapter III

PLANNING FOR WAR

DETAILED planning for the Second World War may be said to have begun in earnest on 3 April 1939,[1] when the Supreme Command issued the first of a series of orders for the invasion of Poland. The series, which continued throughout April and May, contained general instructions for the Armed Forces and gave the intended date of the invasion as 1 September 1939.

There was to be no declaration of war, and the aim of the operation was " to destroy Polish military strength, and to create a situation in the East which satisfies the requirements of defence." [1] Hitler also outlined his policy: " Policy aims at limiting the war to Poland. This is considered possible in view of the internal crisis in France and consequent British restraint. Should Russia intervene, then this would imply Poland's destruction by Bolshevism."

In the first week of May, however, Hitler became less certain of his ability to isolate the war in Poland. On 10 May further instructions were issued as an appendix to ' Fall Weiss ' (the code-word for the operation). These instructions stated that the German Navy and the Luftwaffe were to make preparations for commencing economic warfare against England, and, as a second

priority, against France. The operations were to be ready by
the date of the invasion of Poland and were to be started as
soon as ' Grenzsicherung '—frontier defence—was ordered.
Special instructions [1] for the Navy followed:

" The Navy is to make its own preparations for the war
against British and French merchant shipping. In co-
operation with the Foreign Office, the legal and military
aspects of the intended form of the war against merchant
shipping are to be regularly examined and co-ordinated
with expected political developments. The problems involved
are to be considered with regard to possible war-time
coalitions of the enemy. . . .

In the event of war with England, apart from single
blockade runners, we cannot count on trade with foreign
countries, so that the protection of merchant shipping will
be limited mainly to the Baltic and the inshore waters of
the North Sea."

It was certain that on the outbreak of war with the Western
Powers, England would take immediate preventive measures at
sea. A naval blockade would be promptly organized, and
attempts would be made either to bottle up the German Fleet
in its home bases or to seek it out and destroy it.

Raeder therefore deemed it of the greatest importance that
German naval units should be at sea and in a position to begin
operations immediately war was declared. By July Raeder and
his staff had tacitly assumed that war with England was inevitable,
although Hitler persisted in stating that England had " no need "
to go to war. By the beginning of August they had completed
their plans for naval operations in the Atlantic. [1]

For the war against merchant shipping the U-boat had been
an obvious choice of weapon, but Raeder had also appreciated
the value of powerful surface ships acting singly against lightly-
defended convoys. Their presence would mean a tremendous
strain on the British Fleet which would have to increase convoy
escorts accordingly, with a consequent decrease in the actual
number of the convoys. This in itself would considerably restrict
the flow of supplies to England, and would be almost as efficacious
as actual attacks on the convoys.

The plans of the Naval Staff were based on these principles.
U-boats were to be grouped around the main sea routes of the

British Isles, while the pocket battleships were to be used as independent striking forces, ranging over both the North and South Atlantic Oceans. The remainder of the Fleet was to be increased as speedily as possible and held in reserve for bigger supporting operations, or to intensify warfare against merchant shipping. The superiority of the British Fleet was to be overcome by surprise attacks in isolated areas.

In the beginning at least, warfare was to be waged according to the Hague Convention,[1] and, in order to maintain the sympathy of neutrals (America especially) U-boat commanders were warned to avoid any incidents which might lead to a charge of ' unrestricted submarine warfare ' being preferred against Germany.

On 4 August, the operational orders for the pocket battleships, *Deutschland* and *Graf Spee*, were issued. Several pages of detailed instructions included the following:

" Top Secret.
Officer Only.

C.-in-C., Navy,   Berlin,
  (Operations Division,   4 *August* 1939.
    Naval War Staff).   7 Copies.

Operational Orders for Deutschland and Admiral Graf Spee.

Political Situation.

(1) The political situation makes it appear possible that, in the event of a conflict with Poland, the Guarantor Powers (England and France) will intervene. In the event of this, Italy will probably be on our side.

(2) Russia's attitude is uncertain, though at first, it can be assumed that she will remain neutral, but with a definite one-sided leaning towards the Western Powers and Poland.

(3) With the exception of Spain and Japan, no benevolent attitude will be expected from any neutral Power.

(4) We can count on support for our commerce—raiding forces, only from these Powers, and in their harbours.

(5) The neutrality of all neutral States is to be fully respected, if restrictions (*e.g.* declaration of danger zones) are not specifically laid down by the Naval War Staff."

" *Task in the event of War.*

' Disruption and destruction of enemy merchant shipping by all possible means.'

For this the following is ordered :

(*a*) Merchant warfare is, in the beginning, to be waged according to Prize Law.

(*b*) If in the beginning or during the course of the war Germany declares ' danger zones ' then unrestricted warfare is permitted in these areas. To avoid attacks from our own U-boats due to mistaken identity, pocket battleships are to keep out of ' danger zones ' unless special areas are named.

(*c*) Enemy naval forces, even if inferior, are only to be engaged if it should further the principal task (*i.e.* war on merchant shipping).

(*d*) Frequent changes of position in the operational areas will create uncertainty and will restrict enemy merchant shipping, even without tangible results. A temporary departure into distant areas will also add to the uncertainty of the enemy.

(*e*) If the enemy should protect his shipping with superior forces so that direct successes cannot be obtained, then the mere fact that his shipping is so restricted means that we have greatly impaired his supply situation. Valuable results will also be obtained if the pocket battleships continue to remain in the convoy area.

(*f*) The enemy is not in a position to carry his complete import requirements in escorted convoys. Independent ships can therefore be expected."

Between 19 and 21 August, twenty-one U-boats put to sea.[1] Three were kept in the Baltic to support the operations against Poland, while eighteen took up waiting positions to the north and north-west of the British Isles.

On 21 August, the *Graf Spee* sailed from Germany north-about the British Isles to ner operational area off South America. Her supply ship, the *Altmark*, had left a few days previously. On 24 August, the *Deutschland* with her supply ship, the *Westerwald*, sailed for her operational area in the

North Atlantic. Both battleships were to be prepared for a prolonged period at sea.

During the same period extensive preparations were begun for minelaying, operations off British ports. The magnetic mine was to be used as soon as a sufficient quantity had been produced.

Meanwhile the German plans against Poland became increasingly clear to the rest of the world. International tension mounted, and on 22 August Hitler summoned his commanders to the Obersalzberg. [1, 2]

In a long speech, Hitler confirmed his intention of attacking Poland, and gave a contemptuous account of the position of England and France, implying that even if they did enter the war it would not signify much. " We need not be afraid of a blockade," he said. " I am only afraid that at the last minute some Schweinhund will make a proposal for mediation." There was no doubt that Hitler intended a world war.

On the day following this speech, Hitler successfully negotiated a non-aggression pact with Soviet Russia, and thus secured himself from the danger of a war on two fronts. On 31 August, he issued his first order for war. It included measures to be taken against the probable intervention of the Western Powers by the German Navy and Luftwaffe, and on the following morning German troops invaded Poland. Two days later the British and French ultimatums expired and war was declared against Germany.

For Raeder, the war had come four or five years too soon. On 3 September 1939, he recorded his views of the gloomy prospect before the German Navy:

" Berlin,
3 September 1939.

To-day, the war against England and France broke out, the war which, according to the Fuehrer's previous assertions, we had no need to expect before about 1944. The Fuehrer believed up to the last minute that it could be avoided, even if this meant postponing a final settlement of the Polish question. (The Fuehrer made a statement to this effect in the presence of the Commanders-in-Chief of the Armed Forces at the Obersalzberg on 22 August.)

At the turn of the year 1944-45, by when, according to the Fuehrer's instructions, the Navy's ' Z ' plan would have been completed, Germany could have begun a war against Great Britain with the Navy at the following strength:

For merchant warfare on the high seas:
  3 fast battleships;
  3 converted pocket battleships;
  5 heavy cruisers;
  several minelaying and reconnaissance cruisers;
  2 aircraft carriers;
  about 190 submarines, including about 6 gun submarines, 6 fleet submarines and 6 minelaying submarines.

Two groups, each consisting of three of the heaviest type Diesel-powered battleships equipped with 40 cm. guns, would have had the task of intercepting and destroying the heavy British forces which, more or less dispersed, would pursue the German forces engaged in merchant warfare.

Two ships of the *Scharnhorst* and two of the *Tirpitz* class would have remained available in home waters to hold down some of the heavy British ships.

In this way, especially with the co-operation of Japan and Italy, who would have held down a section of the British Fleet, the prospect of defeating the British Fleet and cutting off supplies, in other words of settling the British question conclusively, would have been good. On 3 September 1939, Germany entered into a war with Great Britain, as the latter—contrary to the Fuehrer's assumption that ' England did not need to fight on account of the Polish question '—thought it expedient to fight now with the Polish question as a pretext. Sooner or later, as she saw it, she would have to fight Germany, and then probably under unfavourable military conditions, *i.e.* against an expanded German Fleet.

As far as the Navy is concerned, obviously it is in no way adequately equipped for the great struggle with Great Britain by the autumn of 1939. It is true that in the short period since 1935, the date of the Fleet Treaty, it has built up a well-trained, suitably organized submarine arm, of which at the moment about twenty-six boats are capable of operations in the Atlantic; the submarine arm is still much too weak, however, to have any decisive effect on the war. The surface forces, moreover, are so inferior in number

and strength to those of the British Fleet that, even at full
strength, they can do no more than show that they know
how to die gallantly and thus are willing to create the
foundations for later reconstruction.

The pocket battleships—with the outbreak of war only
the *Deutschland* and the *Graf Spee* are ready for operations
in the Atlantic—if skilfully used, should be able to carry
out cruiser warfare on the high seas for some time. The
Scharnhorst and the *Gneisenau*, which are still by no means
ready for action or reliable in operation, will have to attempt
to hold down enemy battle cruisers in home waters and
keep them away from the pocket battleships. The pocket
battleships however cannot be decisive for the outcome of
the war either.

(Signed) RAEDER.
(Countersigned) ASSMANN."

At 9 o'clock on the evening of the same day (3 September)
the passenger liner, *Athenia*, was torpedoed and sunk without
warning some 200 miles due west of the Hebrides.

The war at sea had begun.

PART II

ATTACK

September 1939–October 1942

Chapter IV

THE BATTLE OF THE ATLANTIC (1)

THE sinking of the *Athenia* was the first act in a campaign which, known as the Battle of the Atlantic, became the largest, most important, and most monotonous battle of the war. In its essentials it was a fight between Germany and the Allies to strangle each other's supplies, and before it reached its long drawn-out end, 4786 merchant ships of over 21 million gross tons, and 635 U-boats had been sunk. The battle began on the day war broke out and lasted until two days before the armistice, five years and eight months later.

Of all Hitler's military advisers, Raeder alone appears to have foreseen how desperate and how long the struggle would be. From the start he wanted to strike at once against all Allied imports, regardless of whether they were carried in Allied or neutral ships, and regardless of International Law.[1] He believed that only by drastic and immediate attacks could the small German Navy overcome the supremacy of the British and French fleets, and possibly prevent the Allies from ever getting their war supplies organized.

But, as it was to be throughout the war, the operations of the German Navy were closely bound up with Hitler's political schemes, and Hitler had given specific instructions that, in the beginning at least, Germany must conform to the Hague Convention. He was intending to isolate the Polish 'incident', and he hoped to lull the West into a sense of false security by refraining from any illegal aggressive acts at sea, the only sphere in which war with the Western Powers was a reality.

The attack on the *Athenia* thus came as a considerable shock to both Raeder and Hitler.[1] British reports of the incident were disbelieved, and, as U-boats maintained radio silence, it was impossible to check what had happened. Doenitz thought that in spite of the orders he had given a U-boat might have been responsible, but, on the advice of the Naval Staff, Hitler decided to deny German responsibility and instead accused Mr. Churchill, then First Lord of the Admiralty, of attempting to engineer atrocity stories against Germany.

The mystery was not solved until the U-boats returned to harbour, when it was discovered that U-30 (Lieutenant Lemp), in the excitement of the first few hours of the war, had in fact torpedoed and sunk the liner. Lemp was severely reprimanded, and he and his ship's company were sworn to observe the strictest secrecy. Very few officers were informed of the truth, and even the Naval Staff was kept in ignorance for some time after the event. *

The world reaction to the sinking of the *Athenia*, in particular the indignation of such powerful neutrals as the United States, alarmed Hitler, and the orders to U-boats not to attack any passenger liners, even when under escort, were repeated by radio as a clear directive. [1]

On 7 September, at a conference with Raeder, Hitler insisted on further restraint in the Battle of the Atlantic:

" The Commander-in-Chief, Navy, discussed the following problems with the Fuehrer:

1. In view of the political and military restraint shown by France and the still hesitant conduct of British warfare, the pocket battleships should for the time being withdraw from their operational areas. Furthermore, it seems that British trade is being stopped and British naval forces are being sent on planned attacks against German merchant raiders. The risk is thus out of proportion with the chances for success.

2. In view of the political situation, the waiting attitude of France, the generally impartial attitude of the neutral countries, and the fact that the United States, at least outwardly, claims strictest neutrality, the following restrictions should be observed in submarine warfare:

(*a*) No offensive action should be taken against the French.

(*b*) Passenger ships should be spared even in convoys.

---

* U-30 was paid off in the autumn of 1940, her officers and some of her ratings subsequently commissioning U-110. This U-boat was sunk on 9 May 1941. Lemp did not survive.

(c) A part of the submarines should be withdrawn from operations at present to be available later as relief.

3. The views of the *C.-in-C., Navy*, on the political situation:

(a) Great Britain is unable to draw France into the war unconditionally.

(b) France fails to see any war aim and is therefore trying to stay out of the war.

(c) After the collapse of Poland, which can be expected soon, it is possible that France and perhaps afterwards Great Britain might be ready to accept to a certain extent the situation which has been created in the East.

(d) Therefore an attack should not be forced and our strength should be saved for the time being.

The Fuehrer agrees with the views and measures of the C.-in-C., Navy, and makes the following decisions in addition:

(a) No attempt shall be made to solve the *Athenia* affair until the submarines return home.

(b) Submarines in the Atlantic are to spare passenger ships and French ships.

(c) The *Graf Spee* and the *Deutschland* are to hold back and to withdraw for the present.

General policy: Exercise restraint until the political situation in the West has become clearer. This will take about a week."

But apart from the successful progress of the war in Poland, nothing happened. The expected diplomatic moves did not take place, and Raeder and his staff were soon chafing at the restrictions Hitler had imposed on naval warfare.

Valuable opportunities had been lost. The British had already instituted the convoy system, and the measures for blockading Germany were quickly gathering momentum. Patrols had been started in the North Atlantic and submarine mine barrages had been laid in strategic areas.

On 23 September Raeder sent his Chief of Staff, Admiral Schniewind, to Hitler's headquarters to plead for the removal of some at least of the restrictions on naval warfare. The visit was successful, and as a result of Schniewind's arguments, Hitler agreed to lift restrictions against French as well as British warships and convoys, and against the seizure of contraband destined for both countries. In his report on the visit, Schniewind added:

> " The intensification of anti-submarine measures by aircraft and armed merchant vessels will apparently make it impossible to search British merchantmen in the future.*
> *The Fuehrer* approved the proposal that action should be taken without previous warning against enemy merchant ships definitely identified as such (with the exception of unmistakable passenger vessels), since it may be assumed that they are armed.
> To offset this, a neutral ship should occasionally be especially well treated in order to show that the system has not been fundamentally altered."

At the same time Hitler agreed to promote the U-boat building programme, even at the expense of aircraft, and declared his approval of the intention to commit the pocket battleships, which were still in their waiting areas, against the Atlantic trade routes.

The chief result of Schniewind's conference with Hitler was the evolution of the policy of gradual, rather than sudden, development of unrestricted naval warfare. It was decided to remove the restrictions against attacking merchant shipping step by step, without proclamations and without an open repudiation of the Hague Convention.

Meanwhile Raeder welcomed the permission to commit the pocket battleships, and on 26 September he ordered the *Deutschland* and the *Graf Spee* to leave their waiting areas and to commence hostilities.

The *Deutschland* operated in the area between the Azores and the North American coast, and by 15 October had sunk two merchant ships and taken in prize the American ship *City of Flint*. It took all the ingenuity of the German Foreign Office to correct the blunder of seizing an American ship, but after a series of Notes and further muddles the *City of Flint* was finally released in Norwegian waters on 3 November and allowed to return with her crew and cargo intact.

---

* Under the Hague Convention a submarine had to surface and issue a warning before attacking a merchant ship. This restriction did not, of course, apply to attacks on warships.

The *Graf Spee* operated in the South Atlantic between the island of St. Helena and the Brazilian coast. She was successful from the start, and by 22 October had sunk five merchant ships. Hunted by British cruisers, she headed towards South African waters, rounded the Cape of Good Hope on 3 November, and entered the Indian Ocean. She sank a small British tanker off Portuguese East Africa and returned once more to her former operating area in the South Atlantic, meeting her supply ship, the *Altmark*, en route. *Graf Spee* then transferred prisoners, refuelled, and carried out minor repairs before beginning hostilities again on 2 December.

Although the U-boats were as successful as the battleships, they were finding it increasingly difficult to maintain their attacks against Allied shipping.[1] British merchant ships were being armed and organized in convoys, and to surface and challenge a merchant ship was a hazardous undertaking. Raeder therefore proposed to take yet another step in removing restrictions on submarine warfare by allowing them to attack and sink without warning all British and French merchant ships, including passenger liners, which were sailing in convoy. In mid-October Hitler agreed, as by then his political moves had clearly failed.[1]

(Following the surrender of Warsaw, Hitler had, on 6 October, made peace overtures to the Western Democracies. Six days later, however, Britain and France had rejected his proposals in terms which made it clear that they intended to fight on until victory was assured. Hitler had, as usual, backed his political schemes with military preparations, and, while waiting for the answer to his peace proposals, he had issued orders for the preparation of an invasion of the Low Countries and France— operation ' Fall Gelb '. When his offer was rejected, therefore, he was quite ready to allow Raeder to take the next step in repudiating the Hague Convention, but, as he still wanted to maintain good relations with the neutrals, he refused to allow attacks on *neutral* shipping until ' Fall Gelb' was well under way.)

Meanwhile, in these opening stages of the battle, Doenitz and his U-boat branch raised Hitler's estimation of the German Navy to enthusiastic heights by a bold assault on the British Fleet. On 14 October U-47, under the command of Lieutenant Gunther Prien, penetrated the defences of Scapa Flow and sank the battleship, H.M.S. *Royal Oak*.

ROUTE CHART OF THE POCKET BATTLESHIPS "ADMIRAL GRAF SPEE" & "DEUTSCHLAND"
— Route ADM. GRAF SPEE
--- Route DEUTSCHLAND

Gotenhafen Arrival "DEUTSCHLAND" 15·11·39

Wilhelmshaven Departure
"ADM. GRAF SPEE" 21·8·39
"DEUTSCHLAND" 24·8·39

Vessels sunk by "DEUTSCHLAND"

Date	Nationality	Name	Tonnage	Result
5·10·39	British S.S	STONEGATE	5044	Sunk
9·10·39	American S.S	CITY OF FLINT	4963	Prize
14·10·39	Norwegian S.S	LORENTZ W. HANSEN 1918		Sunk

Total 3 Ships of 11,925 tonnage
The CITY OF FLINT was taken into Norwegian waters on 3·11·39 and later released.

Vessels sunk by "ADMIRAL GRAF SPEE"

Date	Nationality	Name	Tonnage	Result
30·9·39	British S.S	CLEMENT	5051	Sunk
5·10·39	British S.S	NEWTON BEACH	4651	Sunk 8·10·39
7·10·39	British S.S	ASHLEA	4222	Sunk
10·10·39	British S.S	HUNTSMAN	8196	Sunk 17·10·39
22·10·39	British Motor V.	TREVANION	5299	Sunk
15·11·39	British Tanker.	AFRICA SHELL	706	Sunk
2·12·39	British S.S	DORIC STAR	10086	Sunk
3·12·39	British S.S	TAIROA	7983	Sunk
7·12·39	British S.S	STREONSHALH	3895	Sunk

Total 9 Ships of 50,089 Tonnage

The operation was personally planned by Doenitz, who selected Prien for the task. A careful survey of Scapa Flow had revealed a weakness in the defences of Holm Sound which was then protected only by three blockships. In his preliminary report to Raeder, Doenitz wrote: " I hold that a penetration at this point on the surface at the turn of the tide would be possible without further ceremony." [1] The attack was ordered for the night of 13/14 October. What happened is recorded in Prien's log:

" *Extract from Log of U-47 (Lieutenant Prien)*
12–17 *October* 1939.

Time.	Position, Wind, etc.	Incidents.
12/10/39		
	Wind SE 7–6, overcast.	During day lay submerged off Orkneys. Surfaced in the evening and came in to the coast in order to fix exact position of ship. From 2200 to 2230 the English are kind enough to switch on all the coastal lights so that I can obtain the most exact fix. . . .
13/10/39		
	E. of Orkney Islands. Wind NNE 3–4, light clouds, very clear night, Northern Lights on entire horizon.	At 0437 lying submerged in 90 metres of water. Rest period for crew. At 1600 general stand-to. After breakfast at 1700, preparations for attack on Scapa Flow. Two torpedoes are placed in rapid loading position before tubes 1 and 2. Explosives brought out in case of necessity of scuttling. Crew's morale splendid. Surfaced at 1915. After warm supper for entire crew, set course for Holm Sound. Everything goes according to plan until 2307, when it is necessary

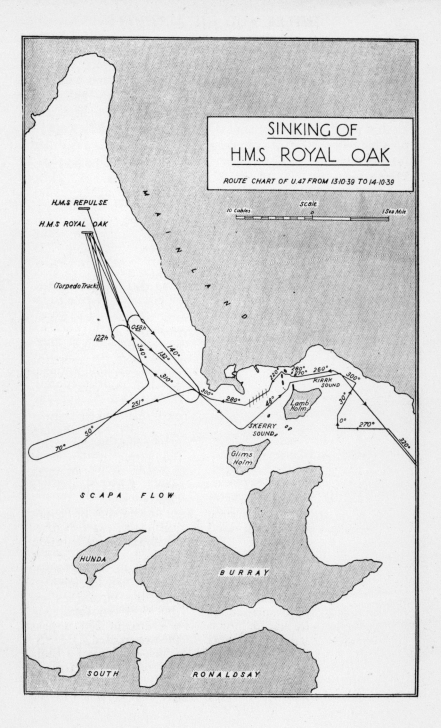

Time.	Position, Wind, etc.	Incidents.

to submerge on sighting a merchant ship just before Rose Ness. I cannot make out the ship in either of the periscopes, in spite of the very clear night and the bright lights. At 2231, surfaced again and entered Holm Sound. Following tide. On nearer approach, the sunken blockship in Skerry Sound is clearly visible, so that at first I believe myself to be already in Kirk Sound, and prepare for work. But the navigator, by means of dead-reckoning, states that the preparations are premature, while I at the same time realise the mistake, for there is only one sunken ship in the straits. By altering course hard to starboard, the imminent danger is averted. A few minutes later, Kirk Sound is clearly visible.

It is a very eerie sight. On land everything is dark, high in the sky are the flickering Northern Lights, so that the bay, surrounded by highish mountains, is directly lit up from above. The blockships lie in the sound, ghostly as the

I am now repaid for having learnt the chart beforehand, for the penetration proceeds with unbelievable speed. In the meantime I had decided to pass the blockships on the Northern side. On a course of 270° I pass the two-masted schooner, which is lying on a bearing of 315°, metres to spare. In the next minute the boat is turned by the

Time.	Position, Wind, etc.	Incidents.
	wings of a theatre.	current to starboard. At the same time I recognize the cable of the northern blockship at an angle of 45 degrees ahead. Port engine stopped, starboard engine slow ahead, and rudder hard to port, the boat slowly touches bottom. The stern still touches the cable, the boat becomes free, it is pulled round to port, and brought on to course again with difficult rapid manœuvring. But, we are in Scapa Flow.
14/10/39 0027		It is disgustingly light. The whole bay is lit up. To the south of Cava there is nothing. I go farther in. To port, I recognize the Hoxa Sound coastguard, to which in the next few minutes the boat must present itself as a target. In that event all would be lost; at present south of Cava no ships are to be seen, although visibility is extremely good. Hence decisions:
0055		South of Cava there is no shipping; so before staking everything on success, all possible precautions must be taken. Therefore, turn to port is made. We proceed north by the coast. Two battleships are lying there at anchor, and further inshore, destroyers. Cruisers not visible,

Time.	Position, Wind, etc.	Incidents.
		therefore attack on the big fellows.
0116 (time queried in pencil, 0058 suggested.)		Distance apart, 3000 metres. Estimated depth, 7·5 metres. Impact firing. One torpedo fired on northern ship, two on southern. After a good 3½ minutes, a torpedo detonates on the northern ship; of the other two nothing is to be seen.
0121 (queried to 0102) (suggested time 0123, in pencil)		About ! Torpedo fired from stern; in the bow two tubes are loaded; three torpedoes from the bow. After three tense minutes comes the detonation on the nearer ship. There is a loud explosion, roar, and rumbling. Then come columns of water, followed by columns of fire, and splinters fly through the air. The harbour springs to life. Destroyers are lit up, signalling starts on every side, and on land, 200 metres away from me, cars roar along the roads. A battleship had been sunk, a second damaged, and the other three torpedoes have gone to blazes. All the tubes are empty. I decide to withdraw, because: (1) With my periscopes I cannot conduct night attacks while submerged. (See experience on entering.) (2) On a bright night I cannot manœuvre unobserved in a calm sea.

Time.	Position, Wind, etc.	Incidents.

(3) I must assume that I was observed by the driver of a car which stopped opposite us, turned around, and drove off towards Scapa at top speed. (4) Nor can I go further north, for there, well hidden from my sight, lie the destroyers which were previously dimly distinguishable.

0128 At full speed both engines we withdraw. Everything is simple until we reach Skildaenoy Point. Then we have more trouble. It is now low tide, the current is against us. Engines at slow and dead slow, I attempt to get away. I must leave by the south through the narrows, because of the depth of the water. Things are again difficult. Course, 058°, slow—10 knots. I make no progress. At full speed I pass the southern blockship with nothing to spare. The helmsman does magnificently. Full speed ahead both, finally ¾ speed and full ahead all out. Free of the blockships — ahead a mole! Hard over and again about, and at 0215 we are once more outside. A pity that only one was destroyed. The torpedo misses I explain as due to faults of course, speed, and drift. In tube 4, a

Time.	Position, Wind, etc.	Incidents.
		misfire. The crew behaved splendidly throughout the operation. . . .
0215		Set SE course for base. I still have 5 torpedoes for possible attacks on merchantmen.
0630	57° 58′ N. 01° 03′ W.	Lay submerged. The glow from Scapa is still visible for a long time. Apparently they are still dropping depth charges.
1935	ENE 3–4, light clouds, occasional rain, visibility bad towards land, otherwise good.	Off again, course 180°. This course was chosen in the hope that we might perhaps catch a ship inshore, and to avoid U-20.
15/10/39 0600	56° 20′ N. 0° 40′ W.	Submerged and lay at 72 metres. From 1000 onwards, depth charges were dropped from time to time in the distance. 32 depth charges were definitely counted. So I lie low, submerged, until dusk.
1823	Wind NE 5, sea 4, swell from E, cloudy, visibility good.	Surfaced. On surfacing, Norwegian steamer *Meteor* lies ahead. W/T traffic from the steamer is reported in error from the W/T office; I therefore fire a salvo far ahead of the steamer which is already stopped. The steamer is destined for Newcastle-on-Tyne, with 238 passengers. Steamer immediately allowed to proceed. It is reported later by the W/T office that the steamer did not make any signals.

Time.	Position, Wind, etc.	Incidents.
16/10/39		
0702	54° 57′ N. 2° 58′ E. Wind NNW 2–2, visibility good.	General course, 180°. Submerged on the Dogger Bank. 3 drifting mines sighted, 54° 58′ N, 2° 56′ E. No measures taken, owing to the proximity of fishing vessels. Proceeded submerged throughout the day.
1856	54° 51′ N. 3° 21′ E. Wind NW 2, light clouds, visibility good.	Surfaced. Course 128°. Steered course of 128° into Channel 1.
17/10/39		
0404		Channel 1 passed. From 0404 to 0447 chased fishing vessel escort ship No. 808 ; gave recognition signal eight times— no reply received. This fool did not react until V/S was used at a distance of 500–600 metres. With such guardships, an incident such as my operation could occur in our waters also.
1100		Entered port Wilhelmshaven III.
1144		Made fast.
1530		Crew flown to Kiel and Berlin.

Raeder reported on the operation on 16 October, when he also obtained the permission to extend naval warfare against British and French merchant shipping.

" *Report of the Commander-in-Chief, Navy, to the Fuehrer on* 16 *October* 1939.

Also present: General Jodl.

1. A report is made regarding the operation by U-47 in Scapa Flow. The Commodore of Submarines is promoted

to Commanding Admiral, Submarines. The Commanding
Officer is to come to Berlin to report and to receive the
Knight's Cross.

2. The Fuehrer is given a memorandum, following which
a report is made regarding the intensification of naval
warfare. *The Fuehrer* grants permission for the following
measures:

(*a*) All merchant ships definitely recognized as enemy
(British or French) can be torpedoed without
warning.

(*b*) Passenger ships in convoy can be torpedoed a short
while after notice has been given of the intention to
do so. (*The C.-in-C.*, *Navy*, points out that passenger
steamers are already being torpedoed when they are
proceeding without lights.)

(*c*) The Italian, Russian, Spanish and Japanese Governments should be requested to declare that they will
carry no contraband goods, otherwise they will be
treated as other neutral nations. (Proceedings to
this effect are under way.)

3. *The C.-in-C.*, *Navy*, reports that the Russians have
placed at our disposal a well-situated base west of Murmansk.
A repair ship is to be stationed there.

(Signed) RAEDER.
(Countersigned) ASSMANN."

Although the action of U-47 and other achievements of the
U-boats and pocket battleships had given the German Navy an
initial advantage in the Battle of the Atlantic, they had made
but a small impression on the vast extent of the Allied supply
organization. Raeder was more aware of Britain's power and
resources than other members of the Supreme Command, who
had themselves been somewhat lulled by the ' phoney ' war, and
towards the end of October he tried to get support for the
German Navy's single-handed effort against the Allies. Hitler
had talked much about creating a New Order for Europe, and
Raeder hastened to point out in a long memorandum, dated
23 October, that this New Order would be an idle dream if
Britain's strength was not destroyed.[1] He insisted that the
Navy alone could not hinder the development of the British
and French war organization and that he must have help from

SURVEY OF THE PLANNED SUBMARINE CONSTRUCTION PROGRAMME

Date.	Additional submarines.	Total submarines at beginning of month.	Submarines withdrawn for training purposes.	Boats at disposal of Com. Ad., Submarines.	Boats operating against enemy.	10% loss.	Total submarines at end of month.
Nov. '39	1	57	12	45	15	5	52
Jan. '40	2	52	18	34	11	3	49
April '40	3	51	24	27	9	3	48
July '40	5	51	37	14	5	1	50
Oct. '40	6	63	42	21	7	2	61
Jan. '41	13	88	55	33	11	3	85
April '41	18	113	55	58	19	6	107
Oct. '41	26	191	75	116	39	12	179
Mar. '42	27	253	75	191	64	19	245
Oct. '42	29	312	75	237	79	24	288
Mar. '43	29	334	75	259	86	26	308
July '43	29	347	75	277	91	27	320

the other branches of the Wehrmacht, particularly from the Luftwaffe.

Hitler was impressed by his arguments, and set up an inter-service and inter-departmental committee for 'Economic Warfare'. This was to be organized by Keitel and to include representatives of the Deputy for the Four Years Plan (Goering), the Foreign Minister (Ribbentrop), the Deputy for German Economy, and of the three Commanders-in-Chief. Committees were alien to the Nazi regime, however, and this one with its conflicting personalities was worse than most. The Luftwaffe continued to disregard naval requests for air reconnaissance and air support; Ribbentrop pursued his own twisted diplomatic course; while in the matter of supply, Funk could hold out no hope of substantially increasing U-boat production for at least another eighteen months. Three weeks later Raeder was complaining to Hitler that although they had only lost six U-boats since the beginning of the war, this loss had already exceeded the supply of new boats for 1939.[1] He presented a table (see previous page) showing that by July 1940, if the present programme and the present rate of sinkings was maintained, they would only have five U-boats operating against the enemy, and that it would not be until March 1942 that they would be able to send enough boats into the Atlantic to achieve an economic advantage (*i.e.* to sink Allied ships faster than they could be built).

Hitler did not react as Raeder had hoped. He was then concentrating on the plans for the invasion of the Low Countries and France, and he had not yet realized the full importance of the Battle of the Atlantic. To him the political aspect of the battle was far more significant, and so long as there were some German warships at sea and able to remind neutrals of what would happen if they were over-friendly towards the Allies, he was content. Moreover he did not want the neutrals to be unnecessarily alarmed, and he considered that the present scale of German activity in the Atlantic struck a nice compromise between the extremes of all-out attack and mere defence. Later, when his preparations on land had been completed, he would be ready to extend German naval operations, and he reminded Raeder of the benefits in store for the German Navy by asking him which ports in France and Holland he would like to have as naval bases.

Raeder was, perforce, satisfied, but he relieved his anxiety by increasing the activities of the German surface fleet. The newly completed battleships, *Gneisenau* and *Scharnhorst*, were sent out on a brief sortie * in which they engaged and sank the hopelessly outnumbered and out-gunned British Armed Merchant Cruiser, *H.M.S. Rawalpindi*, on 23 November.

The *Graf Spee* recommenced her activities on 2 December, and sank three merchant ships, bringing the total number of ships she had sunk to nine) approximately 50,000 tons in all), before the three British cruisers, H.M. Ships *Exeter*, *Ajax* and *Achilles*, under the command of Rear-Admiral Harwood, finally tracked her down on 13 December.

The end of the first phase of the Battle of the Atlantic may be said to have come with the action off the River Plate which followed, and few incidents show more clearly that battle's political nature.

The captain of the *Graf Spee*, Hans Langsdorff, thought at first that he had been sighted by only one cruiser and hence turned immediately to attack. Too late he realized the true situation, and a running fight ensued throughout the day. Damaged, and a considerable distance from his home bases, Langsdorff decided to make for a neutral port where he could carry out temporary repairs before attempting to break through once more into the North Atlantic and so back to Germany. [1] Unaware of the pro-Allied feeling in Uruguay, he shaped course for Montevideo.

Graf Spee reached Montevideo on the evening of the same day, 13 December, and began a prolonged diplomatic argument in an effort to remain in port beyond the legal seventy-two hours. Meanwhile skilful British propaganda created the impression of a large fleet in the vicinity of the La Plata estuary waiting to annihilate the *Graf Spee*. H.M. Ships *Ark Royal* and *Renown* were reported to be at Rio de Janeiro while in reality they were many thousands of miles away. The cruiser force had in fact been reinforced by only one more ship, another cruiser, H.M.S. *Cumberland*.

Langsdorff signalled his appreciation of the situation and his intentions to Berlin. On 16 December Raeder consulted Hitler.

* The sortie covered the return of the *Deutschland*, which had been ordered by Hitler, as, due to her name, her loss would have had serious repercussions on German morale. Her name was later changed to *Luetzow*.

" *Report of the Commander-in-Chief, Navy, to the Fuehrer on* 16 *December* 1939, *at* 1300.

Also present: Brig. General Jodl.
Commander von Puttkamer.

The C.-in-C., Navy, reports that at least two weeks are needed to make the *Graf Spee* seaworthy, and that the Government of Uruguay has granted only 72 hours. The Foreign Office is requested to continue efforts to obtain an extension of the time allowed; this appears hopeless, however, as Britain and France are exerting great pressure, and Uruguay will conform to their wishes. Uruguay is unreliable as a neutral, and is not able to defend her neutrality. Internment in Montevideo is therefore out of the question. A break-through to Argentina, which is stronger, could be considered, since this would permit us to retain greater freedom of action. The Commander of the *Graf Spee* has proposed a break-through to Buenos Aires, and he requests a decision as to whether, if the prospect is hopeless, he should choose internment in Montevideo or scuttle the ship in the fairly shallow waters of the La Plata River.

The Commander's telegram of 16 December follows:

' 1. Strategic position off Montevideo: Besides the cruisers and destroyers, *Ark Royal* and *Renown*. Close blockade at night. Escape into open sea and break-through to home waters hopeless.

2. Propose putting out as far as neutral boundary. If it is possible to fight our way through to Buenos Aires, using remaining ammunition, this will be attempted.

3. If a break-through would result in certain destruction of *Graf Spee* without opportunity of damaging enemy, request decision on whether the ship should be scuttled in spite of insufficient depth in the estuary of the La Plata, or whether internment is to be preferred.

4. Decision requested by radiogram.

(Signed) Commander, *Graf Spee*.'

The C.-in-C., Navy, cannot recommend internment in Uruguay, and he considers the right course to be an attempt to break through, or, if necessary, to scuttle the ship in the La Plata River.

The Fuehrer is also opposed to internment, especially since there is a possibility that the *Graf Spee* might score a success against the British ships in the break-through. The Fuehrer entirely approves of the instructions the C.-in-C., Navy, proposes to send to the Commander of the *Graf Spee*.

The text of the instructions follows (sent as Radiogram 1347/16 to *Graf Spee* at 1707):

' 1. Attempt by all means to extend the time in neutral waters in order to guarantee freedom of action as long as possible.

2. With reference to No. 2: Approved.

3. With reference to No. 3: *No* interment in Uruguay. Attempt effective destruction if ship is scuttled.

(Signed) RAEDER.'

Note: The envoy in Montevideo reports in the afternoon, that further attempts to extend the time limit were without result.

Confirmation was therefore sent by radiogram to the Commander of the *Graf Spee* that the instructions in Radiogram 1347 with reference to No. 2 and No. 3 remain in force.

The text of the radiogram is as follows:

' 16 December, Radiogram 2239/16 to Commander, *Graf Spee*.

As envoy reported impossibility of extending time limit, instructions according to Radiogram 1347/16 Nos. 2 and 3 remain in force.'

Sent at 0040 on 17 December."

On the following morning, watched by a vast crowd of sightseers, *Graf Spee* put to sea. The British ships cleared for action, but, before they could engage the enemy, their spotting aircraft reported that the *Graf Spee* had been scuttled and blown up by her own crew.

Three days later, on 20 December, Captain Langsdorff committed suicide, leaving this letter addressed to the German Ambassador and meant for onward transmission to Germany and his Fuehrer.

" 19/12/39.

To the Ambassador, Buenos Aires.

YOUR EXCELLENCY,

After a long struggle I reached the grave decision to scuttle the pocket battleship *Admiral Graf Spee*, in order to prevent her from falling into enemy hands. I am still convinced that under the circumstances, this decision was the only one left, once I had taken my ship into the trap of Montevideo. For with the ammunition remaining any attempt to fight my way back to open and deep water was bound to fail. And yet only in deep water could I have scuttled the ship, after having used the remaining ammunition, thus avoiding her falling to the enemy.

Sooner than expose my ship to the danger that after a brave fight she would fall partly or completely into enemy hands, I decided not to fight but to destroy the equipment and then scuttle the ship. It was clear to me that this decision might be consciously or unwittingly misconstrued by persons ignorant of my motives, as being attributable entirely or partly to personal considerations. Therefore I decided from the beginning to bear the consequences involved in this decision. For a Captain with a sense of honour, it goes without saying that his personal fate cannot be separated from that of his ship.

I postponed my intention as long as I still bore responsibility for decisions concerning the welfare of the crew under my command. After to-day's decision of the Argentine Government, I can do no more for my ship's company. Neither will I be able to take an active part in the present struggle of my country. I can now only prove by my death that the fighting services of the Third Reich are ready to die for the honour of the flag.

I alone bear the responsibility for scuttling the pocket battleship *Admiral Graf Spee*. I am happy to pay with my life for any possible reflection on the honour of the flag. I shall face my fate with firm faith in the cause and the future of the nation and of my Fuehrer.

I am writing this letter to Your Excellency in the quiet of the evening, after calm deliberation, in order that you may be able to inform my superior officers, and to counter public rumours if this should become necessary.

(Signed) LANGSDORFF,
Captain.

Commanding Officer of the
sunk pocket battleship *Admiral Graf Spee*."

Chapter V

THE INVASION OF NORWAY AND DENMARK

WHILE the German Navy was trying its mettle in the preliminary bouts of the Battle of the Atlantic, Raeder had been considering plans which were later to tax to the limit its entire resources. These plans centred round Norway.

To Germany the importance of Scandinavia, both economically and strategically, could not be exaggerated. Out of a total annual consumption of 15 million tons of iron ore, Germany imported more than 11 million tons from Sweden and Norway.[1] Four and a half million tons alone were shipped by sea from Narvik and Kirkenes. Further, the geographical position of Norway was such that not only could the Allies interfere easily with this iron-ore traffic, but, if they were to obtain the free use of Norwegian ports, they would be able to block the Baltic and the North Sea, thus preventing entirely the movement of German ships into the Atlantic. And if, at the same time, Sweden were to join the Allies, Germany's position would be desperate. Without supplies of iron ore she could not long continue the war.

This situation was indelibly impressed upon Raeder, who, in his early struggles to build up the German Navy, had come to realize how dependent Germany was upon her imports of iron ore. He and his staff had debated the Scandinavian problem in the months before the war, but they had then decided that it would be impossible for the German Navy to defend the long Norwegian coast-line, and that the best solution would be to keep Norway neutral. Germany's vital supplies would be protected by Norwegian territorial waters, and it was thought that

Norway would be unlikely to abandon her rights as a neutral by ceding her ports to Britain.

But in the month following the outbreak of war, friendship between Norway and Britain noticeably strengthened. Raeder became greatly alarmed, and on 10 October 1939 he reported to Hitler, suggesting that Norway should be invaded and occupied. [1, 3]

Hitler had just made his plans for the invasion of Holland and France, and his first thoughts were that to undertake the invasion of Norway as well would impose too great a strain upon the Wehrmacht. He had not previously considered the Scandinavian situation, and, as the approaching winter would make operations in the Baltic impossible for some months, he shelved Raeder's suggestion. Two weeks later the *City of Flint* * case, when Norwegian pilots delayed the ship until the U.S.A. had had time to protest, made Hitler realize that Germany did not have a monopoly over the use of Norwegian territorial waters. He began to reconsider Raeder's ideas.

On 30 November Russia invaded Finland. There was violent indignation in Britain and France, and aid for the Finns was immediately organized. The event might not have disturbed Germany but for the fact that the Allied troops had to pass through Norway, and the subsequent arrival of British and French detachments brought Raeder's invasion schemes immediately to the fore.

Meanwhile Raeder had been considering political rather than military methods of bringing Norway to heel, and he had discussed the problem with Rosenberg of the German Foreign Office. [1]

Rosenberg, the Nazi 'philosopher', was in charge of the organization of Nazi activities in foreign countries. His contacts in Norway were particularly good, and he was able to put Raeder's Chief of Staff, Admiral Schniewind, in touch with two ardently pro-German and pro-Nazi Norwegians—Quisling and his deputy, Hagelin. Schniewind began cautious negotiations with Quisling. The Germans hoped that either Quisling would be

---

* The U.S. ss. *City of Flint* had been captured by the *Deutschland*, and the Prize Crew had tried to sneak the ship into Germany through Norwegian territorial waters. Norwegian pilots had informed the U.S. Consul at Haugesund who had taken prompt diplomatic steps to free the ship.

able to seize power himself and then invite them in, or that he would so assist them in their occupation that the minimum number of troops would be required.

Schniewind's preliminary talks indicated a reasonable chance of success, and in the first fortnight of December he and Rosenberg reported their impressions to Raeder, suggesting that Quisling and Hagelin should be invited to Berlin for discussions and a possible meeting with Hitler. Rosenberg's report was as follows:

" *Memorandum*   (Undated—about 8 December 1939.)

Reference visit of Hr. Quisling from Norway:

Supplementary to earlier information, I wish to report that Quisling is one of the best-known Norwegian general staff officers. He was Military Attaché in Finland, and from 1927 to 1930, before diplomatic relations between the Soviet Union and Great Britain were broken off, he represented British interests in Moscow. From 1931 to 1933 he was Norwegian War Minister, representing the Norwegian Peasant Party; he then resigned and formed a radical national and socialist party called the National Unity Party. This party had, and still has, anti-semitic views and it recommends closest co-operation with Germany. It has 15,000 registered members, and Quisling estimates the number of his direct followers at two to three hundred thousand; this comprises that ten per cent of the population which is in favour of co-operation with Germany even at the present time, when the general attitude in Norway and Sweden is definitely anti-German. His party also did not participate in voting for the Storthing.

The Storthing, contrary to the constitution, has decided to extend its own period of office from 12 January. Quisling suggests that this fact could be used as pretext for action. Quisling, as an experienced officer and a former War Minister, still maintains very close relations with the Norwegian Army. He showed me the original of a letter which he had recently received from the commanding officer in Narvik, Colonel Sunlo. In this letter Colonel Sunlo openly stresses the following: If present conditions continue, Norway will be destroyed. He only hopes that enough will be left of the nation to form a people which can rebuild Norway on a sound basis. The present generation is doomed, and rightly so; it must be admitted that they deserve nothing better, for, as he sees it, the Norwegians have violated the unalterable laws of the world. These laws call for work and idealism, and stupidity has never been considered a legitimate excuse. ' I will do nothing for the old soak Madsen (Minister of Commerce), for that pacifist Monsen (War Minister), it will be good and useful to risk one's bones for the national uprising. Signed: Konrad Sunlo.'

Amtsleiter Scheidt, who has been in Norway several times and has a number of acquaintances there, has stated that the commanding officer of the largest troop training grounds, Hroslev, has expressed himself in a similar manner, likewise the Senior Officer of the War Academy in Halden, Captain Fritzner.

Quisling knows the King very well from the time when he was in office and he believes that the King holds him in esteem, even though the latter is on the whole pro-British. The Jew, Hambro, who is President of the Storthing, and at the same time President of the Committee for Foreign Affairs, is regarded as the greatest enemy of Germany and as perhaps the most powerful political personality. For all practical purposes the politics of Scandinavia rest in his hands at the present time. At the same time he is leader of the delegation to the League of Nations and leader of the strongest political party, the so-called ' Conservatives ', who control the fate of the present minority government. Hambro also controls the press in Norway. It is to be feared that the anti-Russian feeling which is fanned by the Russo-Finnish conflict will very soon result increasingly in greater sympathy for Britain and greater antipathy against Germany.

A plan for possible procedure has been suggested.

According to this plan a number of picked Norwegians will be given training in Germany for this particular task. They will be told exactly what to do, and will be assisted by seasoned National Socialists who are experienced in such matters. These trained men are then to be sent back to Norway as quickly as possible, where details will be discussed. Several focal points in Oslo will have to be occupied with lightning speed, and simultaneously the German Navy with contingents of the German Army will have to put in an appearance at a pre-arranged bay outside Oslo in answer to a special summons from the new Norwegian Government. Quisling has no doubt that such a coup, achieved instantaneously, would at once meet with the approval of those sections of the Army with which he now has connections. Of course he has never discussed political action with them. As regards the King, he believes that he would accept such a *fait accompli.*

Quisling's estimate of the number of German troops needed for the operation coincides with the German estimates.

(Signed) A. ROSENBERG."

The reports of Rosenberg and Schniewind satisfied Raeder, and in view of the urgency of the matter no time was lost in inviting Quisling and Hagelin to Berlin. They arrived on 11 December, and went into immediate conference with Raeder at the Navy Office.[1] Quisling announced his complete readiness to assist Germany, but asked that he should be given secret German help in bringing off his planned *coup d'état.* With such help, he expressed his firm confidence that his party would be able to seize power.

On the following day, 12 December, Raeder reported to Hitler.[1] Keitel and Jodl were also present.

Raeder said that Quisling had impressed him as being reliable. Quisling had told him that as a result of the Russo-Finnish war public opinion in Norway was even more hostile to Germany than before. He had said: " England's influence is very great, above all through the President of the Storthing, Hambro, a Jew and a friend of Hore-Belisha." There was a danger that Sweden would also turn against Germany, and that Britain would probably occupy Norway soon. Raeder added that Quisling was also ready to discuss military measures.

He went on to point out that it was impossible to find out how much Quisling was concerned with his own interests, and that caution was advisable. " On the other hand," he told Hitler, " it must be made impossible for Norway to fall into British hands, as this would be decisive for the outcome of the war."

Hitler agreed, and Raeder continued: " German occupation

of Norwegian coastal bases will naturally cause strong British counter-measures. Severe naval warfare off the Norwegian coast will result, and the German Navy is not yet prepared to cope with this for any length of time. If we invade, this will be the weak spot."

Hitler did not make up his mind immediately; he would see Quisling himself first, and hear the opinions of Rosenberg and others. Then he would decide.

During the following week Quisling was duly interviewed, and Hitler, too, was favourably impressed. He gave orders to start preparations for the invasion, but at the same time he decided that political methods should be attempted first.[1] Quisling and Hagelin were to be encouraged in their efforts to gain control of the Norwegian Government, and, when this had been achieved, Quisling was to offer Germany the free use of Norwegian ports and air bases. Rosenberg was to look after the political details, while Raeder, or his Chief of Staff, Schniewind, was to act as liaison officer for military matters. Quisling was to be provided with money, coal, and special Nazi political troops. These last would serve the double purpose of helping Quisling and at the same time watching him in case he tried to double-cross Germany.

Hitler also ordered a small planning staff to be formed to prepare a military operation, for, if the political measures failed, force was to be used. He detailed one Army Group for the invasion, but he stated that the Navy was to have the major share, and that, if necessary, all naval forces were to be committed. On no account was Norway to be allowed to fall into the hands of the British.

The occupation of Denmark was also to be considered as an essential part of the operation against Norway. As there was no equivalent to Quisling's party in Denmark, force alone was to be used, but it was hoped that, during the development of political tension in Norway, the Danes would be lulled into believing that they would be by-passed. Danish defences were weak; they could be easily surprised; and strong resistance was not expected.

The whole plan was given the name of ' Weseruebung ' (Weser exercise) and, as it would be almost entirely a naval matter, Raeder and his staff were given the principal task of organizing the invasion. The small planning staff was nominally under the chairmanship of Keitel, but the naval demands came first, and, unlike previous inter-service staffs, this one worked harmoniously from the beginning. By the first week in January 1940 planning was well under way, and Raeder had the satisfaction of the complete acceptance of his advice by his Fuehrer. It was later to condemn him at Nuremberg.

Meanwhile Britain and France had also been considering the strategical position of Norway. Admiral Darlan confessed to Raeder in January 1942,[1] that he had suggested to the Allied Governments, even before the war, that they should occupy or at least obtain the use of Norwegian ports: the arguments which led to the German action applied equally well to the Allies. But, more scrupulous than Germany, the Allies had decided that no moves were to be made against Norway unless a German invasion became certain. Preparations were made to counter a German assault, however, and this gave rise to German fears of the imminence of an Allied operation. The *Altmark* incident on 15 February increased these fears, and further strengthened Hitler's determination to act.

The *Altmark*, homeward bound with prisoners of war and survivors from the British merchant ships sunk by the *Graf Spee*, had been intercepted in Norwegian territorial waters by H.M.S. *Cossack*. With the Admiralty's permission, Captain Vian of the *Cossack* had infringed Norwegian neutrality, boarded the *Altmark*, and rescued the prisoners. Norway protested, but only half-heartedly, and to Hitler the incident was an ominous sign of how close Anglo-Norwegian relations had become.

Later, in February, Hitler learnt that Rosenberg's political measures were not being as successful as anticipated.[1] Hagelin's reports for the past two months showed that a new wave of sympathy with, and friendliness towards, England was sweeping Norway. The chances of Quisling being able to seize power were dwindling. The promised German help had, for some reason, not been given, and the German Foreign Office had further bungled the matter by encouraging other Norwegians, who, though friendly to Germany, were strongly opposed to Quisling. Hagelin appealed for support for Quisling alone and for stronger German action.

The combination of these events and reports decided Hitler to concentrate on a military operation, and on 1 March he issued the following directive:

" The Fuehrer and   Berlin,
    Supreme Commander of the Armed Forces.   1/3/1940.

Top Secret.   9 *Copies.*
                                                        3rd Copy.

Directive.
' FALL WESERUEBUNG.'

1. The development of the situation in Scandinavia
requires all preparations to be made for the occupation of
Denmark and Norway by a part of the German Armed
Forces (' Fall Weseruebung '). This operation should prevent
British encroachment on Scandinavia and the Baltic, further
it should guarantee our ore base in Sweden and give our
Navy and Air Force a wider start-line against Britain. The
part which the Navy and the Air Force will have to play,
within the limits of their capabilities, is to protect the
operation against the interference of British naval and air
striking forces.

In view of our military and political power in comparison
with that of the Scandinavian States, the force to be employed
in ' Fall Weseruebung ' will be kept as small as possible.
The numerical weakness will be balanced by daring actions
and surprise execution. On principle we will do our utmost
to make the operation appear as a peaceful occupation, the
object of which is the military protection of the neutrality of
the Scandinavian States. Corresponding demands will be
transmitted to the Governments at the beginning of the
occupation. If necessary, demonstrations by the Navy and
the Air Force will provide the necessary emphasis. If, in
spite of this, resistance should be met with, all military means
will be used to crush it.

2. I put in charge of the preparations and the conduct of
the operation against Denmark and Norway the Commanding
General of the XXI Army Corps, General von Falkenhorst
(Commander of ' Group XXI '). . . .

3. The crossing of the Danish border and the landings in
Norway must take place simultaneously. I emphasise that
the operations must be prepared as quickly as possible.
Should the enemy seize the initiative against Norway, we must
be able to apply immediately our own counter-measures.

It is most important that the Scandinavian States as well

as the Western opponents should be taken by surprise by our measures. All preparations, particularly those of transport and of readiness, drafting and embarkation of the troops, must be made with this factor in mind.

If the preparations for embarkation can no longer be kept secret, the leaders and the troops will be deceived with fictitious objectives. The troops may be acquainted with the actual objectives only after putting to sea. . . .

(Signed) A. HITLER."

Within a few days of this order, Raeder completed his plans. In view of the size of the British Home Fleet he had decided to use all serviceable units of the German surface fleet for the operation. The attack was to be launched in six main areas between Oslo and Narvik; transports were to be heavily escorted; and the High Seas Fleet, in two groups, was to cover the flank of the long Norwegian coast-line against attacks by the British Fleet. No support was to be given to the German Army once the troops had landed—this was to be the responsibility of the Luftwaffe—as the entire German Navy would be needed to defend the invasion areas from sea attacks.

Raeder knew well the risk of such an operation in waters where the German Navy lacked control of the sea, but he relied on tactical surprise, speed, and air support to defeat Allied counter-attacks.

On 9 March Raeder bolstered Hitler's determination to attack, and told him of the naval plans.

" *Report of the Commander-in-Chief, Navy, to the Fuehrer. 9 March* 1940, at 1200.

Also present: General Keitel.

OPERATION ' WESERUEBUNG.'

1. *The C.-in-C., Navy*, states that he has always been, and still is to-day, of the opinion that the occupation of Norway by the British would have a decisive effect against Germany, since then Sweden might also be drawn into the war against Germany and all the ore supplies from Sweden would cease. The British now have the desired opportunity, under pretext of supporting the Finns, to send troop transports through Norway and Sweden and therefore to occupy these countries

if they wish. Therefore operation ' Weseruebung ' is urgent. The C.-in-C., Navy, feels it his duty, however, to present to the Fuehrer a clear picture regarding the character of the naval operation.

The operation in itself is contrary to all principles in the theory of naval warfare. According to this theory, it could be carried out by us only if we had naval supremacy. We do not have this; on the contrary, we are carrying out the operation in face of the vastly superior British Fleet. In spite of this the C.-in-C., Navy, believes that, provided surprise is complete, our troops can and will successfully be transported to Norway.

On many occasions in the history of war those very operations have been successful which went against all the principles of warfare, provided they were carried out by surprise. The critical moment is the penetration of the harbours while passing the coastal fortifications. It is to be expected that this will succeed if carried out by surprise, and that the Norwegians will not make the decision to fire quickly enough, if they decide to do so at all.

The most difficult operation for the ships is the return voyage, which entails breaking through the British naval forces. The main British force has lately again been stationed in Scapa Flow; at present there are two battle cruisers, three battleships, and at least three or four heavy cruisers there. Light naval units will shadow our forces and attempt to direct the main British force to them. All modern naval forces must combine for this break-through, *i.e.* battleships, the *Hipper* and all destroyers from Narvik and Trondheim. The forces at and south of Bergen (small cruisers and special service ships) must break through along the coast with the support of the *Luetzow*. Not one destroyer may be left behind, let alone a cruiser (the *Hipper*) either in Narvik or in Trondheim, at a time when the fate of the German Fleet is hanging in the balance. Strongest co-operation on the part of the Air Force is necessary. Four large submarines will be stationed in Narvik and two probably in the other bases; a number will be disposed along the advance routes of the British Fleet.

In the period immediately following occupation, escort of transports to Oslo will be of primary importance, as well as the establishment of safe bases for naval forces in the harbours on the south-west and west coasts. Subsequently, operations can be carried out from these. The transport of ore from Narvik will be interrupted until further notice, because the problem of whether and in what manner the extensive coastal waters can be defended against British attacks must be clarified first.

2. *The C.-in-C., Navy*, suggests that the Russians be informed, following the occupation, that Tromsoe has not been occupied by the Germans. This could be interpreted by the Russians as constituting some consideration for their interests. It is better to have the Russians in Tromsoe than the British.

The Fuehrer does not wish to have the Russians so near, and is of the opinion that Tromsoe will also have to be occupied by us.

3. *The C.-in-C., Navy*, requests permission for the Naval Air Force to lay about six aerial mines in Scapa Flow, in order to inflict damage on the British capital ships, which might subsequently withdraw to the Faroes.

The Fuehrer gives his full consent, and considers an agreement with the Air Force necessary, since the latter is planning bombing attacks soon.

4. *The C.-in-C., Navy*, gives a survey on the execution of the naval operation by the various groups.

(Signed) RAEDER.
(Countersigned) ASSMANN."

However soberly Raeder weighed up the risks for Hitler, the prime motive for ' Weseruebung ', the security of the iron-ore traffic, made the operation necessary. Events during the following week caused a fever of anxiety in the German Supreme Command—British submarines concentrated off the Skagerrak on 13 March; on the next day a radio message was intercepted ordering transport ships to be ready to move; and on 15 March numerous French officers arrived at Bergen. It seemed to the Germans as if the Allies were about to smash their plans. The German Army was not yet ready, and there was nothing the Supreme Command could do.

But, also on 15 March, the Russo-Finnish peace treaty was suddenly ratified, and Allied preparations reverted to normal. By 26 March Raeder was able to inform Hitler that " the danger of a British landing in Norway is no longer acute." He anticipated that the British would probably make further attempts to disrupt the iron-ore traffic, however, and he suggested that ' Weseruebung ' should be carried out on about 7 April. Hitler agreed, but would not give the actual order. [1]

No sooner had Raeder announced the end of the first false alarm than another crisis began to develop. The German Naval Attaché in Oslo reported that Norwegian anti-aircraft units had been given permission to open fire without waiting for orders from a higher command, and it was believed that similar instructions had been given to the coastal defence batteries.

This could only mean that something of the German plans had leaked out, and on 1 April Hitler ordered the invasion of Norway and Denmark to begin at 5.15 a.m. on 9 April. [1] The postponement of two days from the original date was not explained, but it is probable that Hitler hoped to create the impression of another false alarm, if, that is, the Norwegians had in fact been warned.

Meanwhile tension mounted rapidly. It is one of the major coincidences of the war that the Allies were planning a mine-laying operation in Norwegian territorial waters just at the moment the Germans were completing their plans for invasion. As they expected German reactions to be violent, the Allies were also preparing troop transports so as to be able to counter a possible German assault.

On 4 April Quisling, who had been kept in ignorance of the details of the German plans, hurried to Copenhagen, where, at a secret meeting with a senior German officer, he appealed for immediate German intervention as his own schemes were not sufficiently matured and the political situation was getting beyond his control. [1]

On 5 April Britain and France sent a strong Note to the governments of Norway and Sweden declaring in effect that they could not allow the iron-ore traffic to Germany to continue, and on 7 April, British and French naval units sailed for Norwegian waters.

Simultaneously the advance portion of the German Fleet—*Gneisenau*, *Scharnhorst* and *Hipper*—sailed from Germany. [1]

At dawn on the following day, 8 April, as the Allied ships started laying their mines, Britain and France announced their actions to the world.

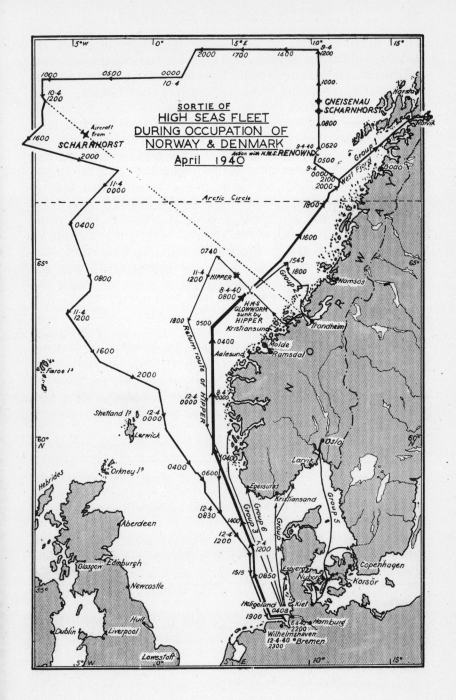

SORTIE OF
HIGH SEAS FLEET
DURING OCCUPATION OF
NORWAY & DENMARK
April 1940

The main body of the German invasion fleet put to sea on the afternoon of the same day, and was intercepted by the British submarine, H.M.S. *Trident*, which sank one of the German transports, the *Rio de Janeiro*. About 300 German troops from the ship scrambled ashore at Lillesand in Norway. They were caught, and the Norwegian Government was warned.

The German battle fleet was also intercepted early on the morning of 8 April by the British destroyer, H.M.S. *Glowworm*, which, although on her own, did not hesitate to attack. Hopelessly outnumbered she rammed the heavy cruiser, *Hipper*, tearing a 120-foot hole in the German vessel's bows. H.M.S. *Glowworm* was destroyed, but managed to give the alarm to the British Home Fleet which raced to hunt down the German battleships.

The landing of troops in Norway and the crossing of the Danish frontier began according to plan shortly after 5 a.m. on 9 April. After sporadic resistance Denmark surrendered on the same day. Her small army was caught by surprise and was overwhelmed. In Oslo Fiord the Norwegian coastal batteries opened fire on the advancing German ships. They sank the cruiser *Bluecher* and damaged another, the *Emden*. In the same area a second British submarine, H.M.S. *Truant*, sank yet another German cruiser, the *Karlsruhe*. Off Bergen, Fleet Air Arm and R.A.F. aircraft attacked and sank a third German cruiser, the *Koenigsberg*.

During these actions H.M.S. *Renown* of the Home Fleet intercepted the German battleships, *Gneisenau* and *Scharnhorst*, but after a short exchange of salvoes, the German ships escaped in the bad weather and mist. British destroyers were more successful and at Narvik intercepted and sank nine merchant ships, two destroyers and damaged one other destroyer. Four days later additional British destroyers, now supported by the veteran battleship, H.M.S. *Warspite*, again entered the fiord near Narvik and sank seven more German destroyers and one U-boat, thus clearing Narvik of enemy shipping and making it possible for the Allies to land troops in Norway to begin their counter-attack.

In all, German naval casualties during the first few days of the Norwegian invasion were:

3 Cruisers sunk,
2 Cruisers severely damaged,

9 Destroyers sunk,
1 Destroyer severely damaged,
and about 12 merchant ships sunk or damaged.

These losses were severe, but they were approximately what Raeder had expected and were a small price to pay for the conquest of Norway.

On land Norwegian resistance, betrayed by Quisling's party, was crippled by the end of the day of the invasion, by which time most of Southern Norway was in German hands.

The German Naval Attaché recorded in his official diary what had happened in Oslo:

" *April 9*
1940
0400   I am in harbour, ready to receive the German warships. Lt. Kempf is in a German ship out in the bay, to serve as pilot. Berths have been arranged so as to be able to carry out the action in Oslo as quickly as possible. Everything that I can do here has been considered and prepared down to the smallest detail.

English and French leave the town of Oslo in the morning hours. The Ambassadors of England, France and Poland will follow. Secret papers are being burnt in the garden of the English Embassy.

0445   The German Ambassador presents the Memorandum.

0800   Shortly after 0800 the first German aircraft fly over the harbour. The Norwegian flak opens fire.

0923   The airfield Fornebo, Oslo, is in German hands.

0930   The Royal Standard is taken down from the Castle. German air attack on fortresses Akershus and Hovedoeya. Paratroops are fetched by the Naval and Air Attachés from Fornebo under flak and machine-gun fire.

The arrival of German fleet units is awaited in vain. Berlin gives no reply to W/T. Panic in the town in consequence of flak defence and the appearance of German aircraft. In the office of the Naval Attaché, the top secret papers are partly destroyed, because the position has become tense owing to the delay in the arrival of the German warships. It is possible that Norwegian soldiers, police, or English defence groups will thrust their way into the house. Pistols have been distributed. The house is secured. I drive unmolested through the town in a German car, my uniform under a civilian overcoat.

1200   About 1200 the first German soldiers land in Fornebo, occupy the Embassy and the most important points of the town. The leader of the action is Colonel Pohlmann of Group XXI.

Telephone communications cut off in the town. The telephone connection between the Naval Attaché Office and the German Embassy is in order. In the late afternoon an aircraft report announces German ship has grounded at the entrance at Oscarsburg. Lt. Pusback in the office of the Naval Attaché receives orders to sail to Oscarsburg. On his arrival the task had already been carried out and the survivors brought to German ships.

The crew of the torpedoed German steamer assemble in great numbers in the offices of the Naval Attaché. Instead of the Norwegian Government which is in flight, there is a new Government formed towards evening by Quisling.

1700   The position in the town has become clear. There are no Norwegian officers at their posts in the Defence Ministry. I help the advancing troops by giving them plans of the town and so on.

My conviction has not changed during the fighting, that the Norwegian operation would have gone through without a shot had the surprise remained secret. Until the late afternoon of 8 April nothing was known to the Government or the Admiralty staff of the operation. I was continually in communication with authoritative powers under the understandable guise of wishing to hear something of the English operation. I should certainly have obtained an impression if the Government at this time had been ready to defend a German action had they seriously believed one was meditated. No, it was not expected. As, however, the torpedoing of German special ships mounted, and as the survivors of the *Rio de Janeiro* gave evidence that they had come to protect Norway, the incidents of *Posidonia* (tanker) and U-21 stood in a new light. During the night of 8–9 April, the Norwegian Government made its weighty decision. The King left the town on the 9th, during the morning."

On 10 April Raeder reviewed the progress of the invasion at Hitler's noon situation conference.

" *Report of the Commander-in-Chief, Navy, to the Fuehrer on* 10 *April* 1940, *at noon.*

Also present: Chief of Staff, Armed Forces High Command.
General Jodl.
Commander von Puttkamer.
Commander-in-Chief, Air.
General Bodenschatz.

1. *The C.-in-C., Navy,* refers to his views on operation ' Weseruebung' expressed in recent conferences. He had said that passage to Norway would with some degree of luck be successful, provided the element of surprise were maintained; the break-through and landing would probably also be successful if a determined thrust were made through the fortification zones, even though a certain stiffening in the attitude of the Norwegians was observed in the last few days; the return passage would be the most difficult part of the operation, and would call for all-out co-operation by the whole German Navy. The first two parts of the operation, the approach and the penetration and landing, were carried out on the whole successfully as anticipated. The losses (*Bluecher* and *Karlsruhe*) are quite in proportion to the risks run and can definitely not be considered high. The third part of the operation is in progress and will probably entail further losses.

2. The situation was made more difficult than anticipated by the fact that the British were also conducting an operation involving minelaying on 8 April, to be followed by occupation of Norwegian bases. This was confirmed by the presence of transports with the British Home Fleet, which were sighted on the afternoon of 9 April in the northern North Sea by attacking aircraft. Numerous British and

French naval forces were thus at sea in the northern North
Sea as far north as the Lofoten Islands.

3. DETAILS:

(a) *Battleships :* Yesterday morning there was an engage-
ment with heavy British forces in the Lofoten Islands area.
The *Repulse* and another battleship were probably involved.
Further details are not known. In the evening the Fleet
Commander reported: Only 25 knots; two heavy turrets
out of action. Further inquiries have not yet been answered.
Losses by the enemy are probable. Radio telegraph com-
munication with the Lofoten Islands is very uncertain.

Plan : Both battleships are to force their way into home
waters as soon as possible.

If a battleship is put out of action or is not ready for
action, the question will arise whether to send the damaged
battleship to Narvik for protection against further attacks,
which are sure to come. Putting into Narvik means that the
ship is eliminated from future operations. She will also be
in great danger from aircraft carriers, without the com-
pensation of any promise of effective operation.

Enemy battleships : Their situation and position this
morning was not yet known. The aircraft carrier *Furious*
put out of Scapa Flow yesterday evening, apparently to join
the Commander-in-Chief, Home Fleet.

Note: According to later reports, three British and two
      German destroyers were sunk; several German
      destroyers have been partially disabled and are serv-
      ing as barrage batteries.

(b) *Situation in Narvik :* According to a garbled radio
message (not in code) received at 0604 to-day, destroyers
were attacked this morning in Narvik by enemy forces,
probably destroyers and several cruisers. The situation is
not clear. At 0830 one destroyer reported a heavy destroyer
engagement off Narvik. The situation must be regarded as
serious, since the troops on land are without artillery. The
most urgent matters are the defence of Narvik and the
question of supplies. No supply vessels have arrived as yet.
It is requested that reinforcements and material be sent
immediately on Swedish railways via northern Sweden.

It is planned to increase the number of submarines in order
to take effective measures against British operations.

(c) *Situation in Trondheim :* The situation regarding the coastal batteries is still obscure; according to information from the Armed Forces High Command, fortifications are safe in German hands and the airfield is out of service. The vessels of the supply group have not arrived, and it is uncertain whether they will arrive. Increased submarine protection is also planned here.

Cruiser *Hipper* and two, later three, destroyers will put out this evening, carrying only a small amount of fuel. They are to refuel at sea, but it is questionable whether this can be accomplished.

(d) *Situation in Bergen :* The cruiser *Koenigsberg* (damaged), the *Bremse* (damaged), the *Carl Peters* and the motor-boat flotilla remain in the harbour. A ship arrived with mines. Three batteries are partially ready for firing this evening. The Commanding Admiral, Scouting Forces, plans to put out this evening with the *Koeln* and torpedo boats.

The situation in Bergen appears to be assured. This base is very exposed to air attacks, however.

(e) *Situation in Christiansand :* The *Tsingtau* and the motor-boat flotilla remain in the harbour. The *Karlsruhe* was torpedoed yesterday while putting out and was later sunk. The crew were taken on board torpedo boats.

(f) *Situation in Oslo :* The *Luetzow* and the *Emden* have not put in because the mine situation is not yet clarified. The *Bluecher* sank yesterday after hitting a mine. It is planned to withdraw the *Luetzow* this evening.

(g) *Urgent Missions :* Reinforcement of the Skagerrak minefield. Submarine hunt is to be carried on in the Kattegat and the Skagerrak with all available means. Sea transports must be escorted.

Supplies to western ports cannot be shipped by sea.

At the beginning and at the conclusion of the conference, *the Fuehrer* expressed his full appreciation to the C.-in-C., Navy, for the great achievement of the Navy.

(Signed) RAEDER."

Twelve days later, on 22 April, when Raeder was writing his full report on the operation, he commented on the political aspects:

" Seizure of the Norwegian Government and political action in general failed completely. One factor which contributed to this was undoubtedly the delay in the arrival of the air-borne troops owing to fog. However, the main reason was the fact that the situation was handled extremely badly on the political side (Minister Braeuer). In such cases the main objective must be to arrest the government at all costs. If energetic steps had been taken it would have been possible to do this and also to bring pressure to bear on the King to form a new government. A diplomat who had previously had very correct relations with the King and the Government was the most unsuitable person for such a task. Before the beginning of the operation I expressed my concern to General Keitel and to General von Falkenhorst at not knowing how the political side was being handled. Both assured me that the matter was being dealt with by the Fuehrer and that the Services were not to be bothered with it. When I mentioned Quisling to von Falkenhorst, I learned to my astonishment that the latter considered the Minister of Foreign Affairs (Koht!) also a very sound man who could be used. After this statement I feared the worst regarding the settlement of political questions.

The situation developed accordingly: Quisling did not obtain the necessary support from General von Falkenhorst and from Minister Braeuer. The Norwegian Government escaped. The reorganization of the government in agreement with the King failed. Quisling was suspected of high treason. An ' Administrative Committee ', which, however, did not constitute a government, was the result. The Norwegian population was split into two camps. It remains to be seen whether the appointment of Terboven as Reich Commissioner and the recall of Minister Braeuer will bring any changes.

(signed) RAEDER.''

However badly the German Foreign Office had bungled the political plans in the beginning, Terboven and Quisling soon proved their ruthless ability. Allied military resistance continued for only another six weeks.

Units of the British Home Fleet were sent to cover the evacuation of Allied troops. Raeder accordingly planned an operation—" Juno "—against them, and on 4 June the *Gneisenau* and *Scharnhorst* sailed for Norway. On 8 June the German battleships surprised and sank the carrier, H.M.S. *Glorious*, her two escorting destroyers, *Acasta* and *Ardent*, two merchant ships and the trawler, *Juniper*. No news of this action was received by the British until twenty-four hours later, by which time the German Fleet had already reached Trondheim and were safe under the protection of the Luftwaffe. The German conquest of Norway was complete.

Chapter VI

OPERATION 'SEA LION'

DUNKIRK AND THE PLANNED INVASION OF ENGLAND

THE attack on the Low Countries and France, which followed the Norwegian operation, did not greatly concern the German Navy. The use of all naval vessels in ' Weseruebung ' precluded any major effort by the Navy in Western Europe, and their share was confined to the continuation of the Battle of the Atlantic. Once the Army's work had been done, however, they were expected to take over the captured ports and to organize the coastal defences.

The offensive against Holland, Belgium and France began on 10 May. Holland was overrun by 15 May, but the Queen of the Netherlands, her Government, and the majority of the Dutch Fleet made good their withdrawal to England. The Dutch Fleet, indeed, became an invaluable and powerful force in the service of the Allies.

In Belgium, King Leopold surrendered on 25 May, and the British Expeditionary Force was left surrounded by the German Army. It was clear that if England was to continue the war this force would have to be evacuated, and, as Ostend was captured on 29 May, the port of Dunkirk was the only one available.

The evacuation started on 26 May, on which day, in a memorandum to the Luftwaffe, Admiral Schniewind stated: " A regular and orderly transport of large numbers of troops cannot take place in the hurried and difficult conditions prevailing." He continued: " Evacuation of troops without their equipment is conceivable, however, if large numbers of smaller vessels, coastal and ferry steamers, fishing trawlers, drifters, and other small craft are used. . . . The German Navy is not in a position to take part successfully in this with the means at its disposal. . . . The best counter-attack will be the use of aircraft on moonless nights with flares."

Four days later, the German Naval Staff conceded that the impossible was taking place. The entry in their War Diary for 30 May stated:

> " The evacuation of English and French troops from the Franco-Belgian coast continues during the day. It is favoured by the extremely bad weather—fog and rain—which does not allow the German forces to attack. . . . By tough resistance the English and French troops have made it possible to hold the Dunkirk area. . . . Thousands of troops wait on the shore for embarkation. Air attacks during the night of 30 May caused several of the transports to be lost;"

and in the entry of the following day there was a hint of admiration for the achievement:

> " The embarkation of troops . . . continues its progress under strong attacks by aircraft and artillery fire from land. . . . The nightly successful appearance of German motor boats heighten the extremely great difficulties of this retreat. The impression remains, nevertheless, that the Western Powers, by a ruthless use of naval forces and transports, will succeed in getting a considerable part of their troops over to England, even though in complete disorder and without heavy arms or equipment. The losses must be enormous. . . ."

The evacuation from Dunkirk ended at dawn on 4 June. More than 335,000 troops had been saved.

During the next two weeks events moved swiftly to a crisis. Italy declared war on 10 June; Paris was occupied on 14 June; and on 17 June France asked for armistice terms. On the following day Mr. Churchill, now Prime Minister of Great Britain, damped Hitler's hopes of a subsequent speedy capitulation of England.

Speaking in the House of Commons, he said:

" What General Weygand called the Battle of France is over. I expect that the Battle of Britain is about to begin. Upon this battle depends the survival of Christian civilisation. . . . The whole fury and might of the enemy must very soon be turned against us. Hitler knows that he will have to break us in this island or lose the war. . . . Let us therefore brace ourselves so that if the British Commonwealth and Empire lasts for a thousand years men will still say, ' This was their finest hour '."

Two days later, on 20 June, Hitler summoned his Commanders-in-Chief to a conference to discuss the armistice terms for France. The question of what to do about England was brought up by Raeder—he had first mentioned the plans for invasion in a previous conference (21 May)—but Hitler, jubilant over his victory in France, paid scant attention. He did not consider that invasion would be necessary, and thought that air attacks and a naval blockade would quickly bring England to defeat.

" *Conference of the Commander-in-Chief, Navy, with the Fuehrer on 20 June 1940, at Wolfsschlucht.*

Also present: Chief of Staff, Armed Forces High Command.
　　　　　　　General Jodl.
　　　　　　　Commander von Puttkamer.

1. FRANCE. *The Armistice.*
The Fuehrer wishes to refrain from taking any measures which would affect French honour. The fleet is therefore to be interned at Brest and Toulon according to peace-time disposition. The ships are to be put out of action in accordance with special instructions. Some naval units must be available for the defence of Indo-China. Bases on the Atlantic coast with all their resources must be completely at the disposal of the German Navy for warfare against Britain. Demands for minesweepers and vessels to defend the harbours and channels are to be made during the negotiations.

The C.-in-C., Navy, points out that the Navy can man only the coastal defences and is not in a position to carry out any land defence. The Army will have to hold troops ready inland.

The Fuehrer is quite aware of this fact. Mechanized forces will be kept in readiness for immediate action at suitable points inland. The Air Force is to take over the air defence. The Navy can provide only two anti-aircraft units.

Brest will probably be the main base for submarine warfare, Boulogne and Cherbourg for motor boats.

The C.-in-C., Navy, draws attention to the importance of bases on the Atlantic coast, *e.g.* Dakar.

The Fuehrer intends to use Madagascar for settling Jews under French supervision. However, he realizes the importance of the proposal made by the C.-in-C., Navy, to exchange Madagascar for the northern part of Portuguese Angola, and he will consider the suggestion.

2. BRITAIN.

(a) *The C.-in-C., Navy*, calls attention to the necessity of starting vigorous air attacks on British bases in order to destroy ships under construction and repair.

The Fuehrer contemplates taking such action soon.

(b) *The C.-in-C., Navy*, reports on negotiations with the Foreign Office concerning a state of siege.

(c) *The C.-in-C., Navy*, makes a report on the preparations for an invasion of England. This report deals with the locality chosen for landing, the question of mines, and shipping available now and in the future.

Special craft (of the type proposed by Von Schell and Feder) are discussed. *The C.-in-C., Navy*, requests that the Navy alone should make and carry out decisions with regard to the construction of special craft. The Armed Forces High Command will receive instructions to ensure this.

The C.-in-C., Navy, states that air supremacy is necessary for an invasion.

The Army must check the composition of the divisions required. All superfluous material must be left behind."

But Raeder's invasion plans fell on deaf ears, and Hitler instead talked airily of reducing the size of the German Army and of creating a New Order in Europe, fit for Herrenvolk to live in.

On the following day, 21 June, the armistice with France was signed in the same railway carriage in which Germany had accepted her defeat in the First World War; but, although the German Army settled down to celebrate victory in champagne and cognac, the Supreme Command knew that they could not neglect England. In the Naval Headquarters a small staff put the finishing touches to their work of the past seven months.

Planning for a landing in England began on 15 November 1939,[1] when Raeder issued an order to his staff to investigate and prepare the operation. This was an order to the Naval Staff only, and neither Hitler nor the other two Services were informed. The plans were apparently prepared not so much because Raeder considered the invasion of England essential, but because he did not want to be confronted with a sudden directive from Hitler ordering the invasion at short notice. Hitler's policy had been to subdue England by 'siege' tactics rather than by direct assault, but Raeder had always believed that Hitler would eventually decide that an actual invasion would be necessary, and he had instructed his staff accordingly.

The discussion about a possible invasion at the conference of 20 June had been noted by Keitel and Jodl, and when it became obvious that, weak as she was, England had no intention of capitulating, the Supreme Command decided to investigate the possibilities of direct attack. Keitel, on Hitler's instructions, issued the following directive:

" Supreme Command. Fuehrer's Headquarters, 2/7/1940.

Top Secret. 5 *Copies.*
2nd Copy.

THE WAR AGAINST ENGLAND.

The Fuehrer and Supreme Commander has decided:

1. That a landing in England is possible, providing that air superiority can be attained and certain other necessary conditions fulfilled. The date of commencement is still undecided. All preparations are to be begun immediately.

2. The Commands of the three Services are to supply the following information:

(*a*) Army
　　(1) Estimates of the strength of the British forces, of losses, and of the extent to which the British Army will have been re-equipped a month or so hence.

(2) An appreciation of the operational strength of our coastal batteries, and their capacity to provide additional protection for our shipping against British naval forces.

(b) Navy

(1) Survey of possible landing points for strong Army forces (25–40 divisions), and estimate of strength of English coastal defences.

(2) Indication of sea routes over which our forces can be transported with the maximum safety. In selecting landing areas, it must be remembered that landings on a broad front will facilitate subsequent deep penetration.

(3) Data of shipping available, with probable date on which this could be ready.

(c) Air Force

An estimate of the chances of attaining air supremacy, and figures showing the relative strengths of the Luftwaffe and R.A.F.

To what extent can the landing be supported by a parachute attack ? (Highest priority to be given to the production of transport aircraft.)

3. The Commands of the three Services should co-operate in evolving a plan for the transport of the maximum number of troops with the minimum of shipping and aircraft space.

The invading forces must be highly mechanized and numerically superior to the opposing armies.

4. All preparations must be undertaken on the basis that the invasion is still only a plan, and has not yet been decided upon. Knowledge of preparations must be restricted to those immediately concerned.

(Signed) KEITEL."

The three branches of the Armed Forces set to work and produced rough plans. The operation was not yet considered necessary, however, and on 11 July Raeder informed Hitler:[1] " that for a speedy termination of the war with Britain the impact of the war must be forcibly brought home to the British public itself." He suggested that heavy air attacks should be made on the principal towns, and in particular pointed out the importance of London : " the great mass of people who cannot be evacuated, difficulties of food supply, and the fact that 40 per cent. of the imports come through the Port of London." On the subject of invasion, Raeder stated: " I consider that an invasion should be used only as a last resort to force Britain to sue for peace. I am convinced that Britain can be made to ask for peace simply by cutting off her import trade by means of submarine warfare, air attacks on convoys, and heavy air attacks on her main centres, Liverpool, for instance. I cannot for my part, therefore, advocate an invasion of Britain as I did in the case of Norway. The prerequisites are complete air superiority and the creation of a mine-free area for transports and disembarkation."

Hitler appeared to agree, but in the next few days he changed his mind, and, on 16 July, issued the directive for the invasion of England—operation ' Sea Lion.'

" The Fuehrer and Supreme Commander of the Wehrmacht.

Fuehrer's Headquarters, 16/7/1940.

Top Secret.

Directive No. 16.

Preparations for the Invasion of England.

As England, in spite of the hopelessness of her military position, has so far shown herself unwilling to come to any compromise, I have decided to begin to prepare for, and if necessary to carry out an invasion of England.

This operation is dictated by the necessity of eliminating Great Britain as a base from which the war against Germany can be fought, and if necessary, the island will be occupied.

I therefore issue the following orders:

1. The landing operation must be a surprise crossing on a broad front extending approximately from Ramsgate to a point West of the Isle of Wight. Elements of the Air Force will do the work of the artillery and elements of the Navy the work of engineers. I ask each of the fighting services to consider the advantage from their respective point of view of preliminary operations such as the occupation of the Isle of Wight or the Duchy of Cornwall prior to the full-scale invasion, and to inform me of the result of their deliberations. I shall be responsible for the final decision.

The preparations for the large scale invasion must be completed by the middle of August. . . ."

On 19 July, Raeder, through his staff, sent to the Supreme Command a long memorandum explaining the difficulties from the naval point of view.

" The task allotted to the Navy in operation ' Sea Lion ' is out of all proportion to the Navy's strength and bears no relation to the tasks that are set the Army and the Air Force.

. . . . . .

The principal difficulties confronting the Navy are as follows:
The transport of Army troops must take place from a coast whose harbour installations and adjacent inland water-ways have been extensively damaged through the fighting in the campaign against France, or are of limited capacity.

. . . . . .

The gaining of air supremacy is vital to the possibility of assembling the requisite Naval Forces and shipping in the relatively restricted area of embarkation.

. . . . . .

So far the enemy has not needed to use his Fleet fully, as a matter of life and death, but the landing operations on the English coast will find him resolved to throw in fully and decisively all his Naval forces. It cannot be assumed that the Luftwaffe alone will succeed in keeping the enemy Naval forces clear of our shipping, as its operations are very dependent on weather conditions.

. . . . . .

These reflections cause the Naval Staff to see exceptional difficulties that cannot be assessed individually until a detailed examination of the transport problem has been made."

Meanwhile German Intelligence was trying to estimate the strength of England's defences. On 17 July an extract from the War Diary of the Naval Staff stated:

" The whole foreign Press, in particular the English Press, comments that a major German attack is expected.

Thousands of barges and vessels are said to be standing by on the Channel and Atlantic coast. The attack is expected in the Dover area, though the defences here are strongest.

Strong air attacks lasting several days will precede the landing."

Two days later a further report was received.

" English defence measures: coastal defence by the Army. Defence is based on mobility and concentration of all available fire-power. No fixed defence line with built-in defences. The task of the Fleet and the R.A.F. would be to render impossible the landing of armoured units or surprise landing by troops. The R.A.F. is so organized that strong units can be quickly concentrated at any danger spot, and also to attack the new German bases in Northern France and Holland and to search for indications of German activity, such as the assembly of ships and barges."

These reports, though lacking in definite information, impressed upon the Naval Staff the difficulties of invasion and on 21 July Raeder reported yet again to Hitler. Only rough notes of this conference are available, but additional information shows that in Hitler's opinion the war was already won, but that England had not yet recognized the situation. From being averse to the landing the German Supreme Command (*i.e.* Keitel and Jodl) had entirely changed its views, and, to the alarm of the Naval Staff, now considered the landing quite a simple operation. Hitler himself was not, however, convinced.

" *Notes of conference on* 21 *July* 1940.

The Fuehrer raised the following points:

What hopes can Britain have for the continuation of the war? She may be expecting the following:

1. A change of policy in America. (America lost $10,000,000,000 in the World War, and got back only $1,400,000,000. She is hoping to become the dominant naval power in any case.)

2. Russia's entry into the war, which would be unpleasant for Germany especially on account of the threat from the air.

Even though Moscow is unenthusiastic about Germany's great successes, she will nevertheless make no effort to enter into the war against Germany of her own accord. Naturally it is our duty to deliberate the American and Russian questions carefully. A speedy termination of the war is in the interest of the German people. There is, however, no urgent need for this, as the situation is far more favourable than it was in the World War. In 1918 the western front was enormously costly. This is not so in the present situation. An abundance of material is available. The fuel problem is the most pressing. This will not become critical as long as Roumania and Russia continue their supplies and the hydrogenation plants can be adequately protected against air attacks. Food supplies are assured for some time, especially if prisoners-of-war are used to a larger extent as farm hands.

In Britain they may have hopes that the fuel situation in Germany will develop unfavourably. It is necessary to clear up the question of whether a direct operation could bring Britain to her knees, and how long this would take. Also diplomatic steps must be taken in regard to Spain, Russia and Japan. Such steps are difficult, though, as long as the world awaits a new miracle which has not yet occurred.

The invasion of Britain is an exceptionally daring undertaking, because even if the way is short, this is not just a river crossing, but the crossing of a sea which is dominated by the enemy. This is not a case of a single crossing operation as in Norway; operational surprise cannot be expected; a defensively prepared and utterly determined enemy faces us and dominates the sea area which we must use. For the Army operation 40 divisions will be required; the most difficult part will be the continued reinforcement of material and stores. We cannot count on supplies of any kind being available to us in England. The prerequisites are complete mastery of the air, the operational use of powerful artillery in the Dover Straits, and protection by minefields. The time of year is an important factor, since the weather in the North Sea and in the Channel during the second half of September is very bad and the fogs begin by the middle of October. The main operation would therefore have to be completed by 15 September; after this date co-operation between the Luftwaffe and the heavy weapons becomes too unreliable. But as air co-operation is decisive, it must be regarded as the principal factor in fixing the date.

The following must be established:

1. How long does the Navy require for its technical preparations?
2. How soon can the guns be in place?
3. To what extent can the Navy safeguard the crossing?

If it is not certain that preparations can be completed by the beginning of September, other plans must be considered.

(Signed) RAEDER."

On the following day it was reported to Hitler that the preparations could not in any event be completed by the middle of August, and that the actual date of invasion could only be determined when air supremacy in the Channel had been achieved.

The Army then sent their theoretical demands to the Naval Staff.

" The General Staff of the Army has given its intentions for carrying out the operation, as follows: about 100,000 men with appropriate equipment, including heavy gear, must be transported in the first wave from the area Dunkirk-Cherbourg to the area between Ramsgate and Lyme Bay. Further waves must follow in quickest succession, so that the formation of a local bridgehead may be followed in the shortest time by a war of movement on the Island. This demands the most rapid turn round of transports after disembarkation of the first echelon."

The amount of shipping required to carry out the Army demands was estimated as: [1]

> 1722 barges,
> 471 tugs,
> 1161 motor boats,
> 155 transports.

The assembly of this armada would impose a severe strain on German economy and, on 25 July, Raeder again reported to Hitler.

" Commander-in-Chief of the Navy.   Berlin,
                                   26 *July* 1940.

Conference with the Fuehrer on 25 July 1940, *at* 1700.

Also present: Chief of Staff, Armed Forces High
                Command (Keitel).
                General Jodl.
                Minister Todt.
                Commander von Puttkamer.
                Colonel Schmundt.

Placement of batteries at the Straits of Dover. (Report by Captain Voss.)

The guns are to be ready by 15 August. The 38 cm. battery will not be ready until the middle of September. Concrete covers will be built later as a protection against air attack.

The C.-in-C., Navy, emphasizes the necessity for making use of the batteries as soon as they are ready in order to protect minesweepers and to close the Straits of Dover. (The 28 cm. Kurfuerst battery will be ready about 1 August.) As British air reconnaissance is obviously closely watching the placing of the guns, firing them will not disclose German plans to any greater degree.

The Fuehrer agrees.

Operation ' Sea Lion '.

The C.-in-C., Navy, describes forcefully once again the effects of these preparations on the German economy: cessation of inland shipping and a great part of maritime shipping, strain on shipyards, etc. *The C.-in-C., Navy,* requests that an order be issued that these preparations be given preference over anything else.

The Fuehrer and the *Chief of Staff,* Armed Forces High Command, agree.

There follows a report on the state of preparations on 25 July, 1940. *The C.-in-C., Navy,* again stresses the necessity of establishing air superiority soon in order to carry out preparations. At the present time, the following can be said:

Every effort is being made to complete preparations by the end of August. Provided that there are no special difficulties and that air superiority is established soon, it will be possible to do the following:

1. Provide and convert barges.
2. Make available the necessary personnel.
3. Prepare ports for embarkation.
4. Reconnoitre the enemy coast.
5. Clear the invasion area of mines.
6. Lay protecting minefields.
7. Set up the organization.

It is still very uncertain whether a sufficient number of ships can be obtained along the Belgian-French coast and how long it will take to convert them. The C.-in-C., Navy, will try to give a clear picture by the middle of next week.

The Fuehrer orders a conference for the middle of next week.   (Signed) RAEDER."

Preparations for 'Sea Lion' now began in earnest. There was intense activity throughout Germany, and signals and memoranda passed incessantly between the various commands. An entry in the War Diary for July 29 stated:

" (*a*) The Army requires the transport of 13 landing divisions (about 260,000 men) . . . a considerable reduction compared with the original requirement of the Fuehrer (on 21 July) of 40 divisions.

(*b*) These 13 divisions must attack the English coast on the widest front (from Ramsgate to Lyme Bay); which means that they must leave the French coast as far as possible simultaneously, and also on the widest front.

(*c*) The landing divisions must be ready for operations in England within the shortest time, that is, within 2 to 3 days. A period of 10 days for the transport as provided by the timetable for the second wave, is unacceptable by the Army.

(*d*) The landing divisions must include sufficient heavy artillery. . . .

(*e*) The Army General Staff requires the landing to take place at dawn."

These demands of the Army started a series of acrimonious disputes with the Navy on the question of landing on a broad or narrow front. From the point of view of the German Navy full security for a landing could only be guaranteed if the landing took place on a narrow strip near Dover or near Beachy Head.

The Army demand for a landing area stretching from Ramsgate to Lyme Regis was regarded as quite impracticable by the Navy.

On 31 July Raeder conferred with Hitler and announced that the earliest date for beginning the operation was 15 September,[1] but planning was almost brought to a standstill by the ' broad ' versus ' narrow ' front controversy.

There was little appreciation by the Army Command of the transport difficulties involved, and on 7 August, at a meeting between the Chief of the Army General Staff, Colonel-General Halder, and the Chief of the Naval Staff, Admiral Schniewind, there was a strong clash of opinions. Halder dramatically stated: " I utterly reject the Navy's proposal; from the point of view of the Army I regard their proposal as complete suicide. I might just as well put the troops that have landed straight through a sausage machine ! "

Schniewind replied as dramatically that it would be equally suicidal, in view of British naval supremacy, to attempt the transport of the troops over such a wide area.

The result was a deadlock between the two services and on 13 August Hitler was asked to decide.

" *Report of the Commander-in-Chief, Navy, to the Fuehrer on* 13 *August* 1940, *at* 1730.

Also present: Chief of Staff, Armed Forces High Command.
　　　　　　　General Jodl.
　　　　　　　Commander von Puttkamer.
　　　　　　　Chief of Staff, Naval Staff.

1. *Operation ' Sea Lion.'* The *C.-in-C., Navy*, requests a prompt decision on whether operation ' Sea Lion ' is to be carried out on the wide front proposed by the C.-in-C., Army, or on the narrow front proposed by *the C.-in-C., Navy*, as otherwise preparations will be held back. *The C.-in-C., Navy*, expresses his opinion on the memorandum of the C.-in-C., Army.

The C.-in-C., Navy, sums up as follows: in view of the limited means available for naval warfare and transport, operation ' Sea Lion ', as emphasized repeatedly, should be attempted only as a last resort, if Britain cannot be made to sue for peace in any other way.

The Fuehrer agrees completely.

Failure on our part would cause the British to gain

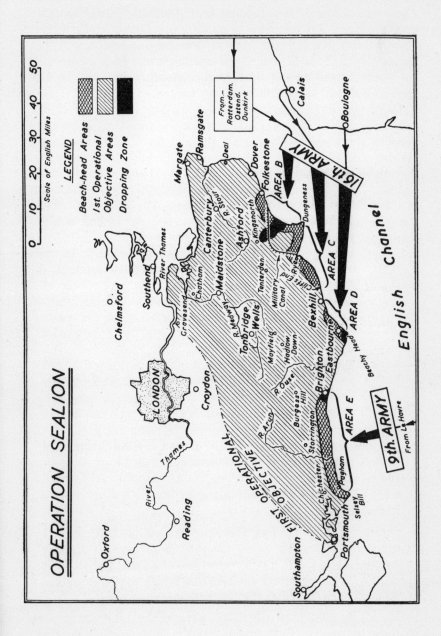

considerable prestige. We must wait and see what effect our intensive air attacks will have.

The Fuehrer will make a decision on 14 August after a conference with the C.-in-C., Army. . . ."

On the following day further discussions were held, and in the end a compromise was reached:

" Supreme Command.   Fuehrer's Headquarters,
Top Secret.   16/8/1940.
Subject : ' *Sea Lion.*'

1. On 15 August the following decisions were made by the Fuehrer:

(*a*) Preparations for the operation to take place on 15 September are to be continued. Final orders will not be given until the situation is clear.

(*b*) Preparations for a landing in Lyme Bay are to be abandoned, on account of the inadequate protection available in that area. Shipping is to be held in readiness along the coast between Ostend and Le Havre, thus avoiding congestion in the ports nearest to the enemy coast, and confusing the enemy as to our exact intentions.

(*c*) Dispositions should be made in such a manner as not to exclude the possibility of an attack on a narrow front, should this be ordered at the last minute, and to leave open the possibility of a single landing in the Brighton area.

2. Suggestions are also invited as to the possible employment of parachute and air-borne troops.

(Signed) KEITEL."

A further directive followed stating:

" Main crossing to be on narrow front, simultaneous landing of four to five thousand troops at Brighton by motor boats and the same number of air-borne troops at Deal–Ramsgate. In addition on D-1 day, the Luftwaffe is to make a strong attack on London, which would cause the population to flee from the city and block the roads."

On 27 August final decisions were made. Landings were to take place in four main areas: Folkstone–Dungeness; Dungeness–Cliff's End; Bexhill–Beachy Head; Brighton–Selsey

Bill. The first operational objective of the Army was a line from Southampton to the mouth of the Thames.

Deception measures were also planned, the principal being a feint landing on the North-East coast. This operation, under the code word ' Herbstreise ' (Autumn Journey), involved four transports escorted by four cruisers which, two days before ' Sea Lion ', were to proceed south from the area Bergen–Christiansand–the German Bight to the area between Aberdeen and Newcastle, and then to retreat at dusk back to the Kattegat. Other diversions were to be made towards Iceland, while the pocket-battleship, *Scheer*, was to make a commerce-raiding sortie into the Atlantic.

Meanwhile the Luftwaffe started their air operations on England. Their strength at the beginning of August amounted to 2669 operational aircraft of which 1015 were bombers, 346 dive bombers, 933 fighters, and 375 heavy fighters. Attacks were concentrated on the destruction of the R.A.F., and targets were selected which were the most likely to force large numbers of R.A.F. aircraft into battle, and only as a secondary consideration were invasion areas ' softened '.

On 1 September the movement of shipping from German North Sea ports to embarkation ports began. The Luftwaffe had announced at the end of August that the air situation was favourable in spite of the effect of bad weather on their operations. They estimated R.A.F. losses since 8 August at 1115 aircraft as opposed to their own losses of 467 aircraft. Control of the air therefore seemed likely, and on 3 September a directive from Fuehrer Headquarters stated the dates for the landing:

" Supreme Command.   Fuehrer's Headquarters,
                                              3/9/1940.
Top Secret.   8 *Copies*.
                                              2nd Copy.

Subject : Operation ' Sea Lion '.

The following dates for the completion of preparations for operation ' Sea Lion ' have been decided:
  (1) The earliest day for the sailing of the invasion fleet has been fixed as 20 September, and that of the landing for 21 September.

(2) Orders for the launching of the attack will be given on ' D. Day minus 10 ', presumably therefore on 11 September.

(3) Final commands will be given at the latest on ' D. Day minus 3 ' at mid-day.

(4) All preparations must remain liable to cancellation 24 hours before ' zero hour '.

(Signed) KEITEL."

German Intelligence, however, continued to give forbidding reports of anti-invasion preparations in England. On 5 September Admiral Canaris' Foreign Intelligence Department sent the following report to the Supreme Command of the Navy:

" *Foreign Intelligence Department.*   Berlin,
                                                        5/9/1940.

To : Supreme Command, Navy,
    Naval War Staff, Section 3.
Re : England. Fortifications on the South Coast.

A secret agent reported on 2 September:

The area Tunbridge Wells to Beachy Head, especially the small town of Rye (where there are large sand-hills) and also St. Leonards, is distinguished by a special labyrinth of defences. These defences, however, are so well camouflaged, that a superficial observer on the sand-hills, bathing spots and fields, would not discover anything extraordinary. This area is extremely well guarded, so that it is almost impossible to reach there without a special pass.

In Hastings, on the other hand, most of the defences can be recognized quite plainly. In the town there are troops of every kind. The presence of numerous small and heavy tanks is most striking.

Numerous armoured cars were also seen in St. Leonards and in a small locality where there is a famous golf-course, probably St. Joseph.

War Organization (*Espionage*) *Appendix* :

The agent was not able to give a clearer account of the number of armoured cars in the different localities, or of the regiments he saw there.

From the position of Beachy Head (west of Hastings) and

Rye (east of Hastings), it can be deduced that the place in question near St. Leonards was the western villa-suburb of Hastings. Tunbridge, which lies on the railway line from Hastings to London, according to the sense of the report, must also lie on the coast, but, as in the case of St. Joseph, this cannot be confirmed from the charts in our possession."

Judging from the standard of this report, it is not surprising to find that the German Intelligence Services miscalculated the size of the British Army.

Intelligence reports in fact assessed the available strength in England as:

320,000	trained troops
100,000	reserves
900,000	recruits
320,000	others (Home Guard, etc.)

Total: 1,640,000

Unconfirmed reports placed the number of divisions in England as 39, of which about 20 were regarded as completely operational, but whose artillery was believed to be at only half the normal strength.

These reports worried the German High Command, and in addition the preparation of barges was behind schedule. It was nevertheless decided to continue with the operation, but there was no longer the same anticipation of easy victory.

It was at about this time (beginning of September) that Hitler began to show his interest in the possibility of attacking Russia. There had been indications throughout the year that he was considering some such move, and on 27 August, while ordering the preparations for 'Sea Lion', he also decided to reinforce the Eastern Front.

(Extract from Supreme Command Directive, 27/8/1940.)

" 3. The present forces in Poland are to be strengthened immediately. For this:

(a) About 10 divisions are to be transferred to the East, but the necessary transport of supplies must not be impaired: and

(*b*) About 2 Armoured Divisions from the Homeland are
to be transferred to the extreme south-east area of
Poland as soon as the material situation permits.
The reinforcement of the new forces is in order to
guarantee the protection of the Roumanian oilfields
in the event of a sudden demand for intervention.

(Signed) KEITEL."

Hitler was still prepared to invade England, if necessary, but
other methods of attacking England had occurred to him and
he and his staff began to doubt whether ' Sea Lion ' was worth
the risk.

On 6 September, the war against England was reviewed:

" Commander-in-Chief, Navy.   Berlin,
Chief of the Naval Staff.   7 *September* 1940.

*Report of the Commander-in-Chief, Navy, to the Fuehrer
on the afternoon of 6 September 1940.*

Also present: Chief of Staff, Armed Forces High
Command.
General Jodl.
Commander von Puttkamer.

1. Current Naval Operations.   (*Details omitted.*)
2. *Operation ' Sea Lion ' :*
Information is given on transport space, the assembly
thereof, clearing of the harbours, fuel supplies, provision of
personnel, minesweeping and minelaying.   Relevant charts
are shown.   In summary: if air supremacy is increasingly
established it will be possible to meet the new deadline.   The
crossing itself will be very difficult.   The Army cannot rely
on being able to keep the divisions together.

The execution of operation ' Sea Lion ' appears possible,
if attended by favourable circumstances regarding air
supremacy, weather, etc.

In the north a diversionary manœuvre (a dummy landing)
is planned with four large ships from the German Bight, ten
ships from the Norwegian area, ?nd escort forces.

The *Hipper* is to operate in the Iceland area, in order to
relieve the dummy landing operation.

3. What are the Fuehrer's political and military directives if operation ' Sea Lion ' does not take place ?

It is hoped that maximum production in German industry will be re-established through release of the capacity now being used for operation ' Sea Lion ', the return of personnel and of the steamers, other vessels and barges. At the same time the appearance of an ' invasion of Britain ' should be kept up.

The Fuehrer agrees.

4. The Naval Staff's deliberations on further possibilities for warfare against Britain in addition to, or instead of, operation ' Sea Lion ' are as follows :

Gibraltar and the Suez Canal have decisive strategic significance for German-Italian warfare in the Mediterranean area.

Britain should be excluded from the Mediterranean. Control of the Mediterranean area is of vital importance to the position of the Central Powers in south-eastern Europe, Asia Minor, Arabia, Egypt and the African area. Unlimited sources for raw materials would be guaranteed. New and strategically favourable bases for further operations against the British Empire would be won. The loss of Gibraltar would mean crucial difficulties for British import traffic from the South Atlantic. Preparations for this operation must be begun at once so that they are completed before the U.S.A. steps in. It should not be considered of secondary import-ance, but as one of the main blows against Britain.

The Fuehrer gives orders to this effect.

5. *The Problem of the U.S.A. :*

In the present significant events, *i.e.* agreement between the U.S.A., Great Britain and Canada, the Naval Staff sees the beginnings of a situation which will necessarily lead to closer co-operation between Britain and the U.S.A. The course of events will be accelerated by the dangerous plight in which Britain finds herself. Britain will probably relinquish her leading position in favour of co-operation with the U.S.A. The British Empire is not expected to collapse, owing to the peculiar innate force of the political objectives embodied in the conception of the Commonwealth of Nations. The Empire will in all probability have to undergo the most drastic changes, but it will very likely re-emerge as an

Anglo-Saxon Empire. Understanding between the U.S.A. and Britain concerning Canada is a prerequisite for this.

This understanding has been reached.

The U.S.A.'s resolution to support the British war effort with the delivery of fifty destroyers represents an openly hostile act against Germany. It is not yet clear whether the United States, even in her present policy, is acting selfishly or in Anglo-Saxon interests. The leased islands are of great significance to the U.S.A. They represent a considerable gain in prestige and a decisive step forward in the pursuit of the Pan-American objective. The possibility of exerting influence on the South American countries is increased.

An examination of the possibilities for active participation in the war on the part of the U.S.A. leads to the following thoughts:

In the interest of her own position, the United States will hardly support the British motherland with significant amounts of material and personnel. Aircraft may be provided after American needs have been satisfied.

The United States may, however, occupy the Spanish and Portuguese Islands in the Atlantic, possibly even the British West African possessions, in an attempt to influence, and if necessary to take over, the French West African colonies.

Preparatory U.S. propaganda accuses Germany of action against French West African colonies, and points out that the German Air Force could take off from West Africa and fly across the South Atlantic to attack the United States.

The C.-in-C., Navy, stresses once more the extreme importance of Dakar for Germany in this war.

The danger of a British or American occupation of the Azores and Canary Islands is particularly great in the event that Spain or Portugal enters the war.

The Fuehrer therefore considers occupation of the Canary Islands by the Air Force both expedient and feasible. The question of supplies for the Air Force would present the only difficulty, as submarines cannot carry petrol. *The C.-in-C., Navy,* believes that tankers can reach the Canary Islands from Spain.

6. *Treatment of the French Colonies:*

In the French possessions in Equatorial Africa there is an open break with Petain's government and a swing over to

General de Gaulle. There is danger that unrest and revolt might spread to the French West African colonies. The economic situation in the colonies, particularly as regards foodstuffs, is used by Britain as a means of exerting pressure. An agreement between the colonies and Britain, and revolt against France would jeopardize our own chances of controlling the African area; the danger exists that strategically important West African ports might be used for British convoy activities and that we might lose a most valuable source of supplies for Europe. The danger of an attack on the part of the U.S.A. is not entirely out of the question, in view of the possibilities for such action.

Far-sighted German measures are necessary to counteract any development of this kind. Therefore the Naval Staff agrees in principle to sending French naval forces to the areas threatened; to the resumption of merchant traffic between the colonies and neutral countries by means of French and neutral vessels, in order to alleviate economic difficulties; and to the attempt to re-establish merchant shipping between France and her colonies.

A condition is that ships must be scuttled in the event of capture by British forces. Germany and Italy must have the possibility to control the vessels. There must be economic advantages to Germany and German right of recall.

7. *Relations to Occupied Territories and Neutral Countries :*
What are the Fuehrer's plans regarding treatment of the occupied northern areas and of Sweden and Finland ?
The Fuehrer conceives a north Germanic union in which the individual members have a certain sovereignty (diplomatic representation, etc.) and have armed forces trained and equipped by them but organized on the pattern of the German Armed Forces. Otherwise, however, they should be both politically and economically closely connected with Germany. These are the views of Quisling, whose standpoint the Fuehrer recognizes to be the correct one as opposed to that of Terboven, the Foreign Office, and von Falkenhorst; the Navy alone, moreover, held these views quite rightly from the very first.

(Signed) RAEDER."

On the day after this important conference (7 September)

the first heavy air raid was made on London. An entry in the War Diary stated: " The Supreme Command intends to bring about the complete destruction of London's harbours, docks, industries, and supplies by means of continuous air attacks, and so hasten the decision." The next day, 300 aircraft again raided London. Violent actions with the R.A.F. ensued, revealing the renewed strength of British fighter defence. The Luftwaffe was still elated and confident, but British sea and air attacks on the Channel ports and on minesweeping operations increased.

On 8 September the Luftwaffe stated:

" The attacks will be continued until the destruction of harbours, supplies and power installations is complete."

On 10 September, the day before Hitler was to have given the executive order for ' Sea Lion ', the Naval Staff reported:

" The weather conditions which for the time of year are completely abnormal and unstable, greatly impair transport movements and minesweeping activities for ' Sea Lion '. It is of decisive importance for the judgment of the situation, that no claim can be made to the destruction of the enemy air force over Southern England and the Channel area. The preparatory attacks of the Luftwaffe have achieved a perceptible weakening of enemy fighter defence, so that it can be taken for granted that the German forces have a considerable fighter superiority over the English area.

The English bombers, however, and the minelaying forces of the British Air Force, as the experiences of the last few days show, are still at full operational strength, and it must be confirmed that the activity of the British forces has undoubtedly been successful, even if no decisive hindrance has yet been caused to German transport movements. . . .

It would be more in the sense of the planned preparation for operation ' Sea Lion ', if the Luftwaffe would now concentrate less on London and more on Portsmouth and Dover, and on the naval forces in and near the operation area, in order to wipe out any possible threat from the enemy. The Naval War Staff, however, does not consider it suitable to approach the Luftwaffe or the Fuehrer now with such demands, because the Fuehrer looks upon a large-scale attack on London as possibly being decisive, and because a systematic and long drawn out bombardment of London might produce an attitude in the enemy which will make the ' Sea Lion ' operation completely unnecessary."

Hitler postponed his decision for three days, *i.e.* until 14 September. On 13 September the R.A.F. sank 80 barges at Ostend. Ships of the Royal Navy bombarded Calais, Boulogne, Ostend and Cherbourg, while light coastal forces attacked minesweepers and barges, and, on the same day as the R.A.F. attacked Ostend, capital ships of the Home Fleet moved south to Rosyth, in readiness to move to the invasion area. The Luftwaffe attacks continued, but weather hampered their activities.

On 14 September Hitler called his commanders together:

" *Conference between the Commander-in-Chief, Navy, and the Fuehrer in the afternoon of* 14 *September* 1940.

The Fuehrer has come to the conclusion that it would be wrong after all to call off operation ' Sea Lion ' altogether as he had apparently planned to do on 13 September. The air attacks have been very effective and would have been more so if the weather had been good. The degree of air supremacy necessary to justify executing operation ' Sea Lion ' has not yet been reached, however. For this reason operation ' Sea Lion ' is not yet practicable. If the pressure of the imminent landing were added to further air attacks, the total effect would be very strong after all. For not one attack is decisive, but the total effect produced. If operation ' Sea Lion ' were called off now, British morale would be lifted and our air attacks would be easier to bear.

The C.-in-C., Navy, agrees. He has always been of the opinion that operation ' Sea Lion ' should be the last resort and that the risk is very great. The situation in the air is not yet such as to reduce the risk involved to a minimum. Should operation ' Sea Lion ' fail, the British would gain a great amount of prestige, and the enormous effect of the air successes would be minimized. In the event of good weather the Air Force must first be given the opportunity to intensify the attacks, especially on London, regardless of operation ' Sea Lion.' These attacks may decide the outcome of the war. Operation ' Sea Lion ' must not be abandoned now, however, for the reasons given by the Fuehrer. The air situation can scarcely be expected to change to any great extent between 24 and 27 September as regards the safety of operation ' Sea Lion '; for this reason the operation should be postponed until 8 or 24 October.

If we wish to avoid loss of prestige, it will be permissible to abandon operation ' Sea Lion ' only at the moment of maximum air successes, on the grounds that it is no longer necessary.

The Fuehrer agrees, but he wishes to decide on 17 September whether the operation is to take place on 27 September or not.

The C.-in-C., Army, declares that the Army no longer attaches such great importance to a landing at dawn, so that the time element involved can be reconsidered. As far as *the C.-in-C., Navy*, can find out, this sudden change in the Army's initial stubborn demand can be traced to the fact that the front-line generals, like the Navy, are opposed to a night crossing.

In discussing the air attacks on London, *the C.-in-C., Navy*, supports the view of the Chief of the General Staff, Air, namely, that the attacks on targets of military importance will not suffice to produce mass psychosis and large-scale evacuation, since the residential areas are some distance from the docks, etc.

The Fuehrer, however, wishes to reserve deliberate attacks on residential areas as a final means of pressure and as reprisal for British attacks of this nature.

The C.-in-C., Navy, points out in this connection what a small area the port and dock installations and industrial sections cover in proportion to the gigantic area occupied by the residential part of London.

As soon as the positions of the heavy British coastal batteries have been established, they are to be attacked by dive bombers of the Air Force.

(Signed) RAEDER."

The result of this conference was a further postponement of the operation. A directive was issued from Hitler's Headquarters:

" Supreme Command.

Top Secret.

Berlin,
14 *September* 1940.
8 *Copies.*
2nd Copy.

At the conference with the Commanders-in-Chief of the Armed Forces on September 14 the Fuehrer had decided:
1. ' *Sea Lion.*'
> (*a*) The start of the operation is again postponed. A new order follows on September 17. All preparations are to be continued.
>
> (*b*) As soon as preparations are complete, the Luftwaffe is to carry out attacks against the British long-range batteries.
>
> (*c*) The measures planned for the evacuation of the coastal area are not to be set in motion to the full extent. Counter-espionage and deception measures are, however, to be increased.

2. *Air attacks against London.*

The air attacks against London are to be continued and the target area is to be expanded against military and other vital installations (*e.g.*, railway stations).

Terror attacks against purely residential areas are reserved for use as an ultimate means of pressure, and are therefore not to be employed at present.

(Signed) KEITEL."

Heavy air attacks by both sides continued for the next two days, and on 17 September an entry in the War Diary stated:

" The enemy Air Force is still by no means defeated; on the contrary it shows increasing activity. The weather situation as a whole does not permit us to expect a period of calm. . . . *The Fuehrer therefore decides to postpone* ' *Sea Lion* ' *indefinitely.*"

On 19 September, a Supreme Command directive was issued confirming the postponement. The Naval Staff summed up the situation:

" 1. The preparations for a landing on the Channel coast are extensively known to the enemy, who is taking more counter-measures. Symptoms are, for example, operational use of his aircraft for attacks and reconnaissance over the German operational harbours; frequent appearance of destroyers off the South Coast of England, in the Straits of Dover, and on the Franco-Belgian coast; stationing of his patrol vessels off the North coast of France; Churchill's last speech; etc.

2. The main units of the Home Fleet are being held in readiness to repel the landing, though the majority of the units are still in Western bases.

3. Already a large number of destroyers (30) has been located by air reconnaissance in the southern and south-eastern harbours.

4. All available information indicates that the enemy's naval forces are solely occupied with this theatre of operations."

Although there was still a possibility of invading in October, shipping was dispersed to prevent further losses. By 21 September the state of the invasion armada was:

	Shipping previously available.	Lost or damaged.
Transports . .	168	21 (*i.e.*, 12·5%)
Barges . . .	1,697	214 (*i.e.*, 12·6%)
Tugs . . .	360	5 (*i.e.*, 1·4%)

Troops and ships were kept at readiness until 12 October, when the operation was postponed until the spring of 1941.

" Supreme Command.   Fuehrer's Headquarters,
Top Secret.   12/10/1940.

1. The Fuehrer has decided that from now until the Spring, preparations for ' Sea Lion ' shall be continued solely for the purpose of maintaining political and military pressure on England.

Should the invasion be reconsidered in the Spring or early Summer of 1941, orders for a renewal of operational readiness will be issued later. In the meantime military conditions for a later invasion are to be improved. . . .

(Signed) KEITEL."

But, by the spring of 1941, Hitler and his staff were deeply involved in the preparations for invading Russia, and operation ' Sea Lion ' was shelved. It was finally cancelled in January 1942.

Chapter VII

PRELUDE TO RUSSIA (1)

" The Fuehrer and   Fuehrer Headquarters,
Supreme Commander.   18/12/40

Top Secret.   9 *Copies.*
                                           2nd Copy.

Directive No. 21

' *BARBAROSSA* '

The German Armed Forces must be prepared even before the end of the war against England to overthrow Soviet Russia in a rapid campaign (operation Barbarossa).

The Army will have to employ all available troops for this, with the limitation that the occupied territories must be secured against surprise. . . ."

So began Hitler's fateful order for the invasion of Russia. It was the result of at least eleven months' careful thought; it was also perhaps the biggest military blunder of all time. All Hitler's Commanders-in-Chief opposed the idea from the moment they realised it had been conceived: it was the only occasion on which they made a concerted stand against him, and Raeder felt so strongly on the matter that even after the order had been issued, he risked dismissal by continuing to protest. And yet, on paper, the plan looked feasible and necessary. The preceding events, the intelligence reports, the strategical considerations, the conflicting ideologies, seemed to Hitler to be reasons beyond dispute.

From January 1940, when Hitler refused to allow Raeder to fulfil some of Germany's naval obligations under the economic agreement with Russia, until the issue of the directive for ' Barbarossa ', Hitler's ideas developed steadily. They centred round two hard facts. The first was the Russo-Finnish war of 1939–40, which, to Hitler, was a striking demonstration of Russian weakness and Russian inefficiency; [1] the second was the Russian seizure of the Baltic states and Russian pressure on Bessarabia in June 1940. [1] The first event, coupled with subsequent intelligence reports disparaging Russian rearmament and the development of Russian industry, convinced Hitler that Russia could not withstand the German Wehrmacht. The second showed the potential dangers of Russian expansion—on the one hand threatening his position in Northern Europe, on the other threatening his principal oil supplies in Roumania. By the Machiavellian principles upon which Hitler based his whole political and diplomatic reasoning, it would have been criminally stupid to allow a potential enemy to increase in strength, if there was an opportunity to defeat him while he was still weak.

Hitler had realized that if he could conquer Britain and the British Empire first, the power and resources resulting from such a victory would have left him secure from any threat of Russian expansion. He had therefore been prepared to try the invasion of England before considering the conquest of Russia, but when operation ' Sea Lion ' virtually failed, operation ' Barbarossa ' became an urgent necessity.

The same reason—the failure of ' Sea Lion '—damned Hitler's plans in the eyes of his commanders. [2] To attack Russia while they were still at war with England seemed to them to be the height of folly. It would mean a war on two fronts, and eventual defeat would be certain. There was no immediate danger from Russia who was being pathetically anxious to sign a second economic agreement with Germany. Matsuoka, the Japanese Foreign Minister, had also indicated his willingness to sign a treaty with Russia, and surely, Hitler's commanders argued, it was only a matter of time before Russia could be included in the recently formed Axis Pact (27 September 1940). " Let us defeat England first," they said, " and then, if it is still necessary, we can attack Russia at our leisure."

But Hitler was adamant. The longer he waited, the stronger

Stalin would become. He felt himself master of diplomatic intrigue, and he was certain that, with proper political and military preparations, the conquest of Russia would be both sure and simple. There were also other considerations. He explained them to his commanders in a speech on 9 January 1941:

" Stalin must be regarded as a cold-blooded blackmailer; he would, if expedient, repudiate any written treaty at any time. Britain's aim for some time to come will be to set Russian strength in motion against us. If the U.S.A. and Russia should enter the war, the situation will become very complicated. Hence any possibility of such a threat developing must be eliminated. If the Russian threat were non-existent, we could wage war on Britain indefinitely. If Russia collapsed, Japan would be greatly relieved; this in turn would mean increased danger for the U.S.A."

Broadly Hitler's plans were to establish a firm control in the Balkans and to strengthen the defences of Western Europe; then, while the Navy and the Luftwaffe attacked England, the Army with additional air support was to carry out a lightning assault against Russia, reaching a front stretching from Archangel to the Caucasus within six months. Italy was to be responsible for the Mediterranean, and Japan was to exert pressure on the United States.

The control of the Balkans was the key to Hitler's offensive preparations. It was not only necessary to ensure the safety of Germany's vital oil supplies, but also an essential prelude to the attack on Russia. It was for this purpose that the movement of German troops towards Roumania had been ordered at the end of August.

In September Hitler continued his preparations by exerting strong pressure on Roumania, then, aided by General Antonescu and his pro-Nazi Iron Guard, German troops entered the country on 7 October, in the guise of a Military Mission and a ' Training Division.'

The next move was to contact King Boris of Bulgaria, and here again Hitler was assured of pro-Nazi support. He intended to entice the King into joining the Axis Pact, but, due to Russian pressure, King Boris demurred and would not accept the same open German infiltration as in Roumania.[2] For the moment,

Hitler agreed not to take any further steps as the preliminary negotiations had been satisfactory. He turned to other political preparations, and arranged conferences with Molotov and Petain—the one to be beguiled with assurances of friendship and a promise of the blessings of an economic agreement, the other to be persuaded or forced into maintaining peace in France.

On the military side, Hitler concentrated for the moment on the defence of Western Europe, partly deceiving his own commanders by his apparent acceptance of their ideas. For, after the postponement of ' Sea Lion ', both Raeder and Goering, strangely united in their efforts to dissuade Hitler from ' Barbarossa ', had suggested a ' great ' plan which involved the conquest of Gibraltar, the expulsion of the British from the Mediterranean, and the subsequent extension of German power to Africa, Egypt and Persia. As parts of this plan fitted in well with Hitler's requirements for the defence of Western Europe, he ordered them to be further investigated—emphasizing the need to conquer Gibraltar and to gain the use of Atlantic bases from Spain.[1] He stated that the French Fleet was to be prevented from breaking out; that attacks on British merchant shipping were to be increased to the fullest possible extent; that air raids on British ports and industries were to be intensified; and that no effort by the German Navy or the Luftwaffe was to be spared in making it impossible for the British to carry out any sort of attack on the continent of Europe. (These measures against the West also contained the germs of an idea for deceiving Russia by making it appear that Germany's real intentions were still directed towards the invasion of England.)

Suddenly, the whole situation was changed. On 28 October, without reference to Hitler, Mussolini invaded Greece.

The effect on Hitler was dramatic.[1] His anger knew no bounds. Not only had Mussolini invited attention where it was least wanted, but he had also undertaken the attack with inadequate and inferior troops. Hitler saw his plans about to be smashed by his closest ally.

Despite his fury, he did not falter. He had no intention of abandoning his attack on Russia, and for the next few days he considered how best to avoid the consequences of Mussolini's action.

By 4 November he had decided. Jodl reported the decision to Raeder's Chief Staff Officer, Operations, Admiral Fricke.[1] They were:

" *Egypt* : The Suez Canal to be mined, and bomber units to be sent to the assistance of the Italians.

Greece : Fighter aircraft to be sent immediately to Roumania, and two divisions of troops to be prepared if support for the Italian offensive was required.

Gibraltar : To be occupied as soon as possible. Co-operation with Franco to be arranged.

Canary and Cape Verde Islands to be occupied as part of the same operation.

France : No final decision. Laval and Ribbentrop to discuss political collaboration and military co-operation. ' The Fuehrer is, in principle, pursuing the definite policy of keeping France weak in order to eliminate any threat to the Axis. There is no doubt that France will be forced to meet the territorial demands of Germany and Italy.'

Russia : Preparations to be made for an Eastern campaign. No directive will be issued until fundamental plan for the Army is ready.

England : ' In the event of a change in the general situation the possibility or necessity of reconsidering operation ' Sea Lion ' might arise in the Spring of 1941.' "

As a result of these decisions, two major military operations were ordered, apart from the plans to attack Russia.

The first—' Marita '—was the invasion of Bulgaria and Yugoslavia, followed by the invasion of Greece. The second— ' Felix '—was the conquest of Gibraltar and the occupation of the Atlantic islands and Atlantic ports of the Iberian peninsula.

Preparations for these plans and Mussolini's action in Greece put the emphasis of the war on the Mediterranean, and Britain was quick to take the opportunity thus afforded. Ever since the Napoleonic wars control of the Mediterranean had been traditional British policy, and even before the attack on Greece, Britain had been building up her strength there at sea and on land. On 14 November, two weeks after the attack on Greece, Raeder presented Hitler with a memorandum [1] pointing out how the Italian offensives in Libya and Greece were being paralysed by British sea power, and how, if Italian naval and air forces were not reinforced, the British Fleet would play havoc with their military operations. They had already damaged a large part of the Italian Fleet at Taranto.

Hitler was unconvinced, and he decided to leave the control of the Mediterranean still in Italian hands. He would not consider any additional moves for their support. The air action against the Suez Canal and the intended transfer of two divisions to Albania were all that he could do for the moment. He hastened his political preparations for the attack on Russia instead.

On 16 November Molotov, the Soviet Foreign Minister, arrived in Berlin. [1] He came for the preliminary negotiations on the second economic agreement with Germany, but the opportunity was taken to discuss many other aspects of Russo-German relations. German activities in the Balkans were explained to him as being in support of Italy, and it was hinted that there would be no German objection if Russia should choose to expand to Persia. Molotov in his turn announced his intention of concluding a pact with Japan. The series of conferences was handled with skill by the Germans, and Hitler himself saw Molotov several times, giving every evidence of his desire for closer relations with Russia.

On 17 November, the day after Molotov's arrival in Berlin, King Boris of Bulgaria attended Hitler at Berchtesgaden, and preparations were made for German military intervention in Bulgaria.

Finally, in Roumania, further political preparations were completed. On 27 November the Iron Guard struck. The ex-Prime Minister, Professor Jorga, was murdered, and Antonescu assumed dictatorial powers. Hitler had set the political stage in the Balkans within four weeks of Mussolini's blunder. Russia had been beguiled, and Nazi puppets were installed in Roumania and Bulgaria. He could send his troops in as soon as they were ready.

Although Hitler was succeeding in the Balkans, his disregard of the Mediterranean was beginning to make itself felt. British sea, air and land forces had been further reinforced, and, on 9 December 1940, General Wavell began the first offensive in the Western Desert, supported by carefully co-ordinated sea and air attacks on Italian shipping and supplies. General Wavell had only 30,000 troops, but these 30,000 drove the Italians before them at a speed which put new heart into the conquered nations of Europe.

The first effect was noticed in France. Reports to the German

High Command indicated an awakening from the apathy which-
had overwhelmed the French after their defeat. General Weygand
in the colonies, and General de Gaulle in England were rallying
supporters to their sides, and it looked as though even the
' non-belligerent ' status which Hitler had imposed on Vichy
France could not be maintained. The following order was
issued :

" The Fuehrer and   Fuehrer
   Supreme Commander of the Armed Forces. Headquarters.
                                            10/12/1940.
Top Secret.   12 *Copies.*
                                              2nd Copy.

Directive No. 19.

OPERATION ' ATTILA '.

1. Should revolts occur in parts of the French Colonial
Empire now under the command of General Weygand,
preparations must be made for the speedy occupation of
the territories of the French motherland which are still
unoccupied. (Operation ' Attila '.)
At the same time, it will be necessary for the French
Home Fleet and that part of the French Air Force which is
on home airfields to be secured, or at least hindered from
going over to the side of the enemy.
Preparations must be camouflaged in order to avoid
alarming the French. . . ."

A second effect of the British operations in the Mediterranean
was to make Spain hesitate to join Germany. Franco told
Hitler early in December that unless Germany could supply
Spain with the goods she had been accustomed to receive from
Britain, Spain would be unable to co-operate with Germany in
the conquest of Gibraltar. Hence, on 11 December, Hitler
postponed operation ' Felix '—the conquest of Gibraltar. He
was further forced to send Luftwaffe formations to Italy to help
in attacks on the British Fleet, and he was also considering the
formation of an ' Afrika Korps '.
By mid-December, however, Hitler felt that he had forestalled
the possible results of the British operations. Plans for the
invasion of Bulgaria, Yugoslavia, and Greece were well in hand,

and he expected to be able to give the order to advance by the end of March. The German Navy and the Luftwaffe were attacking Britain with such force that he thought British intervention in Europe unlikely, while the military preparations for the occupation of Vichy France would ensure the suppression of a rising of the French. He decided that he could begin planning the military moves of his principal operation, ' Barbarossa,' without further ceremony.

But the situation was not as favourable as Hitler supposed. Raeder reported on 27 December 1940:

" The enemy has assumed the initiative at all points and is everywhere conducting successful offensive actions—in Greece, Albania, Libya, and East Africa; in addition an imminent and effective attack on the Italian Dodecanese islands may be expected—all the result of Italy's serious blunder. The Axis threat to Egypt, and thus to Britain's position in the entire Eastern Mediterranean, in the Near East and in the North African area has been eliminated with one stroke."

Raeder went on to explain that it was a question of defeating British naval and air power, and he attempted to drive home to Hitler the meaning of Italian losses and defeats. He insisted that the German Navy and Luftwaffe should be given priority over everything else for their attacks against England. He suggested that it would be folly to carry out ' Barbarossa ' before England had been defeated.

Hitler agreed only to increase U-boat production. He stated emphatically that it was essential to eliminate Russia ' at all costs '—a phrase which was to become increasingly familiar—before beginning the assault on Britain. Later, when Russia had been conquered, everything would be concentrated on the needs of the Luftwaffe and the German Navy.

Raeder's doubts were probably voiced by others as well, in spite of the fact that the directive for ' Barbarossa ' had already been issued, and on 8 and 9 January 1941 Hitler held a general conference with his Commanders-in-Chief and Reichministers at the Berghof, his mountain retreat at the Obersalzberg. He spent most of the two days talking to them. Raeder's notes give an outline of what was said:

" The Fuehrer is of the opinion that it is vital for the

outcome of the war that Italy does not collapse, but remains
a loyal member of the Axis. The Duce is emphatically
pro-Axis. . . . The well-known Italian mentality makes it
difficult for the Germans to influence the Italian leaders,
but he (the Fuehrer) must not go too far in the matters of
leadership. We should not make demands; too great
demands may cause even Mussolini to change his attitude.
. . . The Fuehrer considers that caution is necessary, and
he does not wish to inform the Italians of our plans. There
is great danger that the Royal Family is transmitting intelligence to Britain ! . . . The Fuehrer is determined to do
everything in his power to prevent Italy from losing North
Africa. . . . German formations are to be transferred as
soon as possible. . . . The Italian line in Albania must be
held. The Greeks must not be allowed to mass against
Bulgaria. The Fuehrer orders that sufficient troops be
transferred, *i.e.*, two and a half divisions."

So much he conceded to his critics. Then he outlined his
intentions to 'carry out operation ' Marita ', the occupation of
Bulgaria and Yugoslavia. From the Balkans he turned to
France :

" If France becomes troublesome she will have to be
crushed completely. Under no circumstances must the
French Fleet be allowed to get away from us ; hence Toulon
must be occupied at the very outset. . . ."

At the end of the two-day conference Hitler summed up his
general opinions of the situation :

" I am firmly convinced," he said, " that the situation in
Europe can no longer develop unfavourably for Germany
even if we should lose the whole of North Africa. Our
position is so firmly established in Europe that the outcome
cannot possibly be to our disadvantage. The invasion of
Britain is not feasible unless she is crippled to a considerable
degree, and Germany has complete air superiority. The
success of an invasion must be absolutely assured, otherwise
it would be a crime to attempt it. The British can hope to
win the war only by beating us on the Continent. I am
convinced that this is impossible. Attacks on Britain must
be concentrated on supplies and the armament industry.

Terror raids by the Luftwaffe have small value and accomplish little; the supplies and the ships bringing them must be destroyed. Combined assaults by the Luftwaffe and the Navy on imports might lead to victory as early as July or August. Even to-day I am still ready to negotiate peace with Britain. However, Britain's present leaders will not consider such a peace.

Britain is sustained in her struggle by hopes placed in the U.S.A. and Russia. British diplomatic overtures to Russia are apparent. Eden is very pro-Russian."

Having convinced his audience of his continued interest in the West and the absence of any real danger from that quarter, he outlined his strategical reasons for attacking Russia—the reasons given at the beginning of this chapter. There were no more protests from his commanders, and on 30 January the draft plans for 'Barbarossa' were submitted, directing the vast German war machine towards the forthcoming attack on Russia.

Chapter VIII

PRELUDE TO RUSSIA (2)

THE activity in the German High Command at this time was intense. The complicated series of operations planned by Hitler involved considerable military and political preparations. The chance of the failure of political moves had to be guarded by complementary military plans. Every effort was being made to avoid a war on two fronts, but the possibility had to be taken into account and resulted in complex schemes covering every theatre of war.

Four principal operations were either planned or prepared. These were:

MARITA—The conquest of Bulgaria, Yugoslavia and Greece.
BARBAROSSA—The invasion of Russia.
Unnamed (later AIDA)—Support for Italians in Tripolitania, possibly leading to conquest of Egypt.
ATTILA—Occupation of unoccupied France.

There were as well the continual naval and air attacks against British imports and British industries; the postponed operation 'Sea Lion', preparations for which were maintained as a deception for both England and Russia; and operation 'Felix'—the conquest of Gibraltar, which was in abeyance, but which had to be kept up to date.

Hitler concentrated on the Balkans and Russia, leaving the defences of Western Europe to the local commanders. In the Mediterranean the policy was laid down that full-scale operations would not begin until the autumn of 1941,[1] which was the estimated date for the completion of 'Barbarossa'. Then Gibraltar, Malta, and Suez were to be taken, and the British were to be finally driven out.

Meanwhile, in Libya, British forces continued their rapid advance. Benghazi was captured on 6 February, and the Italian position became desperate. The German High Command had to act, and orders were issued for the Afrika Korps and Luftwaffe squadrons in Sicily to be reinforced—the Luftwaffe in particular was instructed to intensify air attacks on British naval forces and on Malta, and to make the Straits of Sicily impassable.

Better news came from France where agents' reports indicated some improvement in the French attitude towards Germany. The following is a typical report sent from Admiral Canaris, head of the Foreign Intelligence Department, to the Naval Staff:

" Foreign Intelligence Dept.   Berlin,
Top Secret.   10/2/1941.
          Subject: *France. Naval Morale.*

Secret agent reported to-day:

My personal impression from Toulon. The morale and mood has been raised considerably since last time, especially by the increase of pay in the Navy. Security and anti-espionage measures are at present rather pronounced. . . .

People hate the English, but hope for the improvement in France's position through the ultimate victory of England. The German war efforts are respected without any friendliness towards Germany being in question. On the whole, however, the average sailor has had a ' belly-full ' and does not wish to hear any more about this war. To speak of a ' good morale ' would certainly be going too far. The food on board ship since the Armistice has been very moderate."

On 9 February Admiral Darlan became Vice-Premier of the Vichy Government, and on 13 February Petain met Franco at Montpelier. No records of the meeting are available, but together with the intelligence reports and the changes in the Vichy Government, they must have given relief to the German High Command, for, on the next day, 14 February, it was decided to disperse the forces which had been assembled for operation ' Attila '.

Hitler's plans for the Balkans were now ready. On 28 February German troops crossed the Danube and, with the connivance of King Boris, completed the occupation of Bulgaria in one day.

Three weeks later final preparations were completed for the second part of operation ' Marita '; but on 27 March, the day the German troops were to have invaded Yugoslavia, there was a sudden revolution, and King Peter took over the government. Hitler temporarily postponed the invasion until new plans to meet this development had been completed, and on 6 April German troops crossed the frontier into Yugoslavia and Greece.

The Germans advanced with the usual speed of the ' blitzkrieg ' and by 17 April the Yugoslav Army had capitulated. King Peter was evacuated by the Royal Air Force from Kotor.

These events in the Balkans caused considerable alarm in Russia. On 4 April, however, Matsuoka, the Japanese Foreign Minister, had visited Hitler in Berlin on his way to Moscow, where he was about to conclude the Russo–Japanese neutrality pact. Hitler, anticipating that Russia would be alarmed by his moves in the Balkans, primed Matsuoka with encouraging words which were to be passed on to the Kremlin. Hitler later told Raeder what he had done: [1]

" Matsuoka was informed that Russia will not be attacked as long as she maintains a friendly attitude in accordance with the treaty (*i.e.* the Russo-German non-aggression pact). If she does not, then I reserve the right to take suitable action. The Russo-Japanese pact was concluded with Germany's acquiescence. The stand I have taken has had a salutary effect on the attitude of Russia, who will now conduct herself with great correctness and who expects no attack for the present."

The effect of this message was to allay Russian fears, especially as she had just concluded a neutrality pact with yet another member of the Axis powers. Nevertheless, the Soviet Council of War under Timoshenko, ordered military preparations to be made along the whole length of what was now the Russo–German frontier.*

The German forces from Yugoslavia joined those in Greece, and on 21 April the Greek Government informed Britain of their inability to resist further. They asked British forces to withdraw. Evacuation began on 22 April, and by 26 April, the German Army had captured the isthmus and town of Corinth. They entered Athens on the following day. British forces rallied on the island of Crete.

An immediate operation against the island was ordered. Goering was placed in command and the attack began on the morning of 20 May. It was at first entirely by air, and the depleted defences of Crete were quickly swamped by the weight of the German parachute and air forces. Ships of the British Fleet fought gallantly in an effort to keep the troops on the island supplied with food and munitions, but by 27 May the situation was hopeless, and by 1 June evacuation of the remaining British troops was completed.

With the conquest of Crete, Hitler completed his campaign in the Balkans. He was at last ready to carry our operation ' Barbarossa '. It had been his original intention to begin the attack on Russia in the middle of May, but the British actions in the Mediterranean and the Balkans had delayed him one month, a delay which was later partly responsible for preventing the German Army from completing its eastern campaign before the onslaught of winter.

* The German Naval Attaché in Moscow reported on 24 April that the British Ambassador, Sir Stafford Cripps, had prophesied that Germany would attack Russia on 22 June. This prophesy subsequently proved to be entirely correct.

Chapter IX

THE BATTLE OF THE ATLANTIC (2)

THE 'BISMARCK' ACTION

IN the Supreme Command's plans for the invasion of Russia Hitler had imposed upon Raeder the responsibility for preventing the British from starting a Second Front. Raeder, with his knowledge of British power and resources, had taken his responsibility heavily. The U-boat branch was still nowhere near what he considered the minimum strength for success—there were only about thirty operational boats—and he could not fulfil his task unless he threw into the battle the whole weight of the German Navy. He had done this in the Norwegian campaign and escaped with comparatively light losses, but in the Atlantic it would be a different matter. To minimize the risk he decided to adopt the hit-and-run tactics of the 'Kreuzerkrieg' (cruiser war) which he had learnt so successfully under his old tutor, Admiral von Hipper.

Beginning in December 1940, Raeder mustered all the available major units of the High Seas Fleet and the total strength of operational U-boats for an all-out attack on Britain's supplies. Harbours and bases in France and Norway were prepared so that attacks could be spread over as wide an area as possible, and an intelligence and supply organization was created. Small merchant ships were sent out into mid-Atlantic as reconnaissance ships to report the presence of Allied convoys to the lurking raiders, while a complicated system of tankers and supply ships was arranged so that the major warships would not have to run the gauntlet in and out of European harbours too frequently. An additional radio intelligence system was established in Germany to help in the location of British merchant shipping; and with its aid the area commanders—Group North, covering the North Atlantic, Group West, covering the Channel and West Atlantic, and the Admiral Commanding U-boats—exercised a loose, general control over the operations from their headquarters on shore.

Raeder's organization and plans met with considerable success.

The battleships, *Scharnhorst* and *Gneisenau*, the pocket battleship, *Scheer*, and the heavy cruiser, *Hipper*, operated in the North and West Atlantic, sinking 187,662 tons (37 ships) in the first quarter of 1941. During the same period, the armed merchant raiders, about six in all, operating in the South Atlantic and Indian Oceans sank 114,905 tons (25 ships), while the 30 U-boats accounted for 554,408 tons (97 ships).

High as this total was, it was not nearly enough to disrupt British imports completely, and the Royal and Merchant Navies of Britain not only fought England's supplies through, but were able to reinforce the Mediterranean as well.

At a conference with Hitler in May, Raeder gave a full description of the progress of the battle and its implications:

" *Conference of the Commander-in-Chief, Navy, with the Fuehrer at the Berghof, on 22 May 1941.*

Also present : Chief of Staff, Supreme Command (Keitel).
General Jodl.
Captain von Puttkamer.
The Foreign Minister (Ribbentrop).

1. SITUATION.

(*a*) *Submarine warfare :* Since the beginning of May there has been a further increase in the number of ships sunk by our submarines. Eleven boats are at present in the northern operational area and seven are in the southern. During the last few days ships totalling about 85,000 tons were sunk from a convoy. The enemy has adopted a very flexible convoy system, combined with a far-reaching and excellent direction-finding network. The reports are evaluated very rapidly for the purpose of convoy control. Enemy defence of convoys has been strengthened; a close watch of the area west of Britain is being kept by air reconnaissance, anti-submarine groups, surface forces, and single ships. The losses incurred by us in March and April made it necessary to move the submarines further out into the Atlantic. Successful U-boat operations have been carried out off the West African coast near Freetown. One boat has been sent on a minelaying mission in the Takoradi-Lagos area.

(*b*) *Cruiser warfare :* Four auxiliary cruisers are still on operations—one in the South Atlantic and three in the Indian Ocean. Ship ' 10 ' (Captain Kaehler) returned to

Hamburg after nearly eleven months' operations. The ship sank 96,000 tons. Actions were fought with three superior enemy auxiliary cruisers, one of which was sunk and the other two badly damaged.

Ship ' 33 ' (Captain Krueder) sank at noon on May 8 in the Indian Ocean west of Somaliland after an action with the heavy British cruiser *Cornwall*, which has eight 20·3 cm. guns. Only 53 survivors were taken prisoner. The enemy himself reported damage to the *Cornwall* during the action.

The Commanding Officer's character is a sufficient guarantee that ship ' 33 ' fought a gallant battle after vainly trying to escape from the enemy cruiser by using deception.

The successes of ship ' 33 ' amounted to 120,000 tons, including several prizes totalling 50,000 tons brought to home waters. Three large whale ships from the Antarctic, carrying 22,000 tons of whale oil, were among the prizes. At least twelve further ships were captured before the action with the *Cornwall*. Minelaying missions in Australian waters were brilliantly executed. The total success of ship ' 33 ' exceeds that of the cruiser *Emden* or the auxiliary cruiser *Wolf* in the First World War.

It is proposed that these facts, together with the name of this outstanding captain, should be mentioned and given recognition in one of the next reports of the Supreme Command.

The Fuehrer agrees. He also agrees to announce the loss of Lieutenant-Commander Prien at a time when substantial U-boat successes are reported.

The supply ship *Dresden* put into harbour in southern France with 140 Americans, some of them women and children, who were taken on board an auxiliary cruiser during the capture of an Egyptian ship. It is inexcusable for the U.S. government to allow American citizens, including women and children, to travel in ships belonging to belligerents.

The captain of the *Dresden* treated the American passengers with great consideration so that no protests are likely.

(c) *Fleet warfare against merchant shipping :* The *Bismarck* and the *Prinz Eugen* task force is en route to its mission in the Atlantic; the ships left Norwegian waters near Bergen on May 21. The purpose of the operation is war against merchant shipping in the North and Middle Atlantic.

(d) *German merchant shipping:* Of the four blockade runners sent to South America, the first is on the return voyage and will arrive at the end of May, the remaining three are discharging and taking on cargo in Brazil. Up to now goods valued at 19 million reichsmarks have been exported.

Two German merchant ships, carrying 7000 tons of rubber in all, are at present en route from Mairen. In a few days a third one will follow with an additional 4000 tons. The first vessel is to arrive about the end of June; she will proceed by way of Cape Horn.

Five vessels put out from Chile to Japan.

2. The enemy's air forces are very active in attacking German convoy and coastal traffic. Until now they have achieved no great success, and our defence forces have had good results shooting down aircraft.

$$. \qquad . \qquad . \qquad . \qquad . \qquad .$$

11. ITALIAN SUBMARINES.

The C.-in-C., Navy, once again requests the withdrawal of Italian submarines from the Atlantic. The time is propitious, since they are urgently needed in the Eastern Mediterranean.

The Foreign Minister proposes to raise this point with Count Ciano or that the Fuehrer should discuss it at his next meeting with the Duce, which is to take place soon.

The Fuehrer agrees.

12. *The C.-in-C.* asks the Fuehrer for his opinion on Japan's attitude, as he is under the impression that the Japanese are rather cool. (Nomura is negotiating in Washington !)

At present *the Fuehrer* has no clear picture of the situation, but obviously there are internal political difficulties in Japan.

The good friendship policy is to be continued.

The C.-in-C. reports on information received from Admiral Nomura regarding new ships built by the Japanese.

The Fuehrer emphasizes the necessity for complete secrecy.

$$. \qquad . \qquad . \qquad . \qquad .$$

14. *The C.-in-C.* states that very careful and detailed preparations have been made for holding back the important materials to be delivered to Russia. The Russian Navy will be informed in the near future that the German Navy is having to draw on some of the things in view of the state

of emergency, so that slight delays will occur, but that deliveries as a whole are not jeopardized.

The Fuehrer agrees. The Foreign Minister has been informed.

15. *The C.-in-C.* reports that it will take eight months to complete the construction of the aircraft carrier, including installations of anti-aircraft guns, if the work is resumed at the conclusion of operation ' Barbarossa '. An additional year will be needed for trials. As soon as it has been definitely decided to continue this work, the Fuehrer should order Reichsmarschall Goering to make the necessary aircraft available in time.

(Signed) RAEDER."

It was instinctive caution that made Raeder play down the operation upon which the *Bismarck* and *Prinz Eugen* had just sailed, and his remarks belied the great hopes which he and the Naval Staff had placed upon this task force. It was the climax of their Atlantic operations. The most modern and most powerful German battleship with the equally modern cruiser were detailed for a three months' sortie which was going to smash Britain's Atlantic trade. The ships had started training at the end of February, as soon as the ice in the Baltic had melted, and no effort had been spared to make them as efficient and as seaworthy as possible. The organization of reconnaissance ships and tankers in the Atlantic had been specially overhauled, and a large number of U-boats had been sent out to support the operation, which had been given the name of ' Rheinuebung ' (Rhine exercise).

The two ships slipped from Bergen on 21 May, and, sheltering close inshore to the Norwegian coast, made their way north about Iceland, intending to break through the Denmark Straits and thus into the Atlantic. The task force was under the command of Admiral Gunther Luetjens who flew his flag in the *Bismarck* and who was one of the most experienced and ablest officers of the German Navy.

The absence of the German Force was reported on the following day by naval air reconnaissance to the British Home Fleet, who promptly made dispositions to meet this serious threat. The patrol of two cruisers in the Denmark Straits was alerted, and a small force consisting of the battle cruiser H.M.S. *Hood* and the battleship H.M.S. *Prince of Wales* sailed to intercept.

The story of what followed is well known. The German ships were sighted on the evening of 23 May by the cruisers who were on patrol. They reported their position and shortly after 5 o'clock on the morning of 24 May the British battle fleet engaged the enemy. H.M.S. *Hood* opened fire first, followed immediately by the *Prince of Wales*. *Bismarck* replied quickly and accurately, hitting the *Hood* with her second or third salvo. After a few moments the *Hood* blew up with a tremendous explosion, and sank within five minutes. Soon afterwards the *Prince of Wales* was also hit and temporarily broke off the action.

For the next two days the British cruisers, *Norfolk* and *Suffolk*, with the damaged *Prince of Wales*, maintained contact until other British warships had time to reach the area. In the *Bismarck's* log, which was reconstructed for Hitler's benefit, the efficiency of the British cruisers is recorded by the most frequent signal *Bismarck* made: 'Gegner haelt fuehlung' (enemy keeps in touch). The British ships made much use of their radar apparatus, but they did in fact lose contact on the second night. Admiral Luetjens, who realized that they were using radar and therefore thought radio silence unnecessary, kept up a continuous stream of radio traffic, and it was comparatively easy for the Admiralty in London to plot her position, informing the British ships, and enabling a Coastal Command aircraft to find her again.

The *Bismarck* was finally brought to bay on the night of 26/27 May after a hit from a naval aircraft torpedo had damaged her rudder. After fighting off destroyer attacks throughout the night and attacks from British battleships and cruisers from dawn onwards, she was sunk at 10.30 a.m. on 27 May by torpedoes from H.M.S. *Dorsetshire*.

Raeder had made every effort to save her. U-boats had been ordered from all parts of the Atlantic to converge on her, and the Luftwaffe had been instructed to organize all possible help. It is recorded by one U-boat that she sighted the British battleship, *King George V*, and the aircraft carrier, *Ark Royal*, within four hundred yards on 26 May, but, as she had fired all her torpedoes attacking merchant ships the previous day, she had been power- less to do anything to stop the British ships. It was an aircraft from the *Ark Royal* that put the *Bismarck's* rudder out of action and so enabled her to be caught.

A few survivors from the *Bismarck*, apart from the odd 150 who were rescued by British ships, were picked up by U-boats and reconnaissance ships which had collected at the scene of the action. They were interrogated on their return to Germany, and the following report was made by one of the survivors:

> " *Statement made by Ordinary Seaman Herbert Manthey*
> *of the battleship* Bismarck.

(Rescued by U-74.)

Friday, 23/5/1941.

About 1700 a smoke cloud was sighted. I was at my action station, No. 5 Starboard 2 cm. gun. Immediately afterwards an enemy cruiser opened fire. The cruiser was astern. *Bismarck* replied with turrets C and D. I don't know how many salvoes were fired. The cruiser thereupon turned off but maintained contact. On the loudspeaker system it was announced that the enemy cruiser had radioed *Bismarck's* position. Half an hour later it was announced that the enemy cruisers were shooting at each other. After that we were relieved. The night was quiet.

Saturday, 24/5/1941.

At about 0600 on Saturday it was announced over the ship's broadcast system that smoke clouds had been sighted. Action stations were sounded. Shortly afterwards the smoke could be seen with the naked eye. A few minutes later the first enemy ship opened fire. Then *Bismarck* and a second enemy ship opened fire. The two forward turrets fired against the *Hood* while the after turrets fired against the *King George V.** The names of the enemy ships were announced after the action. While the firing was going on, the anti-aircraft crews were sent under cover because of splinters and blast from our own guns. Out of interest in the battle, however, many of my shipmates remained on deck amidships and in the superstructure. I myself was under cover (deck house). Soon after our second salvo had been fired it was announced: 'enemy is burning'; after the third salvo: 'enemy has exploded'. During this engagement with the *Hood*, the after turrets had been scoring hits on *King George V* which thereupon turned off. *Hood* was sunk at about the same time. The general enthusiasm was

---

* Really *Prince of Wales*. She was mistaken for her sister ship throughout the action.

great. It became still greater when it was announced from the bridge that the enemy were the largest British battleships. Now I heard that yet another enemy cruiser was firing on us. The engagement lasted for another ten minutes. At the end of the action we learned that *Bismarck* had received three hits. In my opinion these three hits were caused by the last enemy cruiser. One hit in the ship's side (bows); the second went through the starboard picket boat and detonated in the water; and shipmates told me that the third hit had gone into the port oil bunker. I went there myself and saw that oil was pouring out and was also spilled on the upper deck. The damage itself was under water and could not be seen. This was about two hours later. The forecastle lay deeper in the water and the ship had a very slight list to port. A gunner's mate who belonged to my gun said that only the ship's side had been torn open; others maintained that the shell had gone through but had not exploded.

The sea was calm and visibility was good. The ship reduced speed and a collision mat was got out on the forecastle and divers went down into the ship to find out the damage. They succeeded in making a pipe connection to the oil bunkers so that the oil could be pumped aft. They also succeeded in stopping the leak. As far as I can remember the outboard work took about two hours. The ship then increased speed again. During this time pumping was started below decks. It went on the whole day and night. During the morning I noticed the forecastle slowly rising again.

At about 2300 three flights (27 aircraft) * tried to attack. First they tried together from port, and then they attacked singly from starboard, ahead, and astern. All available guns including the main turrets participated in the defence. The attack lasted about an hour and altogether five aircraft (according to my shipmates) were shot down. This was confirmed on the order transmission system. I do not know how many aircraft were actually shot down. They only scored one torpedo hit, starboard amidships, below the aircraft catapult. The torpedo detonated on the ship's side and left merely scratches on the paintwork. Leading Seaman Kirchberg was thrown by the blast against the hangar and

* From H.M.S. *Victorious*.

killed. This was the first fatal casualty on board. I do not know if any other shipmates were injured.

Shortly after the engagement with the aircraft, *King George V* opened fire on us. *Bismarck* returned the fire with one or two salvoes. As far as I know no hits were scored by either side. The night was quiet.

On the warning telephone it was announced that the enemy were maintaining contact.

Prinz Eugen * I saw for the last time during the action with the *Hood*. At noon nothing could be seen of her.

Sunday, 25/5/1941.

At about 0300 it was announced through the warning telephone that of the 27 aircraft which had attacked us only one had returned to the carrier.

The forecastle was again low in the water. Owing to the violent manœuvres during the air attack the collision mats had broken. Speed was again reduced. The sea was fairly rough.

At about noon the Fleet Commander † spoke to the crew. As far as I can remember he said among other things: ' We did not intend to fight enemy warships but to wage war against merchant shipping. Through treachery the enemy managed to find us in the Denmark Straits. We took up the fight. The crew have behaved magnificently. We shall win or die.'

After the speech of the Fleet Commander the situation became clear to the crew and the mood became serious.

On Sunday afternoon a second funnel was built. On this occasion the spirits of the crew rose again. It was piped that the non-duty watch was to go into the second funnel to smoke.

Otherwise nothing special occurred on Sunday.

Monday, 26/6/1941.

After the air attack on Saturday both watches ate and slept on their stations. The stations were not left again until the sinking.

Enemy shadowing aircraft (2) maintained contact from Monday morning onwards. Sometimes they tried to approach closer but were each time forced to turn off by

* *Prinz Eugen* was detached during the afternoon of 24 May to carry out merchant warfare on her own.
† Admiral Luetjens.

anti-aircraft fire. In the evening between 2100 and 2200
' repel aircraft ' stations was sounded. There were 16 enemy
aircraft. They did not try to attack but flew off again. We
did not open fire. About 10 minutes later I saw three enemy
aircraft (bi-planes) approach our ship from the clouds.
Immediately afterwards aircraft approached us from all
sides. I do not know the exact number. I felt two heavy
shakings in the ship, one shortly after the other. The attacks
were dive-bombing attacks coming from the clouds down to
about 10 to 20 metres above the water. We thought the
attacks were made very pluckily. Seven aircraft were shot
down.

It was announced: ' Rudder jammed hard to starboard.
Ship goes in circles '. In my opinion one torpedo hit went
aft into the steering compartment and another hit near
compartments VII–VIII. Through the telephone I heard
that divers were trying to couple in the hand rudder. After
20–30 minutes we heard that the hand rudder had been
coupled in. Shortly afterwards a second report: ' Rudder
absolutely clear again '.

Enemy destroyers attacked at about midnight. Action
stations were sounded. I remember the action started on
the port quarter and shifted to the starboard side. At this
time it was announced that one destroyer was sinking and
two more were burning.* I myself did not see anything of
this. During action stations the enemy continuously fired
starshells. Occasionally it became as light as day.

On Monday night various congratulatory telegrams arrived,
among them one from the Fuehrer awarding the Knight's
Cross of the Iron Cross to the senior Gunnery Officer.†
The Captain read these telegrams to the crew. Furthermore
81 aircraft were promised for the next day. One U-boat
was supposed to be very near us and all U-boats had been
warned. One tanker and two tugs were also on the way to
help us.

These announcements lifted the morale of the crew again.
Many sang. Otherwise nothing on Monday.

* Apart from H.M.S. *Hood*, no British ships were sunk during this
action.

† There was also one from Hitler to Admiral Luetjens. It was the
admiral's birthday.

Tuesday, 27/5/1941.

The action with the destroyers lasted until about 0600. No torpedo or shell hits were scored. *Bismarck* was making way until this time. I do not know the speed.

About the same time (0600) a stand-easy was ordered. I do not know why. An attempt was made to start the ship's aircraft, but did not succeed. It drifted into the water with its floats uppermost.

During the stand-easy it was piped: ' All non-duty officers to the chart-house '. Immediately afterwards action stations were sounded. Nothing could be seen of the enemy. It was said that smoke clouds had been sighted. Before our own guns fired, enemy shells dropped close to the ship. After about one hour the first hits were scored on our ship. The connection on my telephone broke, and no more orders could be given to my gun. As the hits increased the anti-aircraft crews went under cover. We had the impression that we were fired on from all sides.

First I was with a group of 20 men in the after gunnery position. After a few hits close by, we fled behind C and D turrets on the upper deck. Before that we threw five or six rafts on the deck below and went with the rafts behind the turrets. All rafts except two were destroyed by a hit. We had now several injured. Turret D was still firing.

At this time my shipmate Herzog came to me. We saw a raft between turret C and D. With the help of several others we released it and pulled it behind the turret. Due to a hit in the water, *i.e.*, from the wave, the raft and we three were thrown overboard. Nobody was actually on the float. We only succeeded in reaching it after about 15 minutes as hit after hit landed in the water. Nearby another raft was drifting with one injured and five or six other shipmates. We drifted astern. We only saw the ship herself when we were on top of a wave. Once I saw the *Bismarck* getting a list to port. It appeared that the ship had made a little way. Shortly afterwards I could see the *Bismarck* no longer, but only a smoke cloud. I did not hear an explosion. Not far from us I saw two cruisers making for the place where the *Bismarck* was. They were firing.

We had nothing to eat or drink in the raft. The other raft which had been near us had gone out of sight. I do not know what time we were washed overboard. When the sun was directly over us and we had practically given up all hope of being rescued, we sighted a FW200. We waved to it, but could not ascertain if we had been seen.

We felt tired. My shipmate Herzog had been injured in the foot. In the evening shortly before 1900 a U-boat suddenly surfaced close to us. We were taken on board and immediately packed into bunks and fed. The U-boat—she was U-74—searched for two days for survivors. Only corpses and wreckage were sighted.

(Signed) HERBERT MANTHEY."

So the *Bismarck* perished. Unsighted and unsunk she might have inflicted crippling losses on British shipping. Her destruction was a major victory for Britain. It was a blow, too, to German naval morale; and, more important still, it induced in Hitler so stubborn a caution in committing the major German ships that they were never again the formidable threat to the Allies which under Raeder's bold leadership they had become.

Chapter X

THE U.S.A. AND A 'SECOND FRONT'

THE ESCAPE FROM BREST

THE Wehrmacht attacked Russia on the early morning of 22 June 1941. Count von Schulenberg, the German Ambassador in Moscow, reported that when he went to Molotov to announce the German attack and to ask for his passports, so great was the surprise achieved by the German forces that Molotov refused to believe him, insisting that there must be some mistake. Schulenberg also maintained that it was not until the evening that the Kremlin received confirmation of the news.

The German Army advanced at 'blitz' speed, and there were high hopes at Hitler's headquarters that the campaign would be over even sooner than they had calculated. Towards the end of June, Hitler issued orders and directives for his future plans which were designed to drive the British from the Mediterranean and to establish German power over the Near East. These plans were based on the assumption that ‘ Barbarossa ’ would be completed by the autumn. By mid-July, ‘ Barbarossa ’ was in fact proceeding so well that Hitler felt he was already able to reinforce Rommel in Africa. He sent him an extra division and additional Luftwaffe squadrons.

But in one respect ‘ Barbarossa ’ did not succeed. Goebbels had started a great propaganda drive representing ‘ Barbarossa ’ as a world-saving Western crusade against Eastern Bolshevism in the hope of thereby getting the Western Democracies to come to terms. Both Mr. Churchill and President Roosevelt, however, made crystal clear at once their determination to aid Russia. The President went even further; on 7 July the United States sent naval forces to Iceland.

Raeder reacted at once to this new threat from the West. The possibility of a genuine ‘ Second Front ’ could not be ignored. Two days after United States marines landed in Iceland, he reported his fears to Hitler:

(*Extract from Fuehrer Conference at Wolfsschanze.**)

“ *The C.-in-C., Navy*, points out emphatically how important it is that France should keep a firm hold on North-West Africa. If the U.S.A. or Britain were to gain possession of Dakar and the rest of the coast, it would be a severe threat to our ability to carry on the war in the Atlantic; the position of Axis forces in North Africa would also be severely menaced. Therefore France must receive all the help necessary to hold North-West Africa.

General Keitel states that all the military requirements of France in connection with Dakar will be met.

The Fuehrer is very distrustful of France and considers her counter-demands excessive.

The C.-in-C., Navy, once again emphasizes the decisive strategic significance of keeping a firm hold on North-West Africa in view of the possible plans of the U.S.A. and Britain to drive the French out of that area.”

Hitler ignored Raeder’s prophetic warning, believing that if there was any danger it was in Norway, not in France or North Africa. In any case he was anxious that America should not be provoked into war until he had completed the invasion of Russia.

* ‘ Wolf’s lair ’—code word for Hitler’s H.Q. at Rastenberg, East Prussia.

Hitler and his Admirals
(Raeder receiving a presentation plaque)

The "Admiral Graf Spee" at Montevideo

The scuttling of the "Admiral Graf Spee"

The battleship "Tirpitz"

Grand Admiral Doenitz inspecting his U-boat crews at St. Nazaire, May 1944

German U-boats surrender at Wilhelmshaven. General view of U-boats in the loch at Wilhelmshaven before entering the harbour to surrender

U-236 coming alongside U-826. Both U-boats are wearing the White Ensign as a token of surrender.

Grand Admiral Doenitz speaking at Bordeaux, February 1944

Roosevelt's policy of 'all aid short of war' considerably embarrassed the German Supreme Command. They wanted to keep at peace with such a powerful neutral as the United States, and yet they could not tolerate the American aid to Britain and to Russia. Raeder persistently sought permission to attack American merchant shipping and was as persistently refused. He complained to Hitler that the blockade of England was being jeopardized by this tame acceptance of American power. Hitler replied (25 July 1941):

" There is absolutely no reason to believe that I have changed my view of the great importance of the blockade against Britain. My original view has undergone no changes whatsoever. I want to avoid, however, a declaration of war by the United States while the Eastern campaign is still in progress, especially as the Army is still involved in heavy fighting. But I will never call a submarine commander to account if he torpedoes an American ship by mistake. After the Eastern campaign I reserve the right to take severe action against the U.S.A. as well."

By the end of August it was clear that the Eastern campaign was not going to be finished as easily and as quickly as had been hoped. Russian resistance had become unexpectedly strong, and although the Supreme Command still hoped for victory before the winter, there was an undercurrent of uneasiness. It was realized that if England and America implemented their promise to help Russia, the Eastern campaign might well drag on indefinitely. It was clear also that they *would* implement their promises. The British had begun to organize convoys to Russia. At the famous 'Atlantic Charter' Conference at Placentia Bay, President Roosevelt and Mr. Churchill decided to send an Anglo-American Supply Mission to Moscow. Hitler still, however, refused to lift the ban on attacking American ships. Unlike his staff, he was convinced that the Eastern campaign would be over before Anglo-American aid could be effective. Japan was expected to intervene, and on 22 August he told Raeder:

" I am convinced that Japan will carry out the attack on Vladivostock as soon as forces have been assembled. The present aloofness can be explained by the fact that the assembling of forces is to be accomplished undisturbed."

On 30 August the first Allied convoy to Russia sailed. On 11 September President Roosevelt further confounded the German Supreme Command by announcing that America would extend her protection over Atlantic shipping as far east as Iceland, thus defending convoys to England for at least half the voyage.

To Raeder the announcement came at first almost as a relief. Surely now Hitler would alter his views. As he told him: " There is no longer any difference between British and American ships." He suggested immediate measures for extending the U-boat campaign. Hitler refused. Both Raeder and Doenitz vehemently protested against his decision. They presented long memoranda and detailed arguments explaining how the German Navy was being given an impossible task. Hitler remained adamant. He said that he expected victory over Russia by the end of September—forces were even now assembling for the assault on Moscow—and that then President Roosevelt would soon change his tone.

Far from gaining victory by the end of September, the Wehrmacht suffered a severe setback. . The Red Army defended Moscow with fanatical determination, and it became obvious during the next two months that the Eastern campaign would last at least throughout the winter. But Hitler was even more insistent that America should not be provoked into the war. He was still waiting hopefully for a move from Japan. On 7 December it came with dramatic suddenness—but not against Russia; against the U.S. Fleet at Pearl Harbour.

Hitler had known of the mounting tension between the United States and Japan, and of the Japanese dreams of ' Greater Asia ', but he had nevertheless expected Japan to attack Russia first. Still, the attack on Pearl Harbour, though it would not directly assist in the war against Russia, would distract American attention from the west. On 12 December Raeder discussed the strategic consequences with Hitler:

" Report of the Commander-in-Chief, Navy, to the Fuehrer in Berlin. 12 December, 1941.

Also present: Field-Marshal Keitel.
General Jodl.

1. *General situation.*

The situation in the Atlantic will be eased by Japan's successful intervention. Reports have already been received of the transfer of some battleships from the Atlantic to the Pacific. . . . The need of transport ships will be very great, so that a withdrawal of American merchant vessels from the Atlantic can be expected; the strain on British shipping will increase. The situation with regard to surface warfare by auxiliary cruisers and pocket battleships will probably also change in our favour. Stationing the *Scharnhorst* and the *Gneisenau* at Brest is a step in the right direction. . . . The danger of a major operation against the West coast will also decrease for the present. . . .

The Fuehrer asks:

(*a*) Does the C.-in-C., Navy, believe that the enemy will in the near future take steps to occupy the Atlantic islands and perhaps even to attack Dakar in order to win back the prestige lost in the Pacific?

(*b*) Is there any possibility that the U.S.A. and Britain will abandon East Asia for a time in order to crush Germany and Italy first?

As regards ' *a* ', the *C.-in-C., Navy*, does not believe such steps are imminent. . . .

As regards ' *b* ', it is improbable that the enemy will give up East Asia even temporarily; by so doing, the British would endanger India very seriously, and the United States cannot withdraw her fleet from the Pacific as long as the Japanese fleet has the upper hand."

Raeder's opinion satisfied Hitler who also agreed that fifty U-boats should be transferred at once to the Mediterranean where British successes at sea and on land were becoming a serious threat to the Axis position.

With American and British interest shifting to the Pacific and East Indies, Raeder began to consider using the German surface fleet in the Atlantic again. In spite of the worsening oil situation, the time was favourable for intensive operations by the big ships. The loss of the British battleships *Repulse* and *Prince of Wales* off Singapore and the concentration of other British naval forces in the Mediterranean and the Far East left the central Atlantic comparatively free. The German ships *Scharnhorst*, *Gneisenau* and *Prinz Eugen* had been stationed at Brest ever since the *Bismarck* had been sunk. They had been heavily attacked by the R.A.F., and Raeder suggested to Hitler, who had himself

pointed out that the protection of these ships from air attack
was proving too difficult, that the Brest Group should be sent into
the Atlantic against Allied convoys. There were no longer any
political objections as far as the United States were concerned,
and Raeder was confident that the ships would be successful.

But, besides being deterred by the precedent of the *Bismarck*,
Hitler had suddenly decided that the Allies were about to land
in Norway. His fears had been aroused by the numerous small
raids which the British had made on the Norwegian coast
towards the end of 1941, and, as Vice-Admiral Fricke, Raeder's
new Chief of Staff, later reported:

(Conference of 22 January 1942.)

" *The Fuehrer* is thoroughly convinced that Britain and the
United States intend to make every effort to influence the
course of the war by an attack on northern Norway. . . .

Sweden's support in a spring offensive is expected; for
which she would receive Narvik and ore deposits near
Petsamo. Finland would be guaranteed her independence
within the old frontiers. . . .

Anglo-Saxon domination of the Swedish area will gradually
eliminate all freedom of action in the Baltic. . . .

The Fuehrer is convinced that Norway is the 'zone of
destiny' in this war. He therefore demands unconditional
obedience to all his commands and wishes concerning the
defence of this area.

The Fuehrer desires the Navy to do everything in its power
to head off the British offensive at the very start. The Navy
must take over adequate reconnaissance in weather not fit
for flying. It must defend the sea lanes to Norway, and must
dislodge with all available forces any enemy troops which
land, entirely foregoing all other warfare, 'except for the
Mediterranean operations'. . . .

The Fuehrer demands that every available vessel be employed in Norway. He endorses our plans to use battleships,
pocket battleships, heavy cruisers, light naval vessels, and
E-boats; increases his demand for U-boats; is of the same
opinion as the Naval Staff regarding the improbability of a
landing in Western France. . . .

The Fuehrer emphasized several times that the greatest
speed and efficiency are vitally important. He is deeply

concerned about the grave consequence which unfavourable developments in the north Norwegian area would have on the entire course of the war. . . ."

For these reasons Hitler had refused to allow Raeder to send the surface fleet into the Atlantic, and had ordered him instead to send the Brest Group north to protect the Norwegian coast and to operate against the Russian convoys.

Raeder protested strongly; he pointed out the difficulties— the Brest Group had only two alternative routes, either by a long voyage round the British Isles when they would almost certainly be attacked by the Home Fleet from Scapa Flow, or by the shorter but equally hazardous route through the English Channel where they would be attacked by the R.A.F. as well as by the Home Fleet. The crews of the German ships were untrained and enervated by their long stay at Brest, and there was no question of their being able to fight a sustained action such as the *Bismarck* had encountered.

Hitler insisted that the threat to Norway was extremely serious and that the ships must be moved. He left it to Raeder to decide how, but he showed himself strongly in favour of the Channel route.

The Naval Staff set to and produced rough plans for operation ' Cerberus ', the code word for the movement of the Brest ships. In view of the state of training of the crews, unfitting them for a long voyage, they decided that the ships should go through the Straits of Dover.

In the second week of January, when the plans were completed, Hitler summoned a general conference to discuss the operation. Members of all three Services were present. Raeder opened the conference:

" The question of the passage of the Brest Group through the Channel has been examined by all parties concerned. In the light of the Fuehrer's opinion, the German Fleet's primary task is to defend the Norwegian coast and ports, and, in so doing, it should use its might unsparingly. . . . I do not believe that I should take the initiative in advocating such a break-through operation, but plans have been worked out which ought to be followed, if the break through the Channel is decided upon.

Since you, my Fuehrer, informed me that you insist upon the return of the heavy units to their home bases, I suggest that Vice-Admiral Ciliax reports on the details of the operation. . . ."

Ciliax then explained that he had decided that the ships should leave Brest under cover of darkness, making the actual passage of the Straits of Dover in daylight, since they would thereby be able to have the maximum air cover.   Lieut.-General Jeschonnek, Goering's Chief of Staff, doubted whether the necessary aircraft would be available, but Hitler ordered him to see to it that they were.   Hitler finally summed up:

" In view of past experience I do not believe the British are capable of making and carrying out lightning decisions. I do not believe that they will be as swift as the Naval Staff and Vice-Admiral Ciliax assumed in transferring their bomber and fighter aircraft to the south-eastern part of England for an attack on our ships in the Dover Straits.   Picture what would happen if the situation were reversed, *i.e.*, if a surprise report came in that British battleships had appeared in the Thames estuary and were heading for the Straits of Dover. Even we would hardly be able to bring up fighters and bombers swiftly and methodically.   The situation of the Brest Group is like that of a patient with cancer who is doomed unless he submits to an operation.   An operation, on the other hand, even though it may have to be drastic, will at least offer some hope that the patient's life may yet be saved.   The passage of our ships through the Channel is such an operation.   It must therefore be attempted. . . .

There is nothing to be gained by leaving the ships at Brest; their ' flypaper ' effect, that is their ability to tie up enemy air forces, may not continue for long.   Only as long as the ships remain in battleworthy condition will the enemy feel obliged to attack.   But the moment they are seriously damaged—and this may happen any day—the enemy will discontinue his attacks.   Such a development will nullify the one and only advantage derived from leaving the ships at Brest.   The operation is to be prepared as proposed by the C.-in-C., Navy."

By the beginning of February, preparations for ' Cerberus ' were completed.   The naval force was under the command of Vice-Admiral Ciliax, and the Luftwaffe squadrons were under the command of the brilliant young staff officer, Colonel Galland, who had ensured full co-operation with the Navy, and, who, in spite of Goering's opposition, had obtained more than 250 aircraft for the operation.

On the evening of 11 February, the *Scharnhorst*, *Gneisenau* and *Prinz Eugen*, accompanied by destroyers and E-boats, left Brest, and, at full speed, began their dash up the English Channel. They were not sighted until shortly before eleven o'clock on the following morning.

The escape had been anticipated in England, but due to the delay in receiving the sighting reports, it was not until 1230 that the first attack by Motor Torpedo Boats was delivered. Naval aircraft attacked a quarter of an hour later, but all were shot down by the overwhelming German fighter escort. During the afternoon destroyers of the Royal Navy and R.A.F. bombers attacked repeatedly, but with no effect. The only damage suffered by the German force was by the *Scharnhorst*, who struck a mine at the end of the voyage. The damage was slight.

" Vice-Admiral Ciliax," wrote the *Times*, " has succeeded where the Duke of Medina Sidonia failed. . . . Nothing more mortifying to the pride of sea power has happened in Home Waters since the 17th Century."

Chapter XI

MALTA AND THE MEDITERRANEAN

THE fear of an Allied landing in Norway was the first sign of the Supreme Command's change from attack to defence. For the first time it was Hitler and not his enemies who began to show signs of ' nerves '. He remained as aggressive as ever, but he was destined to make only one more bid for world domination before going irrevocably over to defensive warfare. That bid consisted of a vast land offensive against Russia, and a combined sea, air and land offensive in the Mediterranean.

Until the beginning of 1942, Hitler had remained peculiarly blind to the importance of the Mediterranean. The German forces he had sent there had been for the sole purpose of helping Italy, and, as an Italian collapse would obviously impede his plans, he had only considered the consequences of failure, never of success. Rommel and the Afrika Korps, the U-boats and the Luftwaffe squadrons, had been sent to the Mediterranean essentially as defensive measures. There had been no question of developing a new aggressive front in that theatre.

On 13 February 1942, however, the day after the Channel operation, Hitler received Raeder in an exceptionally friendly audience. He was greatly pleased by the German Navy's achievement—it had been his idea that the Brest Group should go through the Straits of Dover—and he was unusually amenable to Raeder's suggestions.

At the conference Raeder began cautiously. He first detailed the steps he had taken for the defence of Norway, discussed next Russia and the Battle of the Atlantic, and then, playing on Hitler's receptive mood, he went on to drive home, successfully at last, the consequences of victory in the Mediterranean. He said:

" The Mediterranean situation is definitely favourable at the moment. If we examine it (*i.e.* the situation) in conjunction with events in East Asia, we can get some indication of the possibilities of launching an attack as quickly as possible on Egypt and the Suez Canal. The Egyptian government has been changed, and the British position in Egypt is precarious, as the British have to depend on the 40,000 Egyptian troops to safeguard their rear communications. . . . With Rangoon, Sumatra, and Java gone, the last oil wells between Bahrein and the American continent have been lost. Oil supplies for Australia and New Zealand will have to come either from the Persian Gulf or from America. Once the Japanese battleships, aircraft carriers, submarines and naval air forces are based on Ceylon, Britain will be forced to resort to heavily escorted convoys, if she wants to maintain her communications with India and the Near East. . . . Suez and Basra are the western pillars of the British position in the East. Should these positions collapse under the weight of concerted Axis pressure, the consequences for the British Empire would be disastrous. . . .

According to reports available, the British are fully aware of the great danger which is threatening them in Egypt. They fear that the German-Italian forces might establish contact with the Japanese. The Japanese, for their part, are making an honest effort to establish contact with Germany by sea and air, since they realize the decisive significance this would have on the outcome of the war."

The picture that Raeder drew of what would result from victory in the Mediterranean—the collapse of the British Empire and the link with Japan, thus enclosing half the world—made an immediate appeal to Hitler. He gave his consent for preparing what later became known as the ' Great Plan '.

Victory in the Mediterranean depended upon two factors—sea power and the closest possible co-operation between naval, air and land forces. The Navy could not operate without the bases which the Army had to win and hold; the Army could not operate without the supplies which the Navy had to deliver; and neither Army nor Navy could operate without the support and protection of the Air Force—which in its turn also depended upon the Navy for supplies and on the Army for bases. Mediterranean strategy, therefore, had to co-ordinate these various factors and to establish the circle: sea power ensuring supplies→supplies ensuring bases→bases ensuring sea power, if success was to be won. The key to the circle was a central base from which to start, and by far the most important base in the Mediterranean was the island fortress of Malta.

The Great Plan was shaped by the early experiences of Mediterranean warfare, and hence Malta was the most important target of the plan,[5] though not its final objective. Situated almost in the geographical centre between Europe and Africa, Malta provided the ideal base for naval and air operations in the Mediterranean. The success of British forces operating from Malta and their effect on the land fighting in Africa may be judged from the following table of Axis merchant shipping losses between Italy and Africa in the last quarter of 1941:

1941.	Tonnage convoyed.	Tonnage sunk.	Tonnage damaged.	Tonnage delivered.
October . .	50,000	18,800	12,800	18,400
November . .	37,000	26,000	2,600	8,400
December . .	36,000	13,000	5,000	18,000
TOTAL . .	123,000	57,800	20,400	44,800

Thus only 36·6 per cent. of the supplies sent to Rommel had reached him during this period. The Afrika Korps had been so weakened, that, when the British 8th Army attacked in November 1941, Rommel's retreat had been almost a rout. Then, in December, U-boats and Luftwaffe squadrons were sent to reinforce the Mediterranean. The U-boats had attacked the British Navy, sinking the *Ark Royal*, the battleship *Barham* and two cruisers; Italian divers had damaged the battleship *Queen Elizabeth*; while the Luftwaffe had concentrated on Malta, severely damaging the docks and harbour installations. The results had been dramatic and conclusive. In January, only one month after all these attacks, not a single Axis ship was lost on the supply route to Africa. The proof of Malta's importance was complete.

The blockade of Malta was therefore tightened, and strong naval and air forces were stationed to prevent supplies getting through, while the combined German-Italian staffs set to work on the Great Plan.

Towards the end of March 1942, however, a British convoy, escorted by only five light cruisers, broke the blockade after a brilliant and audacious action against the Italian Fleet. The Italians had sent one battleship, six cruisers, and a large number of destroyers to intercept the convoy just east of the Straits of Sicily. Using smoke screens, the British cruisers made frequent attacks on the Italian Fleet, keeping them away from the convoy, and finally, as the Italians were loth to continue fighting at night, drove them off. As the German Admiral at Rome, Vice-Admiral Weichold, reported: [5] " Although a considerable quantity of ammunition was used, not a single ship was sunk."

The effect of this action was to discredit for ever the Italian Navy in the eyes of the Germans, and although the Italian ships were still a powerful factor on paper, more and more reliance was placed upon U-boats and the Luftwaffe to achieve mastery in the Mediterranean. U-boats and aircraft, however, were not in themselves sufficient, and Raeder carried his point with the Supreme Command that nothing less than the capture of Malta would suffice to overcome British supremacy at sea. [1]

Out of these experiences the Great Plan was evolved. Its eventual objective was the conquest of Egypt and Persia, but it stated that this objective was dependent upon the capture of Malta. Two operations were planned; the first—' Hercules '—

was the actual conquest of Malta, while the second—' Aida '—was the direct offensive against Egypt. It was realized that the capture of Malta would be made more difficult while air support could be given by British forces in Cyrenaica, so it was decided that operation ' Hercules ' would not begin until the Afrika Korps had driven the British beyond Tobruk, during which period Luftwaffe attacks were to keep Malta subdued. When this area had been cleared, the Afrika Korps was to stop its advance until ' Hercules ' had been completed. By carrying out the operations in this order, it was hoped to remedy the early mistakes of both Germany and the Allies of advancing too quickly on land. With Malta conquered, Rommel's supplies would be assured, and he would then be able to throw the full weight of his forces against the bastions of Egypt.

Such was the broad outline of the Great Plan at the beginning of April. It was later to be changed with disastrous results for the Axis, but for the moment the special staffs which had been set up at Rome and at Hitler's headquarters worked with passionate fervour, confident that they were contriving the collapse of the British Empire.

As a preliminary move, while the ships were being prepared in Italy and Rommel was gathering his strength for the big attack, all available units of the Luftwaffe in Southern Italy and Sicily were ordered to bomb Malta. The air attacks had been heavy in the first three months of 1942, but in April they were the heaviest which had been made anywhere up to that time. More than two hundred raids were made during the month—an average of six air raids per day. Field-Marshal Kesselring, on a personal reconnaissance of the area at the end of the first week, reported:

" The planned air attack on Malta between 1–9 April, has, in my opinion, eliminated Malta as a naval base. The shipyards and dock installations have been so badly damaged that there can be no question of using Malta as a base for a long time; the last surface forces have left, and the British submarine base has been transferred to Alexandria. . . .

I intend to continue the attack, if weather permits, until April 20, and then, by continual harassing raids, to prevent the enemy from repairing the damage. . . .

In view of the considerably improved situation in the

Mediterranean, the successful defence of the Eastern Front, and the favourable developments in East Asia, the Duce has expressed his great confidence in the further development of the war."

While the success of the air attack on Malta was an incentive to the combined staffs in Rome to hasten the capture of the island, to Hitler it was an excuse for postponing it. He was as loath to attempt the conquest of Malta as he had earlier been to attempt the invasion of England. To him the two situations were parallel: both islands would be defended fanatically, both required the final assault to be made by sea. " On land I am a hero, but at sea I am a coward," he had told Raeder, and he remained consistent. He decided now to postpone operation ' Hercules ' until Rommel had reached the frontiers of Egypt. This postponement was still acceptable to the planning staffs. They regretted it, but they thought that Malta could be kept down until then. Beyond that point, however, the conquest of Malta was essential if Rommel's supplies were to be secure.

At the end of April, Mussolini visited Hitler at the Berghof to discuss the final details. Captain Junge represented Raeder at the conferences, and he reported the main decisions in a letter to a fellow staff officer, Captain Wangenheim of the Operations Division, Naval Staff:

" Berghof,
May 1, 1942.

DEAR WANGENHEIM,
Here, in haste, is my latest news of the Mussolini discussion at the Berghof:
General impression: most satisfactory—the atmosphere was especially so. (At the last meeting, last summer, this was not markedly the case.) Agreements were finally reached on the Libya operation and on Malta. First Libya—end of May or beginning of June—then Malta—mid-July, since to attempt both simultaneously would cancel out each, particularly as regards air cover. . . .
Malta: Fuehrer agrees that Germany should participate to a great extent . . . (details of troops, ships, etc.). But, in spite of these intentions . . . Luftflotte III is to be transferred—to benefit the West principally. Kesselring was of

the opinion that the transfer could be made without risk of Britain regaining supremacy.

Well, we shall see. He ought to know.

To sum up, I consider the outcome satisfactory. Even though the postponement of the Malta operation is not a welcome move, still I am glad to see the increased interest displayed by the Fuehrer in this important area and the consequent increase of German fighting spirit there. The whole business is now assuming importance after having been regarded hitherto as a subsidiary matter in which victories were looked upon as gifts from Heaven, but in which nobody bothered to do anything seriously for the 'Italian theatre of war'.

Hearty greetings,
JUNGE."

On 26 May Rommel launched the first part of operation 'Aida' and the Great Plan got under way. The Afrika Korps advanced at great speed, and Rommel's successes in Cyrenaica together with the heavy losses suffered by the British in their efforts to relieve Malta, further persuaded Hitler that the conquest of Malta was unnecessary. Raeder, supported by Kesselring and the Italian Command, pointed out that, according to the experience of the previous year, if Malta was in any way allowed to recover—and Hitler had been discussing removing the air squadrons to the Eastern Front where they were also needed—Rommel's situation would be precarious. Hitler hedged, and in a conference with Raeder on 15 June shifted the blame on to the Italian 'lack of leadership' for a further postponement of 'Hercules'. He said:

" I quite recognize how important it is to capture Malta. However, I do not believe that this can be done while the offensive on the Eastern Front is in progress, and especially not with Italian troops. The Luftwaffe cannot spare any transport aircraft. Once Tobruk is taken, most shipments will be routed to Tobruk via Crete (thus by-passing Malta). On the other hand the British efforts to get convoys through to Malta from the East and West testify to the plight of the island. These convoys, incidentally, give us the opportunity to inflict much damage on the enemy. Once Malta has been bled white by the continuous air raids and the total blockade, we could risk the attack."

Meanwhile the German Naval Staff in Rome, under the command of Vice-Admiral Weichold, were once more doing their best to make the Italian Navy act. Rommel's rapid advance in Libya meant, as Hitler had said, that supplies could now go through the Ægean, via Crete, to Tobruk, and this meant that the main weight of naval warfare, and hence the Italian Fleet, would be transferred to the Eastern Mediterranean. The Italians agreed to this proposal, but, being short of fuel, they refused to move their ships unless Germany would supply them with more oil. This Germany could not do; they were already giving the Italians all the oil they could spare. The Italian commanders shrugged their shoulders and remained in harbour.

In the meantime the Afrika Korps continued their speedy advance. Tobruk was captured on 21 June, Bardia on 22 June, Sollum on 23 June, and Mersa Matruh on 28 June. By 30 June they were halted by the defensive lines of the 8th Army at El Alamein. Heavy units of the British Fleet were withdrawn from Alexandria to Suez, and the situation was ripe for the long-delayed conquest of Malta.

On 1 and 2 July Rommel made an attempt to penetrate the 8th Army's defences. He was unsuccessful, but he considered that he had been able to gauge their strength exactly. He flew back to Germany to see Hitler and then his doctors.*

At the Berghof, Rommel had a long private conference with Hitler.[1] He was excited and talked with infectious enthusiasm of the prospects of the Afrika Korps. Raeder and Kesselring had warned him of the danger of continuing his campaign without securing his supply line, but he was full of confidence in his own ability and judgment. Goebbel's propaganda machine had built him up as Germany's most brilliant young general and he himself believed what Goebbels had said. Rommel spoke to Hitler of the stupidity of such old-fashioned ideas as guarding his supply lines when Egypt and the stores of the 8th Army lay before him ready for looting. He was prepared to strike now; why waste time capturing Malta? Hitler, who had always shied

* It is interesting to note how many of the German leaders suffered from various bodily ailments. Rommel's was stomach trouble; Raeder had a disorder of the blood and had at one time been given only a year to live; von Brauchitsch also had some chronic illness; Hess, when he landed in England, carried in his pockets practically every known preventative drug; Goering was a confirmed drug addict; while Hitler always had two doctors in attendance.

away from operation ' Hercules ', seized upon Rommel's idea. Without reference to anyone else on his staff or to the Italians, Hitler postponed the conquest of Malta until after the conquest of Egypt.

Raeder, Kesselring, Weichold, the Italians, indeed all who had been concerned with drawing up the Great Plan were aghast at the news. All previous experience in the Mediterranean had shown the folly of disregarding Malta. If one convoy could succeed in fighting its way through to the island, Malta would be restored, with disastrous consequences for the Axis forces. And from 10–15 August one convoy did fight its way through.

When the convoy was first sighted, staff officers of the German and Italian Navies argued hotly with staff officers of the Luftwaffe and Regia Aeronautica as to whether the main attack on the convoy should be by sea or air.[5] In view of the previous record of the Italian Navy, the Air Forces refused to co-operate and attacked alone. They attacked continuously for four days, but part of the convoy succeeded in breaking the blockade. From Rome, Vice-Admiral Weichold described the action:

" A strong British force left Gibraltar for the Central Mediterranean on 10 August. In spite of considerable losses during the approach, essential units of the convoy succeeded in forcing the Straits of Sicily. Two Italian cruiser squadrons (three heavy and three light cruisers) with destroyer escort sailed to intercept the convoy. They were to attack and destroy it on the morning of August 13, south of Pantellaria. As there was a considerable danger of air attack from Malta in this area, the cruisers had to be provided with air cover. The available German and Italian fighters, however, were only sufficient either to give protection to the bombers or to the cruiser squadrons. . . . I made every effort at the German and Italian headquarters to get air cover for the cruisers, as only they could be in a position to complete the destruction of units of the convoy which had broken through. There was a heated difference of opinion between the headquarters of the different services, during which the representatives of both navies stood alone against the other leaders.

Mussolini was rung up for a decision and decided in favour of employing the Air Force. Thereupon the cruiser operation

which had already started, was cancelled. On the return
voyage two units were torpedoed. A more useless waste of
fighting power cannot be imagined."

The convoy was actually attacked off Cape Bon by very strong
air forces, but as it was protected by three aircraft carriers (one
of which, H.M.S. *Eagle*, was sunk) the damage was not as great
as it might have been. Nevertheless, only five out of fifteen
merchant ships reached Malta.

Weichold continued his report:

" To the continental observer, the British losses seemed to
represent a big victory for the Axis, but in reality the facts
were quite different, since it had not been possible to prevent
a British force, among which were five merchant vessels,
from reaching Valetta. . . .

Thanks to these new supplies Malta was now capable of
fighting for several weeks, or, at a pinch, for several months.
The main issue, the danger of air attack on the supply route
to North Africa, remained. To achieve this objective no price
was too high, and from this point of view the British operation, in spite of all the losses, was not a defeat, but a
strategical failure of the first order by the Axis, the repercussions of which will one day be felt."

The result was noticed almost at once. British submarines
returned to Malta, the island made a prodigious recovery to
some 60 per cent. of its former efficiency within two months, and
even by the end of August—a bare two weeks after the delivery
of supplies—38,000 tons * of Axis shipping had been sunk out
of a total of 114,000 tons on the supply routes from Italy to
Africa.

The recovery of Malta and the gallant stand of the 8th Army
at El Alamein made nonsense of Rommel's vain boasting and
fully justified the fears of Raeder and Kesselring. By mid-
September nothing was left of the Great Plan but the paper on
which it had been written.

On 26 August, Raeder conferred with Hitler. Little was said
about the Mediterranean, but Raeder had seen the defeat which
was in store for Germany. He also saw how it would probably
start. He said:

* German figures.

" I continue to regard the possible attempt of the Anglo-Saxons to occupy North-West Africa and get a foothold in North Africa with the aid of the French as a very great danger to the whole German war effort. They would attack Italy from there and endanger our position in North-*East* Africa. Therefore Germany must maintain a strong position in the Mediterranean. . . .

The Fuehrer concurs in this opinion. He does not conceal his increasing dissatisfaction with the Italians and alludes to plans which he is not yet able to discuss."

However much Hitler agreed with Raeder and whatever new plans he was conceiving, he was too late. The 8th Army was preparing its great offensive; the Russians were mustering their forces for the relief of Stalingrad; and in England and America a vast armada of ships and men were assembling for the first big sea-borne invasion of the war.

The Great Plan had been smashed by the tiny, sandstone island of Malta, whose stubborn and courageous people withstood more than 1400 air raids during the two years they were under attack, and who were so justly awarded the highest civilian honour that England can bestow—the George Cross.

Chapter XII

THE BATTLE OF THE ATLANTIC (3)

ALTHOUGH Axis naval power was waning in the Mediterranean, in the Atlantic the German Navy achieved spectacular success, due principally to Doenitz and his U-boats. Throughout 1942 these U-boats so damaged Allied shipping that they came nearer than any other Axis forces to strangling the Allied war effort.

Doenitz was favoured by the fact that America's entry into the war coincided with the new expansion of the U-boat fleet.* The one opened up new hunting grounds where the prey was unprepared and inexperienced; the other enabled this advantage to be exploited to the full. Within one month of the United

* Nearly 250 U-boats were now available, compared with 56 on the outbreak of war.

States' declaration of war, Doenitz was able to send strong forces
of U-boats to the Caribbean (between 60 and 80 U-boats operated
at one time), and, by May 1942, he had achieved ' economic '
superiority—he was sinking Allied ships faster than they could
be built.

Such an achievement was in striking contrast to the failures
in other war theatres and caused Hitler to take a more personal
interest in the U-boat branch. He began to request verbal
reports from Doenitz, and more than once voiced his belief that
the U-boats were the perfect answer to the strong surface fleets
of the Allies. It was Doenitz's opportunity, and he seized it as
readily as he had taken the advantage to attack unprotected
American shipping. From this time onwards he never lost a
chance of pushing himself forward into Hitler's notice, and by
his breezy and confident manner, gradually began to replace his
senior, Raeder.

Doenitz's first major report to Hitler was made on 14 May
1942:

" *The Admiral Commanding U-boats* reports on all matters
pertaining to submarine warfare:

Statistics : 124 submarines were in the operational zones
on May 1. Of these, 85 were stationed in the Atlantic, 19 in
the Mediterranean, 20 in the Arctic. On the other hand
114 submarines, exclusive of training boats, were in the
Baltic preparing for duty. A submarine is normally supposed
to be ready for operations about 4 months after commissioning; 49 of the 114 submarines mentioned above have
been commissioned for longer than that, and therefore should
have been in their operational zones by May 1. Everything
possible must be done to relieve this congestion.

Submarine operations : Submarine warfare is war against
enemy merchant shipping. We must sink ships wherever
the greatest number can be sunk at lowest cost to us, and we
should not concentrate in one certain area if that means
sinking fewer ships. This principle applies unless other
military factors have to be considered, as, for instance, in
the case of our attacks on the convoys to Murmansk, which
serve the purpose of relieving pressure on the Army. From
the point of view of operational cost, our submarine
actions in the American area are justifiable. Sinkings

from January 15 to May 10 amounted to 303 ships or a total of 2,015,252 tons *. . . . Shipbuilding and other allied industries depend mostly on oil for fuel and the most important American oilfields are found near the Gulf of Mexico. Consequently, most American tankers are used in coastal traffic, transporting oil from the oilfields to the industrial area. During the same period, January 15 to May 10, we sank 112 tankers, totalling 927,000 tons. Every tanker we sink not only means one tanker less for carrying oil, but also represents a direct setback to America's shipbuilding programme. America will have to depend on transporting her oil by sea for at least another year, and it will take a long time to lay an additional pipe-line overland. . . .

I do not believe that the race between the enemy shipbuilding programme and the submarine sinkings is in any way hopeless. The total tonnage the enemy can build will be about 8,200,000 tons in 1942 and about 10,400,000 tons in 1943. This means that we would have to sink approximately 700,000 tons per month in order to offset new construction; only what exceeds this amount constitutes a decrease in enemy tonnage. We are already sinking 700,000 tons per month now—'we' meaning Germany, Italy and Japan: submarines, air forces, surface vessels, and mines. Moreover, the construction figures quoted are the maximum amounts ever mentioned in enemy propaganda as the goal of their shipbuilding programme. Our experts doubt whether this goal can be reached and consider that the enemy can build only about 5,000,000 tons in 1942. That would mean that we would only have to sink about 400,000 to 500,000 tons per month to prevent an increase. Anything above that amount cuts into the basic tonnage of the enemy.

I intend to operate submarines in American waters as long as it is profitable, but one day the situation in the American zone will change. Even now everything points to the fact that the Americans are making strenuous efforts to prevent the large number of sinkings. They have organized a considerable air defence and are also using destroyers and patrol craft off the coast. However, these are all manned by inexperienced crews and do not constitute a serious threat

* This figure is approximately correct.

at present. The submarines with their greater experience in warfare are mastering these counter-measures. The American fliers see nothing; the destroyers and patrol vessels ~ travelling too fast most of the time even to find the U⁻ or they are not persistent enough in their pursuit ~ charges.

In fact, the shallow American coastal waters ~ very easy to safeguard and protect shipping which could b done either by establishing a ' war channel ' protected fror seaward by net and mine barrages, or by ~ shipping into convoys. The second meth be chosen, and the convoys will be led ai ~ ast in shallow waters. The daily traffic will the ~ he lighter and our chances of success will be fewer, but a~ ~g as their escorts are inexperienced, I believe that we will be able to continue to attack the convoys in the usual manner.

I will then also resort to the use of mines against American shipping. So far mines have not been used because it was more economical to equip the submarines with torpedoes, but, in anticipation of the expected decrease in shipping, it is planned to mine Chesapeake Bay, Delaware Bay and New York harbour during the new moon period in the middle of June. U-boats equipped with mines will leave on missions within the next few days.

If operations in the American area should prove unprofitable, we shall resume warfare against the convoys in the North Atlantic with a large number of U-boats. The production of U-boat tankers also allows us now to operate U-boats in other, more remote areas. Our U-boat losses are extremely light at the moment, but there is no doubt that the number of losses will rise again once attacks on convoys are resumed and the defences in some zones become stronger. We must therefore strive with all the means at our disposal to improve U-boat weapons in order to keep abreast of the anti-submarine devices of the enemy. The most important thing in this respect is the development of the torpedo with the non-contact pistol. This device would speed up the sinking of torpedoed ships whose crews would thus be unable to save themselves. This increase in personnel losses will no doubt make it difficult to man the many ships America is building.

The U-boat branch has faith in its equipment and believes in its fighting ability. The first thing to do, therefore, is to ⸱⸱t the U-boats out of the Baltic as fast as possible, and in ⸱l to keep as many U-boats as possible at sea and ⸱n operations.

(Signed) DOENITZ."

⸱esides th⸱ ⸱attacks on American coastal shipping and convoys ⸱ritain, the Battle of the Atlantic also embraced Allied con-⸱⸱ ⸱⸱ ⸱⸱⸱⸱⸱. Hitler had recognised the importance of these ⸱⸱⸱⸱⸱ start, and the major part of the surface fleet ⸱hich ⸱⸱ ⸱⸱ ⸱⸱ to the Arctic, though intended principally ⸱⸱r the def⸱ ⸱⸱⸱ Norway, was also intended for attacks on the ⸱ssian con ⸱y⸱⸱

The war in the Arctic during the spring and summer of 1942 was an outstanding example of what could be done when the Luftwaffe and the German Navy worked together. In one respect this theatre of war was similar to the Mediterranean, in that convoys had to pass within less than two hundred miles of the land in order to reach their destination. It was, therefore, an ideal position for the combined use of land-based aircraft and surface or submarine forces. Nor was there any ' Malta ' to complicate the issue—the use of the Arctic islands such as Spitzbergen or Jan Mayen for military bases was impracticable.

Even so, Raeder only obtained Goering's co-operation with difficulty. The two Commanders-in-Chief had fought continually for the control of naval air forces, Goering being loath to sub-ordinate any part of the Luftwaffe to the demands of the Navy, and Raeder insisting that only the Navy should say how and when air power was to be used at sea. Both acknowledged the necessity for air power at sea, and the dispute was simply who should control it. It was a deadlock which was only partially resolved in the Arctic and never resolved in any other war theatre.

In March British carrier-borne aircraft had strongly attacked the *Tirpitz* * off Northern Norway in the Arctic. The *Tirpitz* had been sent on a sortie against a Russian convoy, but she had been sighted by a British force which was covering the convoy at a distance. The *Tirpitz* narrowly escaped destruction and was driven back to her base. This short action brought up

* Battleship of the *Bismarck* class.

sharply the question of giving naval forces air support.   Raeder
went to Hitler and demanded that work on their own carrier,
the *Graf Zeppelin*, should be completed as soon as possible, and
that the Luftwaffe should be ordered to co-operate with the Navy
Hitler strongly supported both of Raeder's demands, and added
that besides the *Graf Zeppelin*, the liners *Potsdam*, *Europa* and
Gneisenau (not to be confused with the battleship) were also to
be converted into auxiliary aircraft carriers.   Goering was
forced to obey Hitler's orders and at the end of March aircraft
destroyers, and U-boats made the first combined attack on a
Russian convoy.   Five out of nineteen merchant ships were sunk
for the loss of one German destroyer.   This attack justified the
air/sea co-operation which Raeder had won with such difficulty
and, from the experience gained, a major attack was planned,
using all the surface, submarine and air forces available.

This operation—' Roesselsprung ' (Knight's move)—was to be
directed against convoy PQ 17 * in June or July, and it was
hoped to sink every ship.   The battleship *Tirpitz*, the pocket
battleships *Luetzow* and *Scheer*, the heavy cruiser *Hipper*, 12
destroyers, about 10 or more U-boats and a large number of
aircraft, were to be used.   The following is an extract from the
operation orders:

> " *Main Task :*   Rapid destruction of enemy merchant
> ships.   If necessary, these should only be crippled and the
> sinking left to the U-boats and air force.   The escort force
> should only be attacked if this is indispensable for accom-
> plishing the main task. . . . An engagement with superior
> enemy forces is to be avoided.   The operation should be
> executed quickly, and should be completed before an enemy
> covering force composed of battleships and carriers—pre-
> sumably stationed in the Faeroes–Iceland area—has a chance
> to intervene. . . .
>
> *The Air Force* will attack only aircraft carriers and
> merchant vessels once our forces have engaged the enemy,
> unless the identity of the ships is unmistakable. . . . It is
> particularly important that the Air Force fulfil the request
> of the Navy with regard to aerial reconnaissance, if necessary
> at the expense of taking part in the battle.   The Navy's request

* Allied convoys *to* Russia were lettered ' PQ '; those *from* Russia,
' QP '.

is justified as it seems possible to achieve total success with the aid of our heavy naval forces."

The convoy PQ 17 was sighted on 2 July and the preliminary moves were started. The *Luetzow* and three destroyers ran aground in fog on their way round to the forward operational base in Alta Fiord, but the remainder of the Fleet got into position without incident. On 4 July a British carrier force was sighted within 300 miles of the convoy and it was debated whether the surface fleet should proceed—it could only do so with Hitler's express permission—but finally, at about midday on 5 July, the order to proceed was given.

The movement of the German Fleet out of Alta Fiord was sighted and reported by a British submarine whose signals were intercepted by the Germans and again caused them to hesitate. In the meantime, U-boats and aircraft carried out a successful and very severe attack on the convoy, which, in view of the presence of the German Fleet, had been scattered to avoid presenting a composite target. The U-boat and air attacks sank 23 out of the 34 ships in the convoy. Then on the evening of 6 July, as the convoy had already been largely destroyed, the German Naval Staff recalled the surface fleet, who accordingly returned to harbour without firing a shot. Nevertheless they had succeeded in causing the convoy to be scattered, and thus simplified the task of the U-boats and Luftwaffe. It was an outstanding example of what could be achieved when there was close air/sea co-operation.

The next Russian convoy, PQ 18, was also heavily attacked at the end of July, losing 13 out of 39 ships. The result of these two actions was that, at a time when the second German offensive in Russia was at its height, the Allies were forced temporarily to suspend supplies to Russia. Here was a very definite success for Raeder and his Navy. Apart from fast ships sailing independently, the next Russian convoy did not sail till September, and convoys on the former scale were not resumed for another three months.

In the Atlantic, Doenitz's successes continued. In June, U-boats sank 145 ships, the highest number for any month during the war.* U-boats themselves were also suffering heavy losses,

* The highest *tonnage* was in November of the same year—well over 700,000 tons.

however, and Doenitz prepared the following table for Hitler
in August:

" U-boat losses up to 24 August, 1942.

Losses in boats :

Total number of U-boats in operation since beginning of war . . .	304 boats.
Total number of U-boats lost since beginning of war	105 boats.
Average monthly loss . . .	2·9 boats.
Average monthly loss to the number in operation	4·9 per cent.

Losses in personnel :

	Officers.	Chief Petty Officers.	Petty Officers.	Ratings.	Total.
Killed . .	185	184	515	1,075	1,959
Captured .	112	113	323	600	1,148
Missing . .	63	59	192	382	696
TOTAL .	360	356	1,030	2,057	3,803

This means a 38 per cent. total loss of operating personnel
each year."

One month later, on 28 September, Doenitz gave a general
account of what had in fact been the most successful period of
the U-boat campaign:

*" Report of the Conference with the Fuehrer in the Reich
Chancellery on Monday, September 28, 1942, from
1630–1830.*

> Present: The Fuehrer
> Grand-Admiral Raeder
> Field-Marshal Keitel
> Admiral Doenitz
> etc.

The Fuehrer opens the conference by saying that he wishes
to be informed about the present state of the U-boat war.

He also desires to form an opinion of the degree with which U-boat warfare is keeping pace with the further demands of war.   He continues by expressing his great appreciation of the achievements of the U-boats and he is convinced that the monthly rate of sinkings will continue to be so high that the enemy will not be able to replace his losses by new construction.   He considers it impossible that the increase in production of enemy shipyards is anything like what their propaganda would have us believe.   Even if the enemy should succeed in launching ships relatively quickly, he would still lack the necessary engines, auxiliary engines, and, most of all, crews for the ships.   With regard to the enemy's manpower problem, he calls attention to the fact that it is very much to our disadvantage if the crews of ships which have been sunk are able to go to sea again in new ships.

The Fuehrer stresses the necessity for putting new technical developments into practical use promptly; only in this way can full advantage be taken of new inventions.   This was demonstrated in the construction of the heavy tank which would have given us a decided superiority in Africa had it been available earlier.

Admiral Doenitz reviews the present state of the Battle of the Atlantic.   He says the U-boat conflict has moved back again from the American coast to mid-Atlantic because fighting off the American coast was no longer sufficiently profitable.   There are still, however, a few ' soft spots ' left along the coast where the enemy can be attacked successfully. He points out that we obtained some results by laying mines off the coast.   Operations around the St. Lawrence River continue to be productive to some extent.

He then touches upon the prospects for success in the South Atlantic, especially along the African coast.   He points out on the map, however, that the chief task of the Navy is attacking convoys in the North Atlantic. . . .

But the great menace for U-boats to-day is aircraft. Admiral Doenitz shows on a map what range enemy aircraft based on the British Isles attained in the years 1940, 1941, and 1942, and therefore in which sea areas effective attacks on convoys by U-boats had to be abandoned.   This illustrates how concentrated attacks against convoys were pushed further and further towards the middle of the Atlantic. . . .

This also shows clearly the necessity for our own Air Force to support the U-boats to a much greater extent than hitherto. . . . Emphasis is laid on the technical improvements of the U-boat and its weapons, not because our losses have greatly increased, but because we wish to attain the same success as before in spite of improvements in enemy defence.

Most important of all is the demand for increased underwater speed. This is to be met by the new Walther U-boat. A U-boat with great underwater speed will be able to come within shooting range of the convoy in spite of enemy escort vessels. It will also enable the U-boat to elude its pursuers quickly. . . .

The Fuehrer fully supports these ideas and adds that, in his opinion, the introduction of a U-boat with high underwater speed would have a revolutionary effect. . . .

Admiral Doenitz brings up for discussion the problem of surface attack on the convoy escort vessels by U-boats. He sees a solution in the remote-controlled rocket.

The Fuehrer warns him against becoming too optimistic about such projectiles with which the Army and Air Force are also experimenting. Nevertheless, it is felt that further research is justified since it may possibly lead to a revolutionary development for the U-boat.

Admiral Doenitz emphasizes once more the necessity for evolving such projectiles for the U-boat. . . .

The Fuehrer mentions the possibility of feigning the destruction of U-boats. He refers to numerous reports of airmen who took it for granted that a U-boat had been destroyed after sighting a big oil slick. He had in mind some kind of torpedo which would explode on the surface and eject oil blubber and similar material.

An objection was made that the loss of one torpedo tube for actual attack would be unfortunate. . . .

In closing, the Walther U-boat was discussed.

Grand-Admiral Raeder reported that . . . mass production of these U-boats is to be started as soon as possible, with corresponding adjustment of the present U-boat construction programme.

The Fuehrer was entirely in harmony with these plans and emphasizes once more the need for quick action. He referred again to his conviction that the U-boat is playing a decisive role in the outcome of the war.

After the conference was adjourned, *Grand-Admiral Raeder* reported to the Fuehrer that a Spanish steamer had unfortunately been sunk by one of our U-boats.

The Fuehrer decided that the sinking is to be admitted, and that Spain is to be fully compensated for the loss of the ship, including the cargo of wheat. He also ordered that a public announcement is to be made that the guilty commander will be court-martialled.

Admiral Doenitz had already issued this order."

The Atlantic was the last theatre in which Germany remained on the offensive. It was not to be for very much longer. In six weeks the U-boats proved themselves powerless to prevent the Allied invasion fleet from reaching North Africa, and in six months they were driven from the Atlantic altogether. They returned later, but they never again exercised the supremacy they held in 1942. The era of attack was over; it was ' the end of the beginning of the war.'

PART III

DEFENCE

October 1942—July 1944

Chapter XIII

MEDITERRANEAN

THE month of October 1942 was the turning-point of the war. It was the last month in which the Axis powers held the initiative and the first month in which the Allies began the series of offensive operations which finally led to the invasion and conquest of Italy and Germany.

Malta—Stalingrad—El Alamein: these were the three rocks on which the Axis plans were wrecked. The relief of Malta and Stalingrad, and the stubborn resistance at El Alamein put an end to the grandiose schemes Hitler had made at the Berghof in the spring of 1942. Then it had all looked so easy. Poring over a large-scale map of the world Hitler had shown with a sweep of his hand how the armies on the Eastern Front would expand the Stalingrad salient and press on relentlessly against the Russians, forcing them to surrender; how Rommel would clear up Libya and Egypt, advancing on to the precious oilfields in Iran; and how by then the Japanese would be in India, ready to link up with Germany and throw an armoured cordon round the continents of Europe and Asia. He had gone on to show how the Axis navies would sweep the Anglo-Saxons from the high seas, how England would be starved and beaten into submission, and how finally even the American continent might be conquered.

It was in the Mediterranean that these world plans first cracked under the gathering weight of Allied power. And when the storm broke on the night of 23 October and the 8th Army began its attack on the Axis positions at El Alamein, it was Allied supremacy at sea which ensured the 8th Army's supplies while at the same time denying them to the Afrika Korps.

On 19 November the Red Army broke through the German armies encircling Stalingrad, and the long retreat from Russia started. Again it was Allied sea power, represented by the convoys to Archangel and Murmansk, which had helped the Red Army to make a recovery which dumbfounded Hitler and put an end to his schemes on the Eastern Front.

This was not all. On 8 November a joint Anglo-American force invaded North Africa. The first major invasion by the Allies, the North African landings met with complete success. All the efforts of the U-boats had failed to prevent the assembling and sailing of this vast armada, which was to mean that Rommel was caught between two Allied armies.

But far more had been gained than a mere tactical advantage over Rommel. The North African landings and the advance of the 8th Army, if successful, meant that Africa would be cleared of Axis forces; meant that Allied naval and air bases could be established on the southern shores of the Mediterranean; meant that Malta would no longer be a defensive stronghold but the advance spearhead of the Allied attack on Europe.

Raeder had warned Hitler at least a year before these events of what would happen, but he had been disregarded because at the time Hitler had been obsessed with the possibility of an Allied invasion of Norway. Nevertheless Raeder had continued to concentrate on the problem of the Mediterranean, so that by the time the 8th Army attacked at El Alamein he was ready with suggestions to repair the damage.

Raeder pointed out to Hitler that next to Malta the most important strategical position was Tunisia. The peninsula stretched far into the Mediterranean, the sea routes to Sicily and Italy were short, and, if German bases could be established and held at Bizerta and Tunis, it should be possible to cut the Mediterranean from north to south. The junction of the Allied armies would be prevented, and hence Sicily and Italy would be saved.

Hitler appreciated Raeder's arguments and some three weeks before the North African landings he initiated operations for taking Tunisia from the French, and, as an additional safeguard, he prepared for the military occupation of Southern France. These plans were carried out immediately after the North African landings. On 9 November the Vichy government formally granted the German request for military, air and naval bases in

Tunisia. On 11 November German troops occupied Southern France.*

Frantic efforts were then made to build up the Tunisian bridgehead. Rommel fought a skilful delaying action back towards the Mareth line, while the German troops already in Tunisia did their best to hinder the Allied advance from the west—as Hitler said: " The bridgehead had to be built up and fortified in a race for time against the Allies in Algeria."

Hitler also feared that attacks would be launched in the Eastern Mediterranean against Crete and the Peloponnesus. Extra men and material were accordingly sent to the Balkans. The Axis prepared to defend the Mediterranean with everything that could be spared from the Eastern Front and Europe.

Naval measures consisted of an increase in U-boats in the Mediterranean, a demand to the Italians to mine the Sicilian Channel,† and a strong, but fruitless endeavour to force the Italian fleet to sea. The refusal to commit the Italian fleet was in part accounted for by the serious shortage of fuel oil, but the main reason was that the Italian Commander-in-Chief, Admiral Riccardi, had little faith in his ability to defeat the British now that they were numerically equal. He did agree, however, to increase sea transport facilities to Tunisia, but insisted that every convoy should be heavily protected by the Luftwaffe.

The weakness of the Italians was a serious defect, but in the main Hitler was satisfied with his defensive measures. Still, he wanted to hear the opinions of his advisers, and on 19 November he summoned Raeder to a conference at the Berghof. Raeder gave his opinions cautiously:

" The landing in North Africa proves that there is as yet no shortage of enemy ships for strategic purposes. . . . The ships used in the North African operation total approximately 1,300,000 tons, according to reports received of ships passing Gibraltar. The enemy can start another operation

* The naval base at Toulon was not occupied until 27 November. The French resisted strongly, and so delayed the Germans that Admiral de Laborde had time to scuttle most of the French Fleet. Hitler gave the port to the Italians, who had long coveted it.

† It is one of the mysteries of the war why the Sicilian Channel was not in fact mined. The Italians accepted the necessity for the operation as strongly as the Germans had recommended it, but for some unknown reason the mining was never actually carried out.

of greater scope by the middle of December if he is able to continue restricting other types of shipping.

Tunisia always was and still is the decisive key position in the Mediterranean. The presence of Axis forces in Tunisia compels the enemy to employ considerable forces which must be supplied by long and vulnerable routes. It is, however, a simple task to supply our own Panzer army since our lines are short. If we are able to hold Tunisia, the enemy will have gained only the advantage of moving his air bases closer to our North African position and to Italy. . . . Should the enemy succeed in dislodging us from North Africa altogether, he will have enough ships and troops to start an all-out attack on the southern flank of Europe. This attack might be launched in any one of three directions:

(*a*) The Iberian Peninsula;
(*b*) Italy;
(*c*) The Balkans.

If the enemy has insufficient forces for operations of such scope, he may possibly occupy the various islands in the Mediterranean—the Balearic islands, Sardinia, and Corsica in the west, and Rhodes and Crete in the east. The following factors cause me to fear a sudden powerful attack on the Ægean from the Suez area: the quiet in the Eastern Mediterranean; the large number of troops landed in South Africa during the last few months; the complete absence of reports from the Indian Ocean; and reports of increased Commando activity in Cyprus. Paralysis of our oil supplies in Roumania will always, of course, be one of the enemy's principal goals."

The tone of the conference was far from defeatist. It had certainly not occurred to Hitler that he was on the defensive, and at the same time he discussed the blockade of Leningrad, the possibility of capturing Iceland, and the intensification of the U-boat campaign. Raeder alone had appreciated the real significance of the Allied victories. They had proved conclusively that the sporadic successes of the U-boats and of the Luftwaffe had been insufficient to wrest control of the sea from the Allies. Without a naval air arm, and without sufficient surface ships, the German Navy was too unbalanced to be able to face the Allied fleets on anything like equal terms. To Raeder it was more obvious than ever that sea power was going to be the decisive factor in the war, and this was Germany's greatest weakness.

Other weaknesses in Germany were also beginning to make themselves felt. German war economy had reached its peak by approximately mid-1942, and it was now impossible to increase production or manpower. All that could be done was to shift the effort from one sphere to another, from ships to tanks, or from bombs to torpedoes. Increased production in one industry meant a reduction in another, and whatever orders Hitler gave, the total level of production remained the same. Of the three services the German Navy suffered most. Only the production of U-boats was increased; every other branch of the Navy was scaled down.

With the Allies in North Africa the position of Spain also had to be reconsidered. An Allied conquest of Spain would put the Axis in as dangerous a situation as the conquest of Tunisia. From Spain the Allies would be able to launch a direct attack against Southern France. On the other hand, if the Axis occupied Spain they would not only be able to isolate the Allied forces in the Mediterranean, but they would also have additional ports from which U-boats would be able to attack the Atlantic convoys. Franco, however, steadily maintained his attitude of benevolent neutrality and resisted all attempts to form an open military alliance.

To Raeder, the occupation of Spain was as essential as holding Tunisia, and when, by mid-December he still saw no improvement in the German position in North Africa, he once more urged Hitler to act:

(*Extract from conference on* 22 *December* 1942.)

" At dinner alone with the Fuehrer, *Grand-Admiral Raeder* discusses the Iberian question: it is a great temptation for the enemy to get the Iberian peninsula in his power. Such a step would be the best way to fight the U-boats. It would also be of the utmost strategic importance to us to take over the entire Iberian peninsula to neutralize or eliminate the Anglo-American occupation of North Africa, and to intensify U-boat warfare and blockade running. Since, however, we do not want to divert either the military or economic forces necessary for such action unless it is imperative, we must strive to maintain the neutrality of the Iberian peninsula.

This, nevertheless, requires extensive military and political measures to be taken immediately. If the enemy should take over the Iberian peninsula we would be confronted by an extremely critical situation from the military point of view. The economic problem would be even worse and almost impossible to cope with. Germany must therefore be ready to seize Spain and Portugal by force . . . at the very moment when the danger of an enemy attack . . . is imminent even if such a step should entail great economic sacrifices for the rest of Europe.

The Fuehrer is of the same opinion. He intends to enter into negotiations with Spain and to prepare for an occupation. For the moment he wants to wait."

During the same private session with Hitler, Raeder pointed out the raw material situation and its effect on the German Navy. He said:

"I must insist that future allotments (of raw materials) recognize the importance of the Navy and the decisive significance of naval warfare for the whole war effort. . . . I cannot find such recognition in the steel allocation to the Navy, which, being 127,000 tons, represents a mere five per cent. of the total of 2,500,000 tons.

The Fuehrer understands the Navy's difficulties. He has also had to reduce greatly the quotas of other branches of the Armed Forces. He explains in detail how he must first prevent the collapse of any front where the enemy could substantially injure home territory. There is still a great deal to be done on this score. He has personally discussed the situation of the Navy with Minister Speer, but he cannot see his way clear to help the Navy at the present time. He hopes that the situation will be better by the second quarter but he can make no promises."

But neither the Allied threat in the Mediterranean, nor the Russian threat against Stalingrad, nor the worsening economic situation in Germany could make Hitler change over to the defensive. Instead he simply regarded these facts as little more than the sort of reverses every military commander experiences. Tunisia was to be held and thus bring an end to Allied ambitions in the Mediterranean; Stalingrad was to be reinforced and

Russian convoys obliterated; and, since he was dictator of a totalitarian state, he would remedy the economic situation simply by ordering production to be increased. The plans he had so confidently made in the spring were by no means cancelled: they were merely postponed until the present obstructions could be removed.

Chapter XIV

RAEDER RESIGNS

THE biggest threat to the German Navy at this time, however, was not from the Allies but from the German High Command itself. Confident in his ability to regain the initiative from the Allies in the Mediterranean, Hitler had listened amicably and even with respect in December to Raeder's ideas for the conduct of the war. Within two weeks, however, his benevolence towards the Navy had turned first to grave displeasure and then to raving, hysterical anger in which he had demanded that all major warships should be scrapped.

The seeds of this sudden change had been planted and fostered many years earlier by Goering, who, disliking Raeder intensely and convinced of the omnipotence of the Luftwaffe, had continually tried to persuade Hitler that the surface ships of the Navy were useless. The events which now occurred gave Goering his opportunity. He skilfully fanned the flames of Hitler's anger and brought about Raeder's downfall.

The affair began in the middle of December 1942, with an inter-Service quarrel between Raeder, Kesselring and Goering over the organization of sea transport in the Mediterranean. Goering had ordered that all matters concerned with the transport of supplies to North Africa should be directed by his nominee in the Department of Sea Transport. As this had implied the direction of naval matters as well, Raeder had protested and had issued instructions to his naval commanders in Italy that the order was not to be obeyed. Goering was incensed and demanded the withdrawal of Raeder's instructions. The matter was taken to Hitler, and, after a slight modification of Goering's orders, Raeder withdrew his objections.

The event was not so serious as might appear. The conflicting jurisdiction of the three Services was a recurring theme and problems of this nature were always solved by a direct appeal to Hitler. The protagonists were occasionally heated in their disputes, but it was recognized that such problems would arise from time to time. There was thus nothing extraordinary about this particular situation. It became, however, the basis for the events which followed.

The next stage in the crisis was brought about by the defeat of the pocket battleship *Luetzow* and the cruiser *Hipper* in the Arctic.

A major attack on the Russian convoys had been planned for December/January. The plan for this operation—' Regenbogen ' (Rainbow)—was much the same as that of the attack on PQ 17, except that, as it was the time of Arctic twilight, the Luftwaffe was not employed.

To begin with, everything went smoothly. The U-boats located the convoy as planned and reported its position to the surface Fleet which promptly sailed to intercept. The big ships made contact in the early hours of 31 December and cleared for action.

The British escort force had been scattered by a gale three days previously, and the convoy was only protected by five destroyers, two corvettes, and one trawler—hopeless odds against the *Luetzow*, the *Hipper* and their six destroyers. The German force split into two groups; the *Hipper* and two destroyers against the escort, and the *Luetzow* and four destroyers against the convoy.

The action which followed was one of the most brilliant fought by the Royal Navy during the whole war. By daring attacks and skilful manœuvring, Captain R. St. V. Sherbrooke, V.C., in command of the British Force and captain of the destroyer H.M.S. *Onslow*, held the German ships at bay for well over an hour. The convoy was covered by a smoke screen, while the destroyers persistently attacked and worried the German battleship and cruiser. Forty minutes after the action had begun, the *Onslow* was hit four times in rapid succession. Captain Sherbrooke was severely wounded in the face, and his left eye was disabled, but he continued to direct the ships under his command until a further hit compelled the *Onslow* to disengage.

Meanwhile two British cruisers, the *Sheffield* and the *Jamaica*,

which had been twenty-five miles away to the north, raced to help
Captain Sherbrooke and his destroyers.   On their arrival, the
German Admiral obeyed his orders to avoid a major action and
retired.   The *Hipper* was severely damaged, and one German
destroyer was sunk.   On the British side, one destroyer, H.M.S.
Achates, was also sunk, while most of the others were damaged.
The convoy, however, succeeded in getting through to Russia
without loss.

Ship for ship the losses were thus about even, but considering
the enormous superiority of the German flee., and the fact that
the convoy escaped unscathed, this action, fought in the dim
light of the Arctic winter, and in waters where human life could
not survive for more than ten minutes, was a major defeat for
Germany.

At Hitler's headquarters, Vice-Admiral Krancke, the newly
appointed naval representative, had told Hitler of the first
sighting reports of the convoy.   At 1145 on the same morning,
Krancke told Hitler that the action was over, that a U-boat had
reported " only a red glow could be seen in the Arctic twilight,"
and that apparently the attack had been successful.

By the evening, however, no definite reports had yet come
through.   This was natural enough since the German ships were
still at sea, and to radio a report would have been to reveal their
position.   Hitler began to grow impatient.   Later, during the
same evening, a Reuter's wireless news item stated that there
had been a naval engagement in the Arctic and that the convoy
had escaped undamaged.   It also stated that one German
destroyer had been sunk and that one German cruiser had been
damaged.   There was still no definite news at Hitler's headquarters and the tension mounted.   Hitler told Raeder to order
the ships to report.   Raeder refused as it would be too dangerous.
Throughout the night Hitler waited for news, but none came.

The *Hipper* arrived at her anchorage early on the morning of
1 January, and the long-awaited report was demanded.   A
breakdown in the teleprinter service, however, delayed the
message further, so that by the time Hitler was ready for the
noon situation conference, there was still no report.   Hitler
exploded.   Vice-Admiral Krancke has described the scene: [7]

" I informed the Fuehrer accordingly (about the breakdown in communications).   He said it was an impudence

that he as Supreme Commander had not received any news
twenty-four hours after the action, and that the British had
already given a report on the previous evening. In a very
excited state he ordered me to send a radio message demanding
a report from the naval forces. . . . Then followed further
remarks from the Fuehrer who was very excited. He spoke
of the uselessness of the big ships, of lack of ability, and lack
of daring on the part of the older naval officers, and so on.
I had to give up any attempt to explain or protest. . . ."

The report was finally delivered to Hitler in the afternoon. It
did not make pleasant reading, and at the evening situation
conference Hitler raged once more. Coupled with the fracas over
sea transport in the Mediterranean, the event decided him. In
a hysterical outburst he ordered the German High Seas Fleet
to be decommissioned, and, except for those ships which were to
be used to train U-boat crews, all major warships were to be
scrapped.

Raeder has given his own account of the events of these two
days: [3]

" The Fuehrer received a purely irrelevant and unsatis-
factory report of the affair and became highly excited—a
condition which was considerably aggravated by the tactless
remarks of the recently appointed naval representative at
Fuehrer Headquarters (Vice-Admiral Krancke). The same
night Hitler declared to his close associates that he was
completely averse to the use of capital ships for such
operations. . . . He dictated his views to be recorded in the
official War Diary as his irrevocable decision on the matter.
I received orders by telephone to report immediately to
Hitler's headquarters, but I requested that I might be
excused until I had collected the necessary and indisputable
facts."

Raeder managed to postpone his meeting with Hitler until
6 January, intending to give him time to cool down and hoping
that then he would take a more balanced view of the situation.
Meanwhile Goering interposed his views. He pointed out how
valuable Luftwaffe squadrons were being tied down in Norway,
protecting the Fleet; how the Luftwaffe could do all that the
warships could do; and how much he, as Deputy for the Four

Years Plan, would welcome the extra steel which the scrapping of big ships would produce.

Practically the whole of Raeder's term as Commander-in-Chief of the German Navy had been spent in trying to obtain a more balanced fleet—more capital ships, aircraft carriers, a Naval Air Arm—and the refutation of his ideas and plans was a slur which he could not overlook. He did not give in easily, however, and he prepared himself carefully for the coming conference with Hitler, determined to restore his Fuehrer's faith in the German Navy.

On 6 January he arrived at Hitler's headquarters—' Wolfs-schanze '—ready for whatever Hitler had to say:

" *The Fuehrer* talks for an hour and a half on the role played by the Prussian and German navies since they came into existence. The German Navy was originally patterned on the British Navy and proved unimportant during the wars of 1864, 1866, and 1870–71. . . .

U-boats constituted the most important branch of the German Navy in the last war and must be considered equally important to-day. The High Seas Fleet made no notable contribution during the last war. It is customary to blame the Kaiser for this inactivity but this opinion is unwarranted. The real reason was that the Navy lacked men of action who were determined to fight with or without the support of the Kaiser. . . .

The revolution and the scuttling of the Fleet at Scapa Flow do not redound to the credit of the German Navy. The Navy has always been careful to consider the numbers of their own ships and men as compared with the enemy before entering an engagement   The Army does not follow this principle. As a soldier, the Fuehrer demands that once forces have been committed to action the battle must be fought out to a decision. Due to the present critical situation where all fighting power, all personnel, and all material must be brought into action, we cannot permit our big ships to ride idly at anchor for months. They require constant protection by the Air Force as well as by numerous smaller surface craft. . . .

Due to the mining of the Baltic the big ships find it more and more difficult to carry out exercises. The Coastal

Defence could use the guns from these big ships very effectively. . . .

It should not be considered a degradation if the Fuehrer decides to scrap the big ships. This would only be true if he were removing a fighting unit which had retained its full usefulness. A parallel with this in the Army would be the removal of all cavalry divisions. . . . The Commander-in-Chief, Navy, is to prepare a memorandum giving his views on the above. These comments will be of historical value. The Fuehrer will examine the document carefully."

During the conference Raeder rarely had an opportunity to comment, but at the end he requested a private interview with Hitler. At Nuremberg Raeder described this interview: [3]

" I then requested to be allowed to speak privately to him, whereupon Field-Marshal Keitel and the two secretaries (who for some time now had been used to take down every word which was spoken at these discussions with the Fuehrer) left the room. I then asked the Fuehrer, who throughout his lecture had proclaimed his disapproval of my leadership of the Navy, if I might be relieved of my command as Commander-in-Chief, stating that I could not continue unless I enjoyed his confidence. I added that I was almost 67 years old, my health was no longer good, and the substitution of a younger and more vigorous man would be both natural and apt. The Fuehrer at once began to mollify me. He had not meant to condemn the Navy as a whole, but only to criticize the big ships; the age of people who worked with him had no significance in itself and he had proved it many times; my resignation at this juncture would only mean that he would have to take on another heavy burden himself. It was the time of the terrible Stalingrad battles; the fall of Stalingrad was imminent. I explained that I could not remain on after his lecture of that day as my authority had been shaken, but at the same time it was clear to me that in our mutual interests—both to avoid imposing an extra burden on the Fuehrer and to guard against giving a severe shock to the Navy—my resignation must not outwardly betray any sign of dissension between us. I therefore proposed that I should hand in my resignation on January 30, 1943, the tenth anniversary of the seizure of

power. Such an arrangement would appear quite natural
and would not give rise to suspicions of disagreement. The
nature of my Farewell Address, too, would have a decisive
influence. The Fuehrer agreed to this proposal and ordered
me to nominate in writing two officers whom I considered
capable of succeeding me."

Raeder nominated first Admiral Carls—a ' big ship ' admiral;
and second Admiral Doenitz—Flag Officer Commanding U-boats.
Hitler chose Doenitz. From the point of view of experience
Carls was much the sounder choice, but Hitler liked Doenitz,
and as he had decided that the German Navy should be reduced
to U-boats and minor escort vessels, the choice of Doenitz was
fairly obvious. Doenitz knew little beyond how to operate
U-boats, but he possessed a certain capability and shrewdness
which allowed him to give at least the appearance of knowledge.
His personality, too, was one that accorded well with the high-
ranking Nazis. He had none of Raeder's overbearing correctness
of manner, and he was able to deal with people like Goering on
their own terms. Head of a branch of the Wehrmacht which
rivalled the Luftwaffe in glamour, Doenitz came to his new office
with all the advantages of a romantic background of heroism and
fanatical loyalty to the Fuehrer.

Raeder's resignation was not effective until 30 January, and
in the meantime Hitler had called for a report on his proposal
to decommission the High Seas Fleet. Raeder ordered his staff to
prepare a memorandum with the utmost care, and he personally
corrected the final draft.[7] It was over 5000 words long and
it was presented to Hitler on 15 January with a covering letter
from Raeder in which he made his final plea for the retention of
the High Seas Fleet. The decommissioning would be, he said,[7]
" a victory gained by our enemies without any effort on their
part. It will cause joy in the hostile camp and deep disappoint-
ment in the camp of our allies, especially Japan. It will be viewed
as a sign of weakness and of a lack of comprehension of the
supreme importance of naval warfare in the approaching final
stage of the war." The memorandum itself presented cogent
reasons for the retention of the big ships. The steel and other
raw materials gained would be but a tiny fraction of the overall
demand in Germany; the ships themselves tied down valuable
British forces which might otherwise be employed in the

Mediterranean or elsewhere; and, most important of all, since Britain depended entirely upon her sea communications, the removal of the threat to these would make it seem to the British that the war was as good as won.

These arguments made no difference to Hitler. Krancke, still the naval representative at Fuehrer Headquarters, telephoned the Naval Staff two days later to say that Hitler had read the memorandum and was still determined to decommission the Fleet. On 21 January Admiral Fricke, Raeder's Chief of Staff, made a more authoritative report, recorded in the Naval Staff's War Diary:

"The Fuehrer made several comments concerning the memorandum which were more or less sarcastic in nature and dealt with minor questions only. . . . It is therefore concluded that the main points of the memorandum have failed to impress the Fuehrer, but to what extent this conclusion is correct only the future can tell."

The future told. On 26 January Hitler ordered:

"1. All work on big ships under construction or being converted is to cease immediately. . . .

2. Unless required for training purposes, battleships, pocket battleships, heavy and light cruisers are to be decommissioned. . . .

3. Naval personnel, workers, etc., becoming available as the result of this directive should be used to accelerate U-boat repairs and construction . . ."

The order ended:

"In view of the political and psychological effect of this order it is only to be communicated to the smallest number of officers."

Although Raeder did not formally resign until 30 January, Doenitz had begun taking over the command of the Navy some two weeks earlier. He had almost joyfully passed the order on to the Naval Staff. He had been in command of the U-boat branch for so long that he thought only in terms of submarine warfare, and at that time the decommissioning of the big ships meant little more to him than that U-boat production would be increased. During each crisis of the war, Doenitz had had but one solution—more and yet more U-boats, and it was thus hardly surprising that he was comparatively unmoved by Hitler's order. He did not see it as Raeder had done—as a bloodless victory for the Allies—but rather as so much extra men, steel and fuel for his U-boats.

But Doenitz did not maintain this attitude for long. His new position brought home to him some of the broader issues of the war and he began to realize what the loss of the big ships would mean. Within three weeks of assuming command, he knew that Raeder had been right, and that the big ships should be kept in commission and operating. He was far more subtle in his dealings with Hitler than Raeder, and in one conference, on 26 February, he won a partial reversal of Hitler's order. Later he was able quietly to cancel the order altogether, and so saved the High Seas Fleet.

When Raeder resigned, Hitler issued a grandiloquent order praising Raeder and appointing him Inspector-General of the Navy—a position without any actual duties—but almost pointedly neglected to confer on him any of the orders or insignias usual on such an occasion. This last slur hurt Raeder deeply, but his loyalty remained unshaken. Although he was never again called in officially to give his advice, he endeavoured from time to time to obtain an audience with Hitler to proffer suggestions for the conduct of the war. He kept in touch with events by arranging for a representative from each of the three Services to bring him three-weekly reports, and thus, in his country house outside Berlin, he was able to continue his interest in the only world he knew.

In estimating Raeder's character one is brought up sharply by the typical sophistry engendered by Nazi Germany. Intelligent and kindly at heart, Raeder nevertheless had believed implicitly in Hitler and had obeyed him without question. Though never a Nazi himself, he was prepared to follow Hitler with the same loyalty with which in earlier days he had followed Kaiser Wilhelm. Both at his trial and during previous interrogations, Raeder denied that he had any knowledge of concentration camps or similar Nazi activities until three months before the end of the war, when a personal friend of his who had himself suffered at the hands of the Gestapo gave him a first-hand account of what he had seen and of how he had been treated. Of other Gestapo activities—informing and spying on Germans themselves—Raeder was well aware. Heydrich, who later became Himmler's principal henchman, had once been a naval officer. Raeder had dismissed him from the Services at the end of 1928 for an offence against a young girl. Ever afterwards Raeder was convinced that his private telephone was tapped and that all his conversations were maliciously reported to Himmler and thus to Hitler. Even during his retirement Raeder was always armed, and carried a small pistol with him wherever he went. Whether because he feared Heydrich and his associates, or whether for some other reason is not known, but it is clear that he suffered as badly as anyone else in Germany from the general persecution mania caused by Gestapo activities.

Raeder was a typical German officer. Brought up under a rigid code of discipline, he obeyed orders as strictly as he himself demanded obedience from his subordinates. In spite of his arrogance and dictatorial manner, Raeder was well liked by the senior officers. His staff had a deep veneration for him, and most naval officers appreciated both his wide grasp of strategy and the extent to which he had resuscitated the German Navy. His resignation was felt as a great loss, particularly by the senior admirals. He was an exceptional strategist and a sound administrator whom Hitler and the German Navy could ill afford to lose.

Against all that has been said in Raeder's favour, however, stands a moral weakness which ultimately sent him to gaol at Nuremberg. Although he could and did resign on account of a military question, Raeder felt no apparent guilt on the wider issue of waging war at all. His representations to Hitler before war began were not that war was wrong, but that the Navy was not yet ready. A bigger man than he, General Ludwig Beck, had given the lead by resigning on the question of invading Czechoslovakia: Raeder, instead, pleaded for speedier rearmament. On all such moral issues Raeder apparently believed that it was not for him to judge. Hitler ordered total war, and Raeder, as his subordinate officer, obeyed the order.

Chapter XV

TUNISIA

RAEDER'S resignation weakened the German position in the Mediterranean. The change in Commanders-in-Chief meant a break in the steady direction of the Axis naval effort in the

Mediterranean. Axis troops were forced into Tunisia, and it became clear, as Raeder had foreseen, that unless the Axis could hold the Allies in Tunisia, Italy would be doomed. Raeder had at least been able to put some spirit into the Italians, and, during his command, supplies to Tunisia had been increased and maintained—so much so that General Eisenhower, on 6 January, reported to the Allied Chiefs of Staff that "unless this (Axis reinforcement) can be materially and immediately reduced, the situation both here and in the 8th Army area will deteriorate without doubt." But, by the beginning of March, the situation had once more become critical for the Axis. The British Mediterranean Fleet, the R.A.F., and the United States Air Force, which had now joined the Allied forces, had taken a heavy toll of Axis shipping and severely damaged the supply ports. More ships were required to transport men and material to Tunisia and these ships required more and more protection. The Italian Navy was available, but would do little to help, so that the onus of convoy protection fell upon the inadequate U-boats and Luftwaffe.

Between 14 and 18 March Hitler held two conferences in a determined attempt to find a solution to the problem, and Doenitz was given his first chance to show what he could do in his new position. Hitler opened the conference:

" Tunisia is strategically of prime importance. Conquest of Tunisia means a saving of 4–5 million tons and more to the enemy. . . . Retention of Tunisia is a question of supplies. The 80,000 tons per month cited as necessary by the Italian Supreme Command are entirely inadequate; rather 150,000 to 200,000 tons monthly are needed. We estimate for each division about 1 train—500 tons are required daily. For the 8 divisions in Tunisia, inclusive of the Italians, this makes a total of 4000 tons daily. . . . It is impossible to supply armies by air. A single 9000 tons ship, for example, can carry as much on one voyage as a whole air fleet can carry over a much longer period. Protection of convoys by the Luftwaffe alone is not possible; ships are still required. The Straits of Sicily must teem with patrol and escort vessels. Good organization is essential. Only the German Navy can organize this. . . . It is therefore necessary to confront the Italians now with the alternative of either making an all-out effort to get supplies through or to lose Tunisia, and with that Italy as well. The Commander-in-Chief, Navy, is to present these views to the Duce. He is to insist on my suggestions being followed as closely as possible."

Hitler then read out a few paragraphs of a letter he intended to send to Mussolini in addition to Doenitz's personal visit. The letter was on much the same lines as his lecture at the conference, and Field-Marshal Kesselring was instructed to deliver it before Doenitz arrived. The conference continued with a suggestion from Kesselring:

"I have arranged with Gauleiter Saukel that from ten to fifteen thousand Italian workers should be sent from Germany to Italy to increase the Italian ship repairing capacity."

Doenitz, too, spoke:

"The German Command must take a strong hand in the convoy conferences. However, in carrying out your orders, my Fuehrer, I will take care lest, due to the Italian mentality, the opposite of what is desired will be accomplished through passive resistance on the part of the Italians. It is not impossible that, even though the Duce should agree, lower officials might sabotage the measures we have planned to put into effect."

Hitler went on to emphasize that he preferred the most drastic solution and that he would only reluctantly agree to anything milder.

Four days later Doenitz returned from Rome. He had obtained complete agreement to the German proposals from Mussolini. He reported to Hitler:

"*The Commander-in-Chief, Navy*, reports the results of his conference with the Duce and of the talks with the Italian Naval Staff in Rome. He submits the signed agreement and gives a step by step description of how the agreement was reached. In so doing he calls attention particularly to the Duce's emphatic approval and the cordial tone of the talks. On the other hand a note of restraint and disapproval was noticeable from the very beginning in his conference with the

Italian Naval Staff, which, according to Admiral Riccardi, was due to the fact that he understood very little of what was said during the conference with the Duce, since the conversation was in German. The proper *rapport* was only established when he, Grand-Admiral Doenitz, spoke in stronger terms after the Italian counter-proposals had not provided a basis for an agreement. Complete agreement was then reached, since the form adhered to by Doenitz gave the Italians the possibility of saving face. . . . The Duce stressed particularly his intention of committing the entire Italian Fleet should the Anglo-Saxons land on Sardinia, but he stated that he lacks the necessary fuel oil. Grand-Admiral Doenitz approved this plan and agreed to investigate the fuel situation as soon as he returned to Berlin, as he is convinced that such an operation might be successful against an enemy who is hampered by his landing operations. What is more he feels that it would be better for the Italian ships to get into the fight even at the risk of heavy losses, rather than fall into the hands of the enemy while still in harbour and perhaps even without fighting."

The promised effort by the Italian Fleet did not materialize. Allied sea and air forces continued their wholesale destruction of Axis merchant shipping and Italian ports, unhampered by the Italian Navy. The Allied control of the sea in the Mediterranean was unbreakable and, as a result, the position of Axis forces in the Tunisian peninsula became precarious. Without supplies there was little they could do against the British 8th and Allied 1st Armies.

The German Navy did what they could, but the mounting U-boat losses and the shortage of steel for shipbuilding in Germany forestalled their efforts. The shortage of steel, indeed, had become extremely serious. On 11 April Doenitz presented Hitler with a long memorandum showing how this shortage was hindering every sphere of naval activity. They had been given a new quota which, at 166,000 tons per month, was still 15,000 tons lower than the lowest amount required—and that excluded the amount required for U-boats. Hitler explained the situation:

" The problem is where can the steel be obtained ? To be sure in a totalitarian state I could order the required amount to be made available, but that would mean exacting it from some other Branch. The pressing needs of the Army for tanks and anti-tank guns, and of the Luftwaffe for AA guns, etcetera, would not permit this for long. The Army must be equipped with the newest types of weapons in sufficient quantities to prevent excessive loss of life. In order not to lose the war in the air, the material of our Luftwaffe should be increased enormously. Finally, the Navy must receive sufficient material not only to prevent submarine warfare from falling off but rather to increase its effectiveness. Something must also be done for the Merchant Navy to solve the supply problem. To this end Minister Speer and Messrs. Roechling and Duisberg are conferring with me during the next few days to discuss the question of increasing the steel production from 2·6 to 4 million tons per month."

But this did not help the immediate situation, and all that Doenitz obtained was a promise that U-boat production would be increased to 27 boats per month by the second half of the year.

Meanwhile, in Tunisia, in spite of sporadic efforts by the Axis, the position grew steadily worse, until on 7 May Tunis and Bizerta were captured simultaneously. Allied control of the sea cut off the remaining enemy forces in the Cape Bon peninsula, and the last remnants of the Axis army in Africa surrendered on 13 May.

The Axis was now unmistakably on the defensive. The Allies were in a position to attack anywhere in southern Europe—from Salonika to Marseilles—and all initiative had passed into their hands. From this time onwards it was the task of the Supreme Command to decide where the Allies were going to strike next and what could best be done to meet the threat. They no longer planned grandiose operations but concentrated on developing the mobility of the Wehrmacht so that speedy reinforcements could be sent to any area of their immense front.

The Tunisian campaign had demonstrated forcibly the meaning of sea power. The Axis had made a serious mistake by its neglect. The Italian Fleet, however, had not been committed and there was still a chance that by mustering all their combined naval resources they might be able to call a halt to the Allied advance.

The immediate problem in the Mediterranean was where were
the Allies going to strike next ? Either Sicily or Sardinia seemed
the most likely objective, and it was obviously a matter of the
utmost urgency that these two islands should be adequately
fortified. Control of the sea would again be the deciding factor,
and Hitler once more sent Doenitz to Italy to find out what
the Italians were doing and to try all in his power to muster the
maximum possible effort. The Italians, however, were near the
end of their tether, and their refusal to co-operate to the extent
necessary was far more marked than before. Doenitz left Berlin
on 12 May, the day before the surrender of the Cape Bon forces,
and he spent four days in Italy conferring with the Italian and
German commanders. His report on these four days shows
clearly the serious breach which had sprung up between the two
major partners of the Axis:

" Naval High Command.

> *The visit of the Commander-in-Chief, Navy, to Rome,*
> 12 *May to* 15 *May,* 1943.

May 12, 1943.

0800.   Departure from Berlin.
1300.   Arrival in Rome.

Conference at Hotel Excelsior with Vice-Admiral Ruge, Rear-
Admiral Meendsen-Bohlken, and Rear-Admiral Loewisch
(the German Naval commanders in Italy).

The commanders give a brief summary of the situation.
The Commander-in-Chief, Navy, very briefly discusses the
immediate problem: which is more important, Sicily or
Sardinia? After lunch Admiral Doenitz asks the commanders
what they think is the best solution for the present situation
where German interests are represented by two naval
commands who thus cannot be effective in dealing with
the Italians and do not guarantee smooth and close
collaboration.

Both commanders are convinced that the present dualism
will have to end. . . . Rear-Admiral Meendsen-Bohlken
does not consider this solution possible for technical reasons.
. . . Admiral Doenitz reserves his decision for the present;
it has already been influenced by the fact that Admiral

Riccardi has asked him through Commander Sestini that Vice-Admiral Ruge should be appointed the sole representative of Germany with the Supermarina (the Italian Navy High Command).

1630 to 1930. *Conference at Supermarina.*

Admiral Riccardi thanks Admiral Doenitz for his visit and expresses the hope that this conference will further the common cause of Italy and Germany. He also welcomes Admiral Doenitz in the name of the Italian Navy.

Admiral Doenitz states that the purpose of his visit is to discuss matters personally and to exchange information, since it is difficult to do this from a distance or by post.

Admiral Riccardi gives a summary of the present situation from the Italian point of view. It is a fact that the enemy is preparing for further operations in the Algerian coastal harbours; at the same time he is systematically destroying the Italian harbours. Since the fall of Tunisia, an attack on the Italian islands has been expected any day. There are three ways of meeting the enemy invasion:

(*a*) Air attack on the African embarkation points.

(*b*) Attack on the approaching invasion fleet at sea.

(*c*) Local defence at the point of invasion.

The enemy will most likely employ forces strong enough to make his first attempt a certain success. It is therefore necessary that our own weak forces should be consolidated. . . . It has become difficult to supply the island of Sicily. Rail traffic to the island has come to a complete standstill and supplies have had to be sent by sea from Naples. The only way to improve transport on the island itself would be by an increased use of lorries.

Before the war Sicily had supplies for 40 days. To-day there is enough for only 7 days. The question of supplies is becoming more and more difficult every day because the enemy Air Force is constantly increasing.

The same situation prevails in Sardinia. Most of the piers at Cagliari have been destroyed. Porto Torres is of very little use, so only Olbia remains. Railways in Sardinia are badly crippled, lorries are the only solution.

Rear-Admiral Sansonetti now explains the plans of the Italian Navy in greater detail. . . . These studies showed that . . . there is no reason to expect an invasion of Sicily. Of course the enemy knows of the minefields between Sicily and North Africa, but these minefields divide his lines of approach. An invasion of Sardinia is more likely at this time. . . . If it is invaded the Italian battle fleet will be used, but . . . Only three large battleships are actually available in La Spezia; there are as well three cruisers and eight destroyers. Four small battleships have been dismantled in Taranto. . . . After hearing the views of the German Admirals stationed in Rome, *Admiral Doenitz* states that he believes the enemy will attack soon. He says that our own forces are too weak to foil the enemy's plans either by destroying his embarkation points or the approaching invasion fleet. He is going to send more U-boats to the Mediterranean although he is convinced that U-boats will never be able to stop an invasion—they would only be of nuisance value. . . . The battle on land alone is decisive; therefore the most important part of the Navy's task is to make battle on land possible which means safeguarding the supply lines across the sea. . . . We must use every available means to get as much material to the islands as possible. Even small vessels will have to be used for shallow harbours and open bays. If there are not enough small vessels, U-boats will have to be used.

Admiral Riccardi interrupts: To transport supplies ?

Admiral Doenitz : Yes, because U-boats are not decisive in battle.

He continues: Cruisers, too, must frequently make fast trips with supplies. . . . Harbour facilities must be exploited to the fullest extent. The responsible Italian officer must have the right to draft civilians for this. It must not happen again as it did in North Africa that we were defeated because our supply system failed. . . . Even though a naval officer would prefer to fight the enemy at sea we must realize that our forces are too limited and that maintenance of supplies is our main task.

Admiral Riccardi states that he will use all available means to help solve the transport problems. However, he asks Admiral Doenitz to use his influence to increase the Air Force.

Admiral Doenitz replies that he had, of course, only taken up naval matters. Upon his return to Berlin he would stress the absolute necessity of increasing the number of aircraft. . . . Once the enemy obtains airfields near the front, it might again be too late for many things. The unique sacrifice of the Italian Fleet might have helped considerably if it had come earlier; later on the effort was dissipated by the increased enemy air force.

(At this point a misunderstanding is caused by the faulty translation of the Italian interpreter which makes it clear that Admiral Riccardi took these remarks as a reproach to the Italian Navy. The reaction of the Admiral as a reflection of the Italian opinion was very enlightening.)

Admiral Sansonetti interjects at this point that the Italian Admiral Borone in Sicily reported yesterday that there would be nothing left on the island in a month's time unless the strongest efforts were made for defence against enemy air attack. . . .

Admiral Doenitz asks Admiral Riccardi if troops were still being transferred to Sardinia.

Admiral Riccardi replies that the transfer itself poses no difficulties. The real obstacle is the availability of ships for heavy equipment.

Admiral Doenitz points out that the main consideration is the cargo space in small ships. . . . Everything shall be done to meet Admiral Riccardi's requirements. . . . He will emphasize that an increase in air power and AA batteries are most urgently needed. He asks if Admiral Riccardi has any further requests.

Admiral Riccardi replies that the above is already a large order. He is convinced that whatever Germany will provide will be most useful. As far as he knows the Duce has already telegraphed the Fuehrer about the question of the Air Force. He is aware that Germany, too, is having great difficulties. . . .

2000. Dinner in the staff quarters of the German Staff with Supermarina.

May 13, 1943. In the morning.

Continuation of the conferences with representatives of various German offices. . . .

1100. Visit to General Ambrosio.

General impression: Polite but formal reception.

Admiral Doenitz explains that, at the moment, the chief weakness in the defence of the large Italian islands is a lack of reinforcements and supplies. No time should be lost in sending these because the enemy is constantly increasing pressure on our supply lines. . . . After establishing numerous unloading positions it may very well be necessary to press into service submarines, cruisers and other vessels in order to complete the transport of men and supplies as quickly as possible. It is more important for the navy to supply transports than to engage the enemy in battle.

General Ambrosio did not fully agree with the above; he felt that submarines and cruisers should fight.

Admiral Doenitz replied that naval forces have already ceased fighting. When the serious need for transport is compared with what may be gained by engaging the enemy, the former takes precedence.

1130.   Interview with the Duce.

General impression: The Duce is well, optimistic, composed, very frank, sincere, and amicable.

The Duce states that he is confident about the future. The only result of British air raids on Italy will be that the people will learn to hate the British which has not always been the case. This helps in carrying on the war. If there is one Italian who hates the British, it is he himself. He is happy that his people are now learning the meaning of the word hate as well. He has answered the Fuehrer's offer of five divisions by stating he only wants three of them. This refusal came as a surprise to Admiral Doenitz. The Duce explains that he had asked that these three divisions should include six panzer battalions with 300 tanks; two of the battalions are detailed for Sardinia, three for Sicily, and one for Southern Italy. He believes that Sicily is in the greatest danger and supports his contention by referring to the British Press which had repeatedly stated that a free route through the Mediterranean would mean a gain in two million tons of cargo space for the Allies.

Admiral Doenitz gives his opinion of the general situation to the Duce on the same lines as he did in the interview with General Ambrosio.

The Duce immediately reacts to this by himself stressing

the necessity for improvisation and considers this easily possible, particularly because of favourable weather conditions during the summer.

1630. *Conference with Vice-Admiral Ruge and Rear-Admiral Meendsen-Bohlken.*

Admiral Doenitz announces his decision that Admiral Ruge is to take over the German Naval Command and still to maintain the Operations Staff at Supermarina. Rear-Admiral Meendsen-Bohlken will be recalled for other duties. Admiral Doenitz explains his reasons for the decision to Rear-Admiral Meendsen-Bohlken.

Later, drive to Nemi Lake; inspection of the old Roman ships

1930. Conference with German Transport Ministry. . . .

2000. Dinner with the German Ambassador.

2200. Conference with Field-Marshal Kesselring.

Field-Marshal Kesselring states that the Fuehrer is considering the transfer of the Hermann Goering Division and the 7th Airborn division to Italy.

2. The Italian Commando Supremo's refusal of the Fuehrer's offer of five divisions was reported direct to the German Supreme Command without informing him (Field-Marshal Kesselring). Kesselring considers this an act of political importance inasmuch as it proves that the Italians want to remain masters in their own house. Relations between him and General Ambrosio are not very cordial. If his person represents an obstacle to better relations with the Commando Supremo, he is going to express his willingness to make way for another German Commander-in-Chief.

3. On his tour of inspection in Sicily, Field-Marshal Kesselring noticed that Italian defence preparations were very incomplete. He impressed this fact on the Italian Commander-in-Chief, General Roatta. A similar tour of Sardinia is planned during the next few days.

4. Kesselring agrees with the Duce that an attack on Sicily is more probable than an attack on Sardinia.

. . . .

7. He considers an attack on the Iberian peninsula the best way of bringing relief to the Mediterranean situation and intends to submit such a plan to the Fuehrer.

Admiral Doenitz repeatedly stresses that the crux of the problem is the transport of supplies and that these must be brought to the islands speedily and in large quantities. . . . The one drawback is that the Italians are accustomed to work in a leisurely manner. . . .

May 14, 1943.

0930.   Audience with the King.

General impression: Warm reception, agreeable, impressive, a wise, experienced person.   The King is lively and vivacious and has a good memory.

Admiral Doenitz gives his opinion of the general situation to the King as previously discussed with General Ambrosio. He is convinced that Tunisia's fall was due only to the lack of supplies.   If we master the supply situation we will defeat the enemy.

The King points out that unfortunately most of the land routes in Italy are also close to the shore and are therefore subject to attack from the sea.   The audience was ended with stories about his travels to Spitzbergen and Norway.

1030.   Departure from Rome.

1630.   Arrival at ' Wolfsschanze '.

1830.   Departure for Berlin.

2045.   Arrival at Tempelhof.

The C.-in-C., Navy, was accompanied by:

> Rear-Admiral Wagner,
> Commander Pfeiffer,
> Lt. Commander Freiwald."

The problem of Sicily or Sardinia was still unresolved.   The Italians for the most part had guessed Sicily, but while Doenitz had been in Italy, some Allied papers, which described Allied plans for invading Sardinia and the Peloponnesus, had been discovered by the Germans in convincing circumstances.   They were immediately shown to Hitler who accepted them at their face value.   He had in any case believed that Sardinia would be the next Allied objective.

Even more important than the problem of where were the Allies going to strike next, was the question of whether the Italians would remain loyal to the Axis, and Hitler awaited

Doenitz's report with some anxiety. He saw Doenitz within an hour of his arrival at ' Wolfsschanze '.

" *The Commander-in-Chief, Navy*, reports the progress and outcome of his conference with the Duce. . . .

The Fuehrer does not agree with the Duce that the most likely invasion point is Sicily. Furthermore, he believes that the discovered Anglo-Saxon order confirms the assumption that the planned attacks will be directed mainly against Sardinia and the Peloponnesus. . . .

The C.-in-C., Navy, has come away from these conferences with the impression that the Italians will do nothing about the all-important matter of increasing shipping facilities. He was therefore very much pleased to note that Captain Engelhardt, Commanding Officer of Supply and Transport, had already begun to make the necessary arrangements.

Captain Engelhardt reports . . .

The Fuehrer asks Admiral Doenitz whether he thinks that the Duce is determined to carry on to the end.

Admiral Doenitz answers that he accepts this as certain, but that he cannot, of course, be sure. He gained the impression that the primary failing of the Italians is their lack of initiative.

The Fuehrer asserts that he does not trust the Italian upper class. He believes that a man like Ambrosio would be happy if Italy could become a British dominion to-day.

Admiral Doenitz states that generally speaking, since his return from Rome, he has come to the conclusion that the plan to hold the Italian islands will result in a purely defensive operation. It will consume much energy without getting the Axis out of its defensive position. It must also be kept in mind that the Anglo-Saxon powers have gained two million tons in shipping space since the Mediterranean was cleared.

The Fuehrer : ' Which our trusty U-boats will now have to sink.'

The C.-in-C., Navy : ' Yet we are at present facing the greatest crisis in U-boat warfare. . . . For the first time fighting has been impossible and we are suffering heavy losses, 15–17 boats per month.'

The Fuehrer : ' These losses are too high. Something must be done about it.'

The C.-in-C., Navy : ' . . . In view of this situation the occupation of Spain, including Gibraltar, would be the best strategic solution. This would constitute an attack against the flank of the Anglo-Saxon offensive, the Axis would regain the initiative, a radical change would take place in the Mediterranean, and U-boat warfare could be given a much broader basis.'

The Fuehrer states that we are not capable of an operation of this kind, since it would require first-class divisions. Occupation of Spain without the consent of the Spaniards is out of the question, as they are the only tough Latin people and would carry on guerilla warfare in our rear. In 1940 it might have been possible to get Spain to agree to such a move. However, the Italian attack on Greece in the autumn of 1940 shocked Spain. The Axis must face the fact that it is saddled with Italy. Therefore the shipping and transport of supplies must be handled according to the suggestions made by Captain Engelhardt."

For the moment, there the situation rested. Preparations were made for receiving the Allies in Sardinia, and Hitler began to turn over in his mind various schemes for dealing with the Italians. Nothing concrete emerged, but he started hinting darkly about the appalling state of Italian leadership and the need for German inspiration. He had not yet decided to intervene actively. Doenitz, for his part, thought he had aquitted himself well in his first major State duty, but his strategical conceptions had been weak, and, for a naval officer, his refutation of sea power had been as incredible as it was to prove disastrous. From Hitler's point of view, however, Doenitz had faced and dealt with the situation realistically. He did not appreciate the fact that had Doenitz offered the Italians adequate supplies of fuel oil and some measure of air protection, they would probably have still been willing to pit their Fleet against the British, even at this late hour. The obvious contempt of Doenitz and the other German officers was the very opposite of what was required to encourage the Italians to fight. But Hitler, too, felt the same contempt for the Italians, and, instead of chiding Doenitz for mishandling his mission, he praised him for his success. He was pleased to see his protégé shaping so well.

Chapter XVI

THE BATTLE OF THE ATLANTIC (4)

WITH the Axis position in the Mediterranean getting more and more precarious, the U-boat campaign increased in importance. It was becoming Germany's only hope of staving off defeat, but in the Atlantic, too, the Allies were at last gaining the advantage. Until the beginning of 1943 the rate of merchant shipping destroyed in relation to the rate of U-boats lost had still been favourable to Germany, and, moreover, the number of ships sunk in 1942 had outstripped the Allied building programme. But Allied counter-measures had steadily improved. The use of long-range aircraft, aircraft carriers, and radar-equipped escort vessels, all working together as a group, had slowly begun to gain the initiative. It had been one of Doenitz's early and unpleasant tasks when he was appointed Commander-in-Chief to explain the situation to Hitler. He said:

" During this month (January) the enemy, surprisingly enough, discovered the positions of our U-boats, and, in some cases, even the exact number of ships. It was confirmed later on that his convoys evaded the known U-boat formations. This detailed information can come from two sources: treason, or undetected reconnaissance aircraft finding the formations. With regard to the possibility of treason all the necessary steps have been taken. If, on the other hand, the enemy found our U-boat formations solely by means of reconnaissance our formations will have to be scattered more widely."

Doenitz had gone on to explain that his U-boats were much hampered by the lack of Luftwaffe support. He pleaded for additional air reconnaissance, and he was promised some assistance. In fact he got little, and the Allies, besides locating the positions of the U-boats, began to organize large-scale attacks.

In February 1943, 19 U-boats were sunk; in March, 15; and in April, 16 U-boats were lost. These losses were high, but in May the Allied Chiefs of Staff initiated a series of combined sea and air offensives against U-boats in the Bay of Biscay. Doenitz was to be attacked in his own waters. The results of these operations were that in May, 37 U-boats were sunk, representing approximately 30 per cent. of all U-boats at sea. Not even Germany could stand losses on this scale, and on 31 May Hitler ordered Doenitz to report.

" *The Commander-in-Chief, Navy*, reports as follows: The substantial increase of the enemy Air Force is the cause of the present crisis in U-boat warfare. By means of sound detection it has been determined that as many aircraft now pass through the narrows between Iceland and the Faeroes in one day as only recently appeared in the course of a week. Aircraft carriers are also being used in conjunction with the North Atlantic convoys so that all convoy routes are now under enemy air protection. But the U-boat crisis would not have happened because of aircraft alone. The determining factor is a new location device also used by surface vessels which enables them to discover the position of our U-boats. When the ceiling is low, visibility poor, or at night, they carry out surprise attacks. . . .

Approximately 65 per cent. of the losses occur while the U-boats are en route or lying in wait; only about 35 per cent. occur near the convoys themselves. That is to be expected, for a U-boat spends most of the six to eight weeks of an operation en route or lying in wait. During this time the danger of sudden attacks from the air, when it is dark or when visibility is poor, by an enemy who cannot be detected beforehand, is very great. . . . The following measures have been taken:

1. I have withdrawn from the North Atlantic to the area west of the Azores in the hope of encountering less air reconnaissance there. I am lying in wait there for a convoy bound for Gibraltar. It is very difficult, however, to find this convoy in so large an area. With new U-boats now becoming available I shall proceed to more distant areas in the hope that aircraft there are not as yet fully equipped with the new device. I intend to resume attacks on North Atlantic convoys at the time of the new moon."

Doenitz continued his report with various practical suggestions. As always when dealing with U-boat warfare, he showed an exceptionally firm grasp of the subject, and his suggestions were both feasible and good. He asked for a radar interception set and other electronic devices to jam the Allied radar apparatus; for increased anti-aircraft armament for the U-boats; and an acoustic torpedo which would improve the U-boat's chances of success. He came out strongly with a demand for air assistance from the Luftwaffe:

> " Our U-boats undoubtedly could have sunk more shipping if we had had naval aircraft. . . . Many of the aircraft in the Atlantic are inferior to our own. . . . Even now it is not too late to give the Navy an air branch. . . . A school for naval airmen must be started at once at Gdynia in direct conjunction with the convoy training flotillas directed by the U-boat Branch, because naval airmen must be trained just as systematically as the U-boat personnel. . . . They must receive their training in the Baltic sea with the U-boat crews so that they will speak the same language and can subsequently fight together. . . ."

Doenitz went on to forecast the future prospects for the U-boats:

> " At the moment our efforts are being frustrated by a technical device against which counter-measures will be found. It is impossible to foretell to what extent U-boat warfare will again become effective. The enemy's anti-submarine defence on water and from the air will be improved. In 1940 a U-boat was able to sink an average of 1000 tons per day at sea; at the end of 1942 it could sink only 200 tons. Nevertheless I am convinced that U-boat warfare must be carried on even if great successes are no longer possible. The forces tied up by U-boat warfare were considerable even during the First World War.
>
> *The Fuehrer :* There can be no talk of slackening off U-boat warfare. The Atlantic is my first line of defence in the West and even if I have to fight a defensive battle there, that is preferable to waiting to defend myself on the coast of Europe. The enemy forces tied down by our U-boats are tremendous, even though the actual losses we inflict are no longer great. I cannot afford to release these forces by discontinuing U-boat warfare.

Grand-Admiral Doenitz : I therefore believe that we must continue the present effort to increase U-boat production. As a matter of fact I do not believe that 30 U-boats are sufficient. Even in what amounts to purely defensive U-boat warfare in the Atlantic we will need great numbers of U-boats. In my opinion we should strive for 40 U-boats per month. In agreement with Minister Speer, I have already arranged for the construction of 30 U-boats and for building auxiliary vessels as previously mentioned. I now request that this order be signed by the Fuehrer.

The Fuehrer agrees, changes the number of U-boats from 30 to 40 per month, and signs.

Grand-Admiral Doenitz proposes a surprise attack on Gibraltar with the Luftwaffe's new weapon.* as soon as these have been stockpiled in sufficient numbers—in other words about the end of June.

The Fuehrer considers that he will then run the risk of some of the new weapons falling on land at Gibraltar and that the British will find out what they are. He is also doubtful of being able to reach Gibraltar, particularly since it is becoming increasingly difficult to fly over Spain, from a political point of view."

Whatever measures Doenitz had designed, the hard fact remained that he had been forced to withdraw his U-boats from the North Atlantic, and on June 24 the British Admiralty allowed merchant ships of 15 knots or over to resume transatlantic passages independent of convoy protection. It was Doenitz's first real defeat in the Battle of the Atlantic. He dealt with the crisis calmly and efficiently, but it took more than Hitler's signature to increase U-boat production to 40 boats per month. It was now realized that there were not enough men either to build or to man the boats.

The shortage of manpower in the whole of Germany had gradually made itself felt from about the middle of 1942. It was then more a question of adequate fighting strength rather than workers, but by the middle of 1943, the shortage of both had become acute. A table, discovered in the German naval archives, shows the situation (in the German Navy only) which was forecast for the period June 1943 to September 1944 :

* Radio-controlled glider bombs—' Chase-me-Charlies '.

```
" Personnel required     .    .   437,822
  Personnel allocated     .    .   102,984
                                  _____
  Shortage     .    .    .   334,838 "
```

The situation was such that the allocation to the Navy, when reduced to monthly figures, barely covered the losses. There was a shortage of 200,000 men before U-boat construction was increased; now it looked as if the building programme would have to be cancelled altogether.

Doenitz appealed to Hitler, but there was little Hitler could do. As he said:

" There are no extra men. The anti-aircraft and night-fighter defences must be increased to protect the German cities. I must also strengthen the Eastern Front. The Army needs divisions for the protection of Europe."

Doenitz suggested that Army and Air Force personnel should nevertheless be diverted to the Navy. He pointed out that, under the present allocation, U-boat warfare would come to an end. Already he was having to use officers who had only entered the Navy in 1939 as U-boat captains.

Hitler's reaction to this statement was, as Doenitz had expected, immediate and decisive. He said:

" The cessation of U-boat warfare is out of the question. I shall have to allocate personnel as they become available."

He ordered Doenitz to draw up a list of the number of men required, and the dates by when they would be needed, promising that he would take appropriate action.

As a result of Hitler's personal order the U-boat branch never again lacked men, but the effects were felt elsewhere. Aircraft production declined (in 1944 it rose again sharply), reserves for the Army had to be reduced, and in many other smaller ways the allocation of men to the U-boats reduced efficiency and production over all Germany.

Doenitz had not yet exhausted his ideas for meeting the U-boat crisis. In the next few weeks he produced three more schemes. The first two were technical—the development of a new type of submarine (the Walther U-boat) which had a very high underwater speed, and the improvement of the anti-aircraft armament

of U-boats; the third was to intensify mine warfare. He planned
to lay 3000 mines per month off the coasts of Britain.

On 8 July Doenitz discussed his new ideas at 'Wolfsschanze'.
Far more than Raeder had ever done, Doenitz tended to bring
Hitler into the internal affairs of the Navy. He encouraged his
Fuehrer's personal interest and frequently took minor operational
or administrative problems to him. Sometimes he did this to
show how well he was running the Navy; at other times it was
because he really did want help. Whatever the reason, the habit
was in striking contrast to other German leaders, who sought
instead to keep Hitler out of their internal affairs as much as
possible. It gained Hitler's marked favour, and Doenitz began
to outstrip his rivals at Hitler's court.

" *The Commander-in-Chief, Navy*, reports to the Fuehrer
the successful design of the 'electro'-submarine and
enumerates its tactical advantages. Entirely new possibilities
are introduced as the U-boat will be able to approach the
convoy quickly and will also be able to escape under water
instead of having to surface. . . .

The C.-in-C., Navy, reports that in very many cases the
present quadruple 20-mm. gun failed to bring down attacking
aircraft in spite of direct hits, while in other cases the aircraft
were not shot down until after they had succeeded in dropping
their bombs. He further reports that our efforts to increase
the number of U-boats in the Mediterranean have met with
great difficulties. Of the last four U-boats which attempted
to pass through the Straits of Gibraltar three were lost. . . .
He is therefore planning to ship the small Walther U-boat
by way of the Rhône from Germany to the Mediterranean.
. . . The first U-boats should be ready by April 1944, since
their small size makes rapid construction possible.

The Fuehrer expresses his complete agreement with the
plan and discusses with Grand-Admiral Doenitz the problem
of organizing the construction of the new submarines. He
says that he is firmly convinced that technical changes will
continue alternately to favour or impede offensive or defensive
warfare. One must therefore not become discouraged but
be ever receptive to new ideas. A man whose mind is closed
thereby admits his defeat. The same is true of the Luftwaffe.
. . . With regard to the general situation, *Grand-Admiral*

Doenitz reports to the Fuehrer that he has transferred U-boats from the North Atlantic after it had had to be abandoned as a result of the lost battle in May. . . . As a result of these changes there were few sinkings in June, but July has begun to show some improvement. It is now quite clear that the enemy is directing his main efforts against the exit lanes of our U-boats, *i.e.*, in the Shetlands passage and the Bay of Biscay. Our losses in these areas are still very high. Most of the losses were caused by the enemy's Air Force but of late apparently also by escort groups and naval forces which are co-operating with the Air Force. Against this combination we have no defence yet, and for the time being the departure of U-boats from home ports has been stopped until all have been equipped with quadruple and twin gun mountings. . . .

(The manpower shortage is discussed.) For the enlarged programme the Navy needs 262,000 men by the autumn of 1944, and they must be young men.

The Fuehrer considers this figure too high but accepts it after a lengthy discussion with Grand-Admiral Doenitz. He decides that in addition to the measures which have already been decided upon, 10,000 technicians of the 1925 age group are to be given to the Navy in exchange for other men.

The C.-in-C., Navy, calls this only a stopgap and presents a summary of the total requirements.

The Fuehrer discusses the present availability of men with Field-Marshal Keitel. . . . He (the Fuehrer) suggests that the C.-in-C., Navy, should investigate the possibility of obtaining men for the Navy from the occupied territories as the SS has done so successfully. He believes that this offers great possibilities for the Navy and that some 20,000 to 25,000 men could be recruited.

The C.-in-C., Navy, declares that he will try it and that he will contact Reichsfuehrer SS Himmler. . . . He then requests to see the Foreign Office reports concerning the enemy.

The Fuehrer agrees and gives the order, but he emphasizes that the reports are exclusively for the personal information of Grand-Admiral Doenitz.

In conclusion, *Grand-Admiral Doenitz* again stresses the importance of the speedy construction of the new submarine.

The Fuehrer agrees heartily and says to Minister Speer

who enters at this moment: ' The construction of this new submarine is of the utmost importance.'

Minister Speer replies: ' There is no doubt about that. I have given top priority to the new submarines.'

(Signed) DOENITZ.
(Countersigned) Lt. RUDOLPH."

But it was too late. Germany's defeat in the Atlantic in the summer of 1943 lasted for twelve months. More than anything else it made possible the great Allied offensives of 1944, for it was during these crucial twelve months that the vast quantities of stores and weapons, without which the assault on Europe could not have been made, were brought to England and the Mediterranean from all parts of the world. They were brought by sea routes from which the German Navy—and the Luftwaffe —had been driven.

Chapter XVII

THE ITALIAN COLLAPSE

On 10 July the Allies invaded Sicily. Hitler had accepted the false signs that the landings would take place in Sardinia or Greece with the result that Sicily was ill-prepared to meet the invasion, and the landings were not strongly opposed.

The invasion made the political attitude of the Italians clearer. They had been unwilling participants in the war from the time of their first big defeats in Africa and Albania, but, while Germany had remained the dominant force in Europe, they had continued to give what assistance they could. Mussolini, indeed, had been and was still an ardent belligerent, but it was the belligerence of a bull frog, full of hot air and fighting words only, and now that the Allies were showing their power, the bulk of the Italians were less willing than ever to continue fighting.

The Allied invasion fleet had not been attacked—principally because Doenitz had advised against a major fleet action—but whatever the reason, such a passive policy killed what fighting spirit was left in the Italian Navy. They still had over a hundred warships and more than 200,000 tons of merchant shipping, but, in the face of German contempt and lack of co-operation, they had remained in harbour, allowing what was the biggest assault in history on their country to pass unchallenged.

In the week following the Allied landings, Doenitz received alarming reports from the German naval commanders in Italy. There were mutterings in the Italian fleet, and it had been impossible to get them to make even minor offensive moves. There was nothing decisive yet to show that they were about to desert with their ships to the Allies, but the signs were becoming increasingly ominous.

Doenitz grew desperate. He had somehow either to boost the morale of the Italian Navy, or to take over the Italian Fleet himself. Neither alternative seemed practicable, and in his dilemma he reported to Hitler on 17 July:

" *The Commander-in-Chief, Navy*, says that he is making this report because he feels that it is his duty to give the Fuehrer his opinion about the situation in Italy. Generally speaking his views are the same as those submitted by Jodl in writing.

He happens to know that the younger officers of the Italian Navy who have really seen action, for example with the Tunisian convoys, and also the young submarine commanders are opposed to the Supermarina. Even when he first visited Rome, these young officers were expecting a change in the high command of the Italian Navy since it was completely out of touch with what was going on at the front and was therefore not recognized by most of the younger officers. What is more, he is of the opinion that the Italian Navy would have been of much greater help to us if it had been under German leadership. This holds true to-day. He believes that there are quite a few Italian officers who sincerely want to fight on our side and who have proved their willingness in action, but who would at the same time welcome a change in leadership. He believes it would be advisable to place a young Italian admiral in command, who has the confidence of the Italian Navy, to be assisted by a German staff. . . . The attitude of the Supermarina is infamous. In spite of all his efforts, he was unable to get Admiral Riccardi to use his light forces to drive the enemy out of the Straits of Messina —an intolerable situation since he has the forces available to do so. Admiral Riccardi is hoarding these light forces in case the battleships should put to sea. Grand-Admiral Doenitz believes that that will never happen. However, he has no way of doing anything about the situation except to send telegrams. Riccardi replies to these that he will submit them to the Duce.

The Fuehrer : ' The Duce is not getting them ! '

Grand-Admiral Doenitz continues: ' Later an answer arrives that for very subtle reasons it is impossible to take the necessary steps. The situation would be greatly improved if the present Supermarina could be done away with and a new command with a good German staff put in its place. . . . If we want to hold Italy, German troops and German naval coastal artillery must take over the harbours. Otherwise Taranto and Naples will meet the same fate as Augusta.'

The Fuehrer replies that he has himself been considering how to do this. The greatest problem is the demoralization of the Italian Army about which nothing has been done. Only very severe measures, like those applied by Stalin in 1941, or by the French in 1917, will be of any use. If only individual units were affected, we could appeal to their sense of honour by offering medals, etc., but the whole army is in a state of collapse and only barbaric measures can help to save the nation. A sort of directorate, tribunal, or court-martial must be set up in Italy to remove undesirable elements. There must still be some capable people in Italy. He has already consulted Ambassador Mackensen, but he could suggest no one capable of taking over the leadership.

Grand-Admiral Doenitz : ' I believe, my Fuehrer, that we must either do without the Italian Army altogether or we must try to strengthen it with German troops.'

The Fuehrer : ' Without the Italian Army we cannot defend the entire peninsula. In that case we would have to withdraw to a relatively short line.'

Lt.-General Jodl points out that this would have very serious repercussions in the Balkans.

Grand-Admiral Doenitz : ' That is why I believe we must infiltrate our men into the Italian Army.'

At this point Field-Marshal Rommel enters and *the Fuehrer* asks him whether he knows of any really capable person in the Italian Army who is fully co-operating with Germany.

Field-Marshal Rommel replies that there is no such person. Ferrari Orsi would have qualified, but he was killed in action. At the moment Roatta would probably come closest, although he is not to be trusted and is without character.

Grand-Admiral Doenitz says that he will ask again in naval circles and see whether they know of a suitable Army man.

The Fuehrer declares that everything depends on a radical change in the Italian situation. If this can be brought about, it will be worth taking the risk. If not, there is no point in throwing in additional German troops and thus committing the last reserves. . . .

Grand-Admiral Doenitz says that Germany ought to give the British something new to worry about. He suggests that they begin laying the new mines in great numbers at the end of August.

The Fuehrer repeatedly asserts that he is very much worried that the enemy in turn might use these new types of mines if he finds them. This could easily happen if the Air Force made a mistake in dropping them. He is willing to let the Navy lay the new mines at any time, but you can never tell where the Air Force will drop them.

Grand-Admiral Doenitz points out that experienced units of the Luftwaffe, for example the IX Fliegerkorps, were very successful in laying mines. . . .

The Fuehrer : ' All right, I agree. But if the British should get hold of these mines and drop them in the Baltic Sea, we shall be finished."

It was in fact too late to save Italy, but on 19 July, two days after the above conference, Hitler met Mussolini at Verona. The Duce renewed his assurances of loyalty to the Axis, and protested his continuing faith in their common cause. They were cheering words to Hitler who did not realize how precarious Mussolini's position was, nor how empty were any promises which the Duce gave. One week later Hitler was given what was probably the heaviest shock of his career. On 25 July, at a full meeting of the Grand Fascist Council, Mussolini was quietly forced to resign by a vote of no confidence. Marshal Badoglio took over the government and issued a proclamation that by the King's order he had also assumed full military powers.

To Hitler the overthrow of Mussolini meant not only that

Italy would almost certainly now surrender, but also that the authority of dictators was being undermined. It was a situation which he could not tolerate, and in spite of every evidence to the contrary he insisted that Fascism in Italy was as strong as ever and that with strong German support, Italy would not collapse. It was for the moment nothing more than wishful thinking, but Hitler was passionately determined to make his wishful thinking come true. Mussolini's quiet resignation was wholly out of character, and Hitler decided that, by sending in German forces, he could restore the fallen Duce to his pedestal and at the same time bring Italy completely within his (Hitler's) power. There would then be no question of Italy's surrender. In two days he drafted four political/military operations designed to retrieve the Italian situation.

The first of these operations—' Student '—was the restoration of Fascism in Italy; the second—' Eiche '—was the rescue and restoration of Mussolini to power; the third—' Achse '—and the fourth—' Schwarz '—provided for the capture of the Italian Fleet and the military occupation of Italy by the German Army, should this be necessary to make the first two operations successful.

The neatness of Hitler's plans was belied by the confusion which persisted in his headquarters. The situation in Italy was still by no means clear. Hitler distrusted Badoglio whom he suspected of intending—if he had not already begun—secret negotiations with the Allies. But he could not be sure that this was true. On the other hand, the operations he had planned would almost certainly precipitate the Badoglio government into an armistice with the Allies. This would make the German position all the more difficult, and Hitler therefore moved with care. He kept his plans broad and flexible, and on 26 July, the day after Mussolini's downfall, he summoned a full conference of all his advisers.

At the conference, which lasted for three days, Hitler first explained the four operations he had planned, and then invited his commanders to comment. To them the all-important question was whether Fascism was really at an end in Italy, or whether it had merely suffered a temporary eclipse as Hitler was suggesting. They were unusually frank in their comments, and on the evening of the second day of the conference, the question was discussed by Hitler in a small, intimate circle of his closest advisers. Doenitz expressed his views:

" 'Italy must under no circumstances be abandoned. There are no doubt a good many people in Italy who feel honour-bound to continue the war on our side. These people must be aligned with us. It is my conviction that this group, which certainly includes a large number of younger Italian naval officers, now feels less bound to the Fascist régime, but it is loyal to the House of Savoy to which it is bound by oath. Our measures must therefore be so designed as not to give the impression that they are directed against the Royal House.

. . . I doubt whether Fascism still means anything either to those who favour continuing the war on our side or to the Italian people themselves. On the other hand, it is quite clear that the present Italian government will not keep on fighting in spite of its pretence. We must forestall by all means any surprise action by the Anglo-Saxons. All will depend on the correct timing of any action against the present Italian government. I believe there is still time and that it can be used by us to strengthen our position in Italy by bringing in more divisions. As the situation develops we may find a better propagandist approach against the present government which, after all, still pretends to be fighting the war on our side and is trying to maintain order and be considered the King's government.'

Rommel and *Richthofen* agree with Grand-Admiral Doenitz; *Jodl* is very outspoken in his doubt that Fascism will be revived. He recommends refraining from any action against the government, but merely reinforcing our troops in Italy. Goering and Ribbentrop take the same stand as the Fuehrer. Kesselring believes that the present government is trustworthy and he is therefore against any interference on our part.

The Fuehrer : ' We must act at once, otherwise the Anglo-Saxons will steal a march on us by occupying the airfields. The Fascist party is at present only stunned and will rise up again behind our lines. The Fascist party is the only one that is determined to fight on our side. We must therefore restore it. All reasons advocating further delays are wrong; if we delay we run the danger of losing Italy to the Anglo-Saxons. These are matters which a soldier cannot comprehend. Only a man with political insight can see clearly. . . .' "

While he was at the conference, Doenitz received a report on the Italian situation from the German commander, Vice-Admiral Ruge. It said:

" The resignation of Mussolini without offering any resistance whatsoever has brought about the almost complete collapse of the Fascist Party. The situation is made worse by an acute food problem and chaotic traffic conditions. The new government is trying to assert itself and has taken positive steps to show its willingness to carry on the war. How long this attitude will last is hard to say. The Navy is backing the House of Savoy. . . . They are in favour of a more vigorous pursuit of the war, but they cannot be counted on to support Fascism, at least not for the present. Fascism has completely lost its hold on the people. . . .

Operation ' Student ' might therefore find some support in scattered places, but it will certainly be opposed by the Armed Forces and the majority of the people. This would lead to complete disruption of communications which are difficult enough to maintain as it is.

Without the co-operation of the Italians, the evacuation of our troops from the islands (Sicily and Sardinia) is out of the question. In brief, I believe that the proposed plans (' Student ', ' Eiche ', and ' Achse ') if carried out now, will alienate the great majority of those Italian forces which are still in existence. Thus Germany will be discredited before history without having been able to change the situation."

Doenitz showed this report to Hitler, who disagreed strongly both with its analysis of the situation and with its defeatist attitude. Vice-Admiral Ruge, the author, retired a few days later with kidney trouble.

During the last week in July the situation greatly worsened. Mussolini, who had only been kept under house arrest, was thrown into prison, the whereabouts of which was unknown to the Germans; the Allies made steady progress in Sicily, further encouraging the anti-Fascist forces in Italy, and Badoglio behaved more suspiciously than ever.

The situation in Italy posed three distinct problems for Hitler:

(*a*) How to prevent the Italians from surrendering to the Allies.

(*b*) If Italy surrendered, how to minimize the effect of the surrender.

(*c*) The tactical problem of whether to abandon Sicily or hold on as long as possible.

From Hitler's point of view, Mussolini was the key to the whole Italian problem. He had been the Fascist figurehead for so long that without him there was little chance of a Fascist revival. If Mussolini could be rescued and restored as Duce, Hitler was sure that he could make short work of Badoglio and the King. With German support, Mussolini should be able to reform the Fascists into a sufficiently effective force to withstand the Allies.

But time was short. By 1 August Hitler was certain that Badoglio had already begun negotiations with the Allies ; so, while the plans to rescue Mussolini (Eiche) and to restore Fascism (Student) were being worked out, other plans to ensure that as little as possible would be lost in the event of a sudden Italian surrender were also prepared. The Italian fleet was the most important single item, and Doenitz was ordered to make all necessary preparations for the capture or destruction of the Italian ships. They were not on any account to be allowed to escape to the Allies.

Meanwhile, Badoglio, too, was in an awkward position. Until he had come to terms with the Allies he had to continue co-operation with the Germans. Hitler took full advantage of the situation, and, under the guise of strengthening the Axis defences against the Allies, poured division after division of German troops into Italy. It was clear to everyone that these troops were for no other purpose than to seize power in Italy, but while the negotiations were still so uncertain there was nothing the Italians could do. Hitler played the Italians with his diabolic skill. He knew that if they chose, they could easily destroy his communications while he was still in the process of building up his forces, but he relied on the natural hesitation of the Allies to come to terms with an ex-enemy to keep the Italians wavering and idle. For his part all the operations he had planned were kept as secret as possible.

Throughout August there was a constant interplay between the threat of open force and the secret methods of the Gestapo.

Doenitz kept a comprehensive diary of the period, and extracts show the development of Hitler's plans. The rescue of Mussolini was the central theme.

" *July* 30, 1943.

Word is received from the Admiral, Fuehrer Headquarters, that relations with Italy are becoming more strained, since there are further indications that the Italian government is double-crossing us. Nevertheless, operation ' Schwarz ' is to be deferred in order to pour as many troops into Italy as possible while co-operation still continues.

August 1.

At a conference with the Fuehrer, information is obtained from Engineer Desauer about the Duce's possible whereabouts. Orders are issued to proceed with operation ' Eiche '. The movement of German troops into northern Italy continues.

August 2.

Reports from Rome. . . . Italian warships can be seized only with the help of strong military forces. Kesselring has not yet decided. . . . The general impression is that the various German officers understand the task in hand. They are, however, somewhat overwhelmed by the difficulties that must be dealt with and overcome by the widely scattered units of the German Navy in the event of operation ' Achse '. In the afternoon, the Fuehrer again sees Engineer Desauer who reports that a column of cars heavily guarded by Carabinieri was sighted, but the Duce himself was not seen. He mentions Petty Officer Laurich as an additional witness. The order is given to bring Petty Officer Laurich unobtrusively from Gaeta to headquarters via Berlin. Reports indicate that the Duce is being held on Ventolene Island.

August 3.

Jodl reports that the Italians have completely ceased resistance to our measures. During the discussion of the possible reasons for this, *the Fuehrer* puts forward the theory that they may be biding their time in order to come to terms with the Anglo-Saxons before an open break with Germany. *Jodl* and the *Commander-in-Chief, Navy*, suggest that the Italians may feel helpless and therefore want to rely on us again. It remains to be seen what the actual situation is, and meanwhile operations ' Eiche ', ' Achse ', and ' Schwarz ' are not to be undertaken yet.

August 6.

The Admiral at Fuehrer Headquarters reports that Himmler has sent information that the Italians are holding a destroyer in readiness to remove the ' valuable object ' (Mussolini) in case of emergency. *The Fuehrer* informs the Commander-in-Chief, Navy, at once, asking him to re-examine the distribution of Italian destroyers. Preventive measures must be taken immediately. He suggests that a submarine should be used to blockade the harbour of Ventolene.

Grand-Admiral Doenitz replies : An inconspicuous blockade of the harbour, even with U-boats, is impossible since it would have to stand just off the harbour entrance. There is no inconspicuous way of rendering the destroyer harmless in its present anchorage. A blockade would therefore be inadvisable in order to prevent our intentions from being recognized prematurely.

August 8.

Petty Officer Laurich * reports to the Commander-in-Chief, Navy, who decides that Laurich shall fly with him the next day to Fuehrer Headquarters. He is put under oath to observe absolute secrecy.

August 9.

At Fuehrer Headquarters. A report was made on the general war situation. The entry of our troops into Italy has been marked by an ever-increasing number of incidents of minor importance. *The Fuehrer* is convinced that both the King and Badoglio are planning treachery. He is struck by the increased activity of the Italian Navy. . . .

In the afternoon, after the noon situation conference, Petty Officer Laurich makes his report before a select few. Besides the Fuehrer and the Commander-in-Chief, Navy, Ribbentrop, Goering, Himmler, Keitel, Ambassador Hevel, and the Admiral at Fuehrer Headquarters are also present.

---

* Laurich had struck up a friendship with an Italian naval officer. who had told him that Mussolini had been taken to Ventolene, Laurich had zealously passed this information on to his Commanding Officer who in turn had informed Doenitz.

The Fuehrer dismisses Laurich with the words, ' Well done, my boy.'

An early execution of ' Eiche ' appears necessary. The general conviction is that Mussolini is on San Stefano. The action will therefore be confined to the island. . . . Parachute troops will probably have to be used. . . .

The Fuehrer expresses his views on the Italian situation in detail. He calls it shameful the way the Duce has been treated after he had directed the destinies of Italy for twenty years and had been hailed by the whole of Italy during this time. He criticizes especially the attitude of the King and speaks about the lack of responsibility among many rulers who rely upon unscrupulous historians to touch up their record and who therefore fail to recognize their accountability to history. The Fuehrer feels the predicament of the Duce all the more because of the close ties of friendship which exist between them. He still considers the Italian government to be extremely unreliable and believes it capable of almost any kind of treason.

August 11.

After the noon situation conference, the Italian problem is discussed again at great length.

The Fuehrer states : ' The Italians will not show their true colours until after Grandi's trip to Lisbon or the meeting of Churchill and Roosevelt in Canada has produced results. The Italians are going ahead with their negotiations at full speed. They will be taken in by any promise of the Anglo-Saxons if only the continued rule of the Royal House is guaranteed. Their negotiations are treasonable. . . .

During our last meeting at the station, the Duce suddenly remarked : " I don't know how my Generals reason, or where they want to defend Italy, or why they keep such strong forces in northern Italy ! " On the other hand they themselves are becoming frightened as they realize that they face two great dangers—capitulation or communism. The one and only point that speaks against treason is the fact that the Crown Prince has sent his children to north-western upper Italy. If the government remains on our side, however, there will still be the danger of an uprising among the people. . .'

Subsequently the Fuehrer discusses indications which point to growing differences between the Anglo-Saxons and the

Russians: the recall of Maisky and Litvinoff, the meeting of Churchill and Roosevelt without Stalin. The Anglo-Saxons do not wish to see Russia in Finland, nor, under any circumstances, that Russia should improve her sea communications in the North. Poland is to be restored; the Russians will not be allowed to come near the Bosphorous, and they will be kept out of the Balkans as well as Iran and Iraq. These reasons are enough to nettle Stalin."

During the following week the situation in Italy remained fluid, and Hitler decided to postpone 'Eiche' once more. It was still not certain where the Italians were holding Mussolini. Reports now indicated that he had been taken to Sardinia, but while his whereabouts were uncertain it was obviously impracticable to carry out an operation against every alternative hide-out.

On 17 August the Allies completed the conquest of Sicily. This brought up sharply the question of a new defence line on the Italian peninsula, and Rommel and Jodl met the Italian generals, Roatta and Rossi, to discuss the position. They achieved little else than an assurance from the Italians of non-interference and the security of the German supply lines.

From Rome came contradictory reports. The German Ambassador, von Mackensen, reported on 19 August:

" There is dissatisfaction in Fascist circles and confidence in the Duce's direction of the war has vanished. The Fascist Council voted without realizing the consequences. Not even the Duce was aware of conditions. It remained for the King to make the Duce aware of the state of affairs that even his Fascist Party had lost faith in him. Following this the Duce offered his resignation and asked for a guarantee of safety for himself and his family. The King agreed, and the Duce was then allegedly placed in protective custody. I do not believe that Badoglio had any previous knowledge of the affair. The longing for peace is widespread among the Italians, but it is realized that the present government will continue the fight because it would be impossible to obtain peace without turning the whole of Italy into a battlefield. The present conditions do not warrant a pessimistic attitude; the Fuehrer is seeing matters in a more pessimistic manner than, in my opinion, is justified. I can of course, offer no proof that I am right and the Fuehrer wrong."

Hitler would not consider even the possibility that he could be wrong, and preparations were continued with speed. By the end of August everything was ready.

On 3 September Marshal Badoglio signed an armistice with the Allies, but it was not to be announced until 8 September. On 9 September the Allies landed in strength at Salerno, some 15 miles south of Naples on the Italian mainland.

Hitler struck back at once. Operations ' Eiche ' and ' Schwarz ' were immediately put into operation. Mussolini, definitely located at the Villa Weber outside Madelena in Sardinia, was rescued by a daring operation by German parachute troops. The German troops in Italy speedily disarmed their former Allies and Badoglio and the King were forced to flee from Rome. A puppet government under Mussolini was set up in Northern Italy with headquarters in Milan.

But one of Hitler's counter-blows failed of its full effect. Though the Italian battleship *Roma* was sunk, the great majority of the Italian fleet escaped down the Adriatic Sea and surrendered to the Allies at Malta. The gain to the Anglo-American forces was considerable, but none the less, by ruthless action, Hitler had managed to prevent the collapse of Italy from becoming a total disaster. He had paved the way for what was to become one of the longest and most bitter campaigns of the war.

Chapter XVIII

DEFENCE AND RETREAT

HITLER had partially retrieved the position in Italy, but now, in different places all over Europe, symptoms of defeat began to appear. They were faint as yet, and it is doubtful whether Hitler recognized them for what they were. He had accepted the fact that he was on the defensive, but he was far from accepting the inevitability of defeat. The symptoms of fear in Germany and of underground movements in Western and Eastern Europe were to Hitler the natural results of the change from offensive to defensive warfare, nothing more. As soon as the various fronts became stabilized—and he had no doubts that they would be—there would be no more talk of defeat. Germany would settle down to regain her strength behind solid defences; he would then once more strike for victory.

Four vignettes of widely separated areas during the last few months of 1943 show how much the situation had changed.

Germany

Germany was now almost a daily target for Allied air forces, and in particular the German ports had been severely hit—so much so that Doenitz became alarmed about civilian morale. He paid a visit to Hamburg during the first half of August, and on 19 August he reported his views to Hitler:

"*The Commander-in-Chief, Navy*, reports to the Fuehrer privately on his visit to the shipyards at Hamburg: 'The general feeling of the people is one of depression in spite of their willingness to work. Everybody sees only the many reverses of Germany. In view of the impressions I gained from my visit to Hamburg and on the basis of many reports and intelligence I believe it is urgent that the Fuehrer should speak to the people very soon. I consider this to be absolutely necessary in view of the current difficulties and the war situation; the entire German nation longs for it.'

The Fuehrer says that he intends to speak, but that he must wait until the Italian situation is clarified.

The Commander-in-Chief, Navy, continues: 'The questions which the workers in Hamburg asked were typical. They wanted revenge for the air raids and they asked: How well prepared are we for defence against further raids? I believe that the workers are willing to work but that they are beginning to ask themselves what there is to be gained, if in future air raids all their work is smashed again. I did not tell the workers when we would start to retaliate or that our defences would be improved in the near future, and I gave as the reason that I would be playing into the hands of the enemy if I were to tell them. I believe it is necessary to tell the German people that they must show patience and fortitude, that they have no right to give up if they are not told these things. The latter would merely confirm the well-established British opinion that they can bear up under air raids because they can endure hardships while the Germans are more like the Italians in this respect. We must appeal to German pride and honour without making promises or raising hopes which later cannot be fulfilled.

I believe that the air raids cannot endanger our essential industries in any material way. I saw machines standing right next to a bomb crater in the machine shops of the Hamburg shipyards. Even though the bomb scored a direct hit on a shop the machines were absolutely undamaged because the effect of the blast seems to be vertical not horizontal. It seems that steel construction with glass roofs is advantageous because the roofs shatter immediately and thus have no concentrating effect. I believe it is possible and necessary to keep our shipbuilding to the large western shipyards in spite of the air raids; and that it is possible on the whole to maintain our armament programme. The most important thing is to keep up confidence, and with that the will to work and the spirit of the worker. We need not succumb to the air raids, but we might if the morale of the workers suffers from them with a consequent decrease in our production. I believe that we must now inspire strength into the people, and I keep telling my officers that this is now our solemn duty towards our soldiers as well as towards the whole German people. In my opinion the greatest danger arises when the intelligentsia starts to utter its opinion in a wise and important manner. These opinions are false most of the time since these people see only part of what is going on and not the overall picture. They do untold harm since they weaken the will to resist. By senseless chatter these people help to bring about the destruction of the very things which are dear to them. Everything should be done to correct this state of affairs.

The Fuehrer listened very intently to these statements from Grand-Admiral Doenitz and agreed with him. The symptoms of weakness must be eradicated, since they strengthen the enemy's will to attack us. The Fuehrer thanked the Commander-in-Chief, Navy, very warmly."

Denmark

Apart from the open Allied attacks, a new threat in the shape of underground movements also began to make itself felt. In mild Denmark the underground increased its activities to such an extent that an ultimatum was sent to the Danes threatening them with full military occupation if these activities did not stop. A joint naval and army operation—' Safari '—was planned against Denmark, and was actually started, though the disturbances had already calmed down by the time the army moved in. The episode was a good example of the confusion which was becoming more frequent at Hitler's headquarters:

(Extract from conferences, 28–29 August.)

" *The Chief of Naval Staff* tells Lt.-General Jodl about the reports which have come in during the afternoon about developments in Denmark. According to these reports the Danish government has rejected the ultimatum of the German plenipotentiary, Dr. Best. The ' Safari ' measures will therefore be carried out. In this connection it is evident that Jodl has received his information about Denmark only through the reports of the Naval Staff. Neither the Ministry of Foreign Affairs nor the Commander, Armed Forces in Denmark, has kept him informed as they considered the matter purely political.

Jodl states that he will take the matter in hand at once as ' Safari ' has already got under way. He hopes to have a full report on the situation during the evening.

Evening situation conference.

The Fuehrer is informed of the latest developments in Denmark. Since the situation seems to be comparatively quiet, *the Fuehrer* asks: ' Why all this to-do about Denmark ? ' He addresses the Foreign Minister who sits somewhat apart: ' My dear Foreign Minister, what have you got to say about this ? '

Ribbentrop replies that the whole thing is purely a political question and it would have been better if the Commander, Armed Forces, had kept out of it altogether.

The Fuehrer dismisses this with the remark that it was a matter of military concern.

Ribbentrop maintains that it is still possible to stop operation ' Safari ' even though the troops are already on the march.

The Fuehrer refuses to consider withdrawal from an action

once it has begun. We cannot keep changing our orders
according to our whims.

Ribbentrop remarks that sooner or later we would probably
have had to resort to these measures anyway.

Afternoon situation conference. August 29.

In Denmark, generally speaking, operation ' Safari ' has
been completed.

The Fuehrer remarks that we had to expect the present
situation in Denmark and that sooner or later we would
have been forced to resort to the measures just undertaken
because the Danes were constantly exposed to enemy propaganda which we are not in a position to counteract."

France

In France, ever since Germany had marched into the unoccupied
territory at the end of 1942, the feeling against Germany had
steadily increased. At the end of August, as part of the security
operations against Italy, Germany had seized the port of Toulon
which had formerly been in the hands of the Italians. The
attitude of Vichy stiffened yet further, and once again what
remained of the French Fleet became a matter of political
importance. Following Raeder's example, Doenitz felt that to
allow the French to have the full use of their fleet might serve
to make them better disposed towards Germany. On 11
September he discussed the matter with Hitler and Ribbentrop:

" At lunch with the Fuehrer.

The Commander-in-Chief, Navy, discusses with Ribbentrop
the problem of how the French Fleet is to be treated after
Italy ceases to be a political factor. The matter is taken up
with the Fuehrer.

The Fuehrer is of the opinion that latest events have
definitely freed France of her rival in the Mediterranean,
i.e., Italy. This might possibly result in an increasingly rigid
French attitude. Caution should therefore be exercised in
dealing with France.

Ribbentrop emphasized that he is aware of the interest
which Grand-Admiral Doenitz has in the careful treatment
of the French Navy since their co-operation is of vital
importance to Germany. He promises to keep this in mind.

He does not consider it appropriate to extend special favours at this time, but he will be careful to avoid cause for friction with the French Navy.

The Commander-in-Chief, Navy, does not yet intend to take any steps regarding a declaration of honour to Admiral de Laborde (who was recently arrested by the Gestapo and released again), or the creation of a ' Flotte Symbolique '."

Russia

While Hitler had been busy saving what he could out of the Italian collapse, the Russians had started the offensive on the Eastern Front which was eventually to end at Berlin. The retreat of the German army was difficult, and had in part to be made with naval assistance in the Sea of Azov and the Black Sea. The Crimea was the key position, and became the first of the ' fortresses ' which later, in every part of Europe, Hitler ordered to be held to the last.

On 28 October Hitler held a full conference of all his military advisers to work out his first essays in the strategy of retreat, but he received little assistance:

" *Goering* calls attention to the great agricultural importance of the Ukraine, urging strongly that the area should be held.

The Fuehrer himself states that the loss of the Crimea would greatly endanger the Roumanian oilfields. He feels that the arrival of strong reinforcements would yet restore the situation on the southern front.

Doenitz requests information about supply requirements in case the Crimea is cut off. . . .

Keitel does not consider the supply problem to be crucial yet. Ammunition on hand will last two or three weeks; food until the middle of December. . . .

The Fuehrer believes that it would be possible to restore the southern front with the help of the eight divisions just transferred to that sector. This attempt must be made since the Crimea is of the utmost strategic importance. The problem is made more difficult by the fact that there are Roumanian, not German divisions in the Crimea. These troops have repeatedly demonstrated that they are poor fighters, if they fight at all.

Keitel dwells on this point with particular emphasis, fearing
a complete collapse of the Roumanian divisions in the event
of a determined Russian landing. . . ."

So the conference continued, reaching no firm conclusions
because no one was prepared to drive home to Hitler the fact
that the ' invincible ' German army was retreating with virtually
no chance of ever regaining the initiative. In Italy Hitler had
acted with ruthless efficiency; in Russia he seemed for the first
time to be overwhelmed by the difficulties of the situation.

Chapter XIX

ANTI-INVASION PREPARATIONS

By the beginning of 1944, the German Supreme Command,
despite Hitler's assurances, were openly on the defensive. They
sought simply to hold the territory they had conquered, and they
did not any longer plan large-scale offensive operations. It was
clear that the Fatherland itself was in danger. Rundstedt's
famous answer to Keitel's frenzied appeal for advice—" What
shall we do? Make peace, you fools. What else can you
do ? "—did not occur until June 1944, but it is obvious that
by the beginning of the year the Supreme Command already
considered an Allied invasion of Europe inevitable and defeat a
real and unpleasant possibility.

In December 1943 Doenitz, after a conference with Hitler,
decided to change the policy that had kept the big ships of the
German Fleet idle. Accordingly the *Scharnhorst*, with escorting
destroyers, had sailed from her Norwegian base on Christmas
Eve. Her target was a large convoy which had been sighted
en route for Russia. The weather was bad, and there was some
hope that the battleship would not be detected. At about midday
on 26 December, however, she was sighted and intercepted by a
scouting force from the British Home Fleet. British destroyers
and cruisers attacked, and the *Scharnhorst* retreated, but heavy
British ships, including the *Duke of York*, caught up with her,
and in the evening of the same day, the *Scharnhorst* was sunk
off North Cape.

Hitler had become accustomed to the results of actions with the British Fleet and he did not comment very much. Doenitz explained the defeat away by pointing out the superiority of British radar and how slack German scientists had been. Hitler's remarks were short and bitter:

" The thing that grieves him (*i.e.*, the Fuehrer) is the unanswered question of how the Admiral could have made the grave error of assuming that he was confronted by heavy ships when only enemy cruisers were involved. Our battleship, in fact, ran away from the cruisers, although it was superior to them both in fighting power and armour. The Fuehrer always suspects that such happenings occur because too much thought is given to the safety of the ships as in the case of the *Graf Spee*."

The loss of the *Scharnhorst* left Germany with only one operational battleship, the *Tirpitz*. The remainder of the major warships of the German Navy (2 pocket battleships, 7 cruisers, and 2 old battleships) were principally concerned with training duties. They were made available from time to time for patrols off the Norwegian coast, but in general they were non-operational.

The U-boat fleet consisted of 419 boats of which 161 were operational, 168 on trial and 90 used for training. There were also a fair number of minesweepers, E-boats and patrol vessels. Only a small number of the U-boats—those fitted with the Schnorkel * device—could be used in the Channel. It was clear that the German Fleet would be able to put up little opposition against the Allied invasion armada.

Ever since the winter of 1941–42, when Hitler became obsessed with the fear of an invasion of Norway, plans had been gradually evolved for meeting a full-scale invasion of the continent. A directive from Hitler in February 1942 (Directive No. 40) had laid down the fundamental organization between the commands of the three Services in the event of invasion; thereafter various supplementary orders had been issued for the construction and strengthening of the defences of France and the Netherlands. By 1944, however, these defences were still paper plans rather than solid obstructions, and Directive No. 40 which had

* The British ' snort '—an underwater ventilation device.

sought to settle once and for all the problems of inter-Service relationships had by its different interpretation by each of the Services, considerably increased the friction between them.

The biggest problem with which the German High Command had to deal, was to estimate the most likely point on the long European coast-line where the Allies would land. If they could do this with any certainty then they would be able to achieve a greater concentration of their limited forces. But German intelligence had become increasingly unreliable with the progress of the war, and from the many reports they received they were totally unable to make a sound appreciation of Allied intentions. Hitler's 'intuition' (probably based on a private intelligence service) further confused the problem. At different times he named Holland, Jutland, the Gironde, the Bay of Biscay, and once even Normandy as the most probable areas for the Allied invasion. This lack of adequate intelligence made the task of defence almost impossible, and Germany's forces were dispersed from Jutland to the Bay of Biscay.

The naval share of these defences was both more realistic and better organized than that of the Army. Appreciating the strength of Allied sea power, Doenitz had decided that it would be impractical and suicidal to use the major warships of the German Fleet. Of the forces at his disposal, two branches of naval warfare appealed to him most. The first was the use of 'small battle units'—midget submarines, one-man torpedoes and similar weapons; the other was mine warfare. A new mine had been developed which, being extremely simple to construct, promised to be very effective in coastal waters. The planned use of both these defence measures was, however, entirely dependent on the numbers of each which German factories could produce. Doenitz, therefore, did not neglect the older form of shore defence—coastal batteries.

The length of the coast of Western Europe made it impossible to cover every area by coastal batteries. Hitler solved the problem by declaring certain towns and ports to be 'fortresses', which simply meant that coastal artillery units were to be concentrated at these points which Hitler had further ordered were to be defended 'to the last'. The batteries were manned jointly by naval and army personnel, and this dual command later caused much difficulty when they went into action.

The whole problem of shore defence was made more difficult

by the attempt of Army commands to employ naval personnel in military defence units. Doenitz was adamant in his refusal to allocate naval units to the Army at this stage, saying that he required them for the U-boat campaign in which he still placed his greatest hopes of victory. The result was a conflict between the Army and the Navy which seriously disrupted the coastal defence organization.

Doenitz also slowed up the U-boat campaign partly in order to have the maximum number of boats available when the invasion actually began, and partly because Allied counter-measures were by now so successful that U-boats had the greatest difficulty in approaching their targets. But with the new types now in an advanced stage of production, Doenitz hoped to restore the position in Germany's favour.

The first of the two new types of U-boat was the normal U-boat fitted with Schnorkel—a device which enabled the U-boat to operate its diesel engines while submerged, thereby increasing its underwater endurance and making detection more difficult. The second new type was that sometimes known as the ' Walther ' U-boat. This was a boat with a specially designed hull and engines which had exceptional underwater speed, and was designed with the hope of overcoming Allied counter-measures.

The value of the new U-boats was considerably offset by heavy Allied air raids on U-boat production centres. Only three ports (Hamburg, Bremen and Danzig) could be used for the final assembly of the new U-boats, and each of these ports was subject to heavy ' carpet ' bombing, with the result that none of the new boats was in fact operational by the day of the Allied invasion. Secondly, the Baltic, which was the only area available for U-boat training, was threatened by the Russian advance.

But, in spite of these difficulties, Doenitz had high hopes for his new U-boat campaign which he proposed to begin in the second half of 1944 against the Atlantic and Arctic convoys. So great was his faith that he appeared to believe that the new U-boats would bring about a stalemate in the war and would make possible a negotiated peace. Meanwhile the new defensive measures were tried out at Anzio.

The Allied landings at Anzio and Nettuno on 22 January 1944, in particular, were regarded by the German High Command as a preliminary experiment by the Allies before their main assault on Western Europe. They were therefore particularly anxious, not only for the sake of German morale, but also to deter the Allies from their bigger plans, that these landings should fail.

On 28 January, six days after the landings had been made, Hitler sent the following message to his commanders in Italy:

" Within the next few days the ' Battle for Rome ' will commence. . . . This battle has a special significance because the landing at Nettuno marks the beginning of the invasion of Europe planned for 1944. Strong German forces are to be tied down in areas as far as possible from the bases in Britain where the majority of the invasion troops are still stationed. The object of the Allies is to gain experience for future operations.

Every soldier must therefore be aware of the importance of the battle which the 14th Army has to fight.

It must be fought with bitter hatred against an enemy who wages a ruthless war of annihilation against the German people and who, without any higher ethical aims, strives for the destruction of Germany and European culture.

As in the battle for Sicily, on the Rapido River, and at Ortona, it must be driven home to the enemy that the fighting power of Germany is unbroken and that the invasion of the year 1944 is an undertaking which will be crushed in the blood of British soldiers."

Thus inspired, the German Army managed to contain the Allies in their bridgehead, and gave the Wehrmacht an opportunity to try out their anti-invasion measures.

Neither the coastal batteries, nor the mines, nor the midget U-boats were of the standard to be used in Western Europe, but nevertheless they proved effective in retarding the Allied build-up on the beach-head. It seemed to the German Supreme Command proof of their probable success against the long expected ' Second Front '.

On 19 February 1944 Doenitz sent the following appreciation and general policy governing naval anti-invasion measures to all naval commands. This order remained in force up to the date of the invasion:

" General direction for the employment of forces in the event of an enemy landing:
1. The enemy is making extensive preparations for the

opening of a second front. Before long he intends to make
a thrust into the heart of the continent and bring the war to
a speedy conclusion. Using bluff and propaganda, he is
endeavouring to conceal his main object and to make full
use of the element of surprise.

2. The enemy will endeavour to break up German resistance by means of small operations preceding or simultaneous
with the large-scale landing. In addition to those areas
mentioned by the Fuehrer, the coast of Southern France and
Biscay have recently come into the picture. Almost all
areas under German domination must now be regarded as
endangered.

3. The enemy's landing tactics are known to us from
experiences in the Mediterranean and from captured information. In future, he will probably carry out the same procedure.
There will be special points of weakness in the following:

(a) In order to guarantee success, the first landing forces
     must be brought up and the landing of the first wave
     carried out according to a fixed time-table.
(b) Superiority in strength can only be effective after a
     strong bridgehead has been formed. In the past this
     has proved the critical time for the enemy.
(c) As the operation progresses the enemy must keep up a
     heavy supply programme . . . this will undoubtedly
     produce snags and weak points."

Doenitz went on to describe the difficulties and requirements
for adequate defence. He stated that although the Navy alone
could neither prevent nor repulse the enemy landing, yet by
delaying tactics they could gain time which would be of decisive
importance to the Army. He ended his message with the
following exhortation:

" The importance of the task demands that special attention
is paid to the spiritual preparation of the troops. When the
enemy begins his decisive attack against our ' Lebensraum '
his troops will be imbued with the will to destroy without
mercy, and will be well trained in the arts of brutal warfare.
Every crew and every man must know that only stubborn
and tenacious fighting will bring success and help us to
pass through the decisive phase of the war which lies ahead
of us."

Chapter XX

INVASION

On 6 June 1944 the Allies invaded Western Europe; and though
the Germans had been expecting invasion ever since the previous
April, when it came they were taken almost completely by
surprise. The fault lay in the main with their meteorologists
who failed to predict the two-day gap in the bad weather that
in the first week of June was coming in from the Atlantic; but
German air reconnaissance also failed at the supreme test. In
the early hours of 5 June the invasion was postponed for
24 hours. Part of the invasion fleet was already at sea in the
Channel. The ships put into Poole Harbour. All that day they
remained undiscovered.

So it happened that the German defences were caught largely
unprepared. During the week or so preceding the invasion there
does not seem to have been any awareness of its imminence.
No special moves were made; Rommel, in fact, was away
visiting Hitler, and his own family.

The landings in Normandy, besides achieving tactical surprise,
also found few of the naval anti-invasion measures completed.
The production of midget submarines and mines was far behind
schedule—due to Allied bombing attacks—while the coastal
batteries were badly sited and unable to cope with the bombardment of Allied battleships. The artificial harbour at Arromanches,
' Mulberry ', upset what few preparations the German Navy had
made in the Seine area. They had presupposed that a large
unloading port would be one of the first objectives of the invading
forces, and they had decided on Le Havre as the most likely
port for this purpose. Their intelligence services had given them
no indications of the Allied intentions to dispense with such a
port, and the vast floating harbour which the Allies built came
as a complete surprise. It totally disorganized the preconceived
defence plan.

Six days after the invasion had begun, Doenitz went to Hitler's
headquarters to learn what further plans Hitler might have. The
news was bad, but by no means altogether disheartening. He
wrote down later:

" Keitel and Jodl consider the situation very serious, although they still see a hope in an unsuccessful enemy landing attempt at another point. . . . The most likely spot would be on the coast between Dieppe and Boulogne, or between Calais and the Scheldt. It is hoped that the long range bombardment of London (with V.1's) which will begin during the night of 12/13 June will on the one hand divert enemy aircraft and on the other induce the enemy to attempt a second landing in Northern France. If the enemy succeeds in fighting his way out of the present bridgehead and gains freedom of action for mobile warfare in France, then France will be lost. Our next line of defence would be the Maginot Line or the old West Wall. Keitel believes that even then there would be a chance to defeat the enemy. Jodl does not commit himself in this respect since everything depends on how the situation develops and on how many troops we can save. . . . It is still too early to abandon altogether the long-range planning policy of the Navy in favour of short-term action. . . . It must be kept in mind that it might become necessary to move all U-boats to Norway."

Although there was confusion among the front-line forces, at Hitler's headquarters all were still cool and calm. They did not realize the extent of the disorganization and continued to plan as though the forces under their command were as clearly defined as pieces on a chess-board. At a series of conferences at the end of June, Hitler summed up his conception of the situation:

" The overpowering air superiority of the enemy and his very effective use of naval bombardment limit the possibilities of a large-scale attack on our part. We cannot fix the time for such an attack; it depends on when troops and supplies can be brought up, and this cannot be calculated in advance. On the other hand we must not allow mobile warfare to develop, as the enemy surpasses us by far in mobility due to his air superiority and his superabundance of motor vehicles and fuel. Everything therefore depends on our confining him to his bridgehead by building up a front to block it off, and then on fighting a war of attrition to wear him down and force him back, using every method of guerilla warfare. . . . We have got to lay more mines and still more mines in the

Seine Bay with the tenacity of a bulldog, imitating the British procedure against our own transport network. Just as they do we must concentrate everything against the enemy supply lines. It is incomparably more effective to sink a whole cargo at sea than to have to fight the unloaded personnel and material on land. Enemy warships must be attacked, especially battleships. Just as we succeeded in Norway in forcing the enemy out of the country by harassing his supply lines with aircraft, U-boats and battleships, so must we do the same thing here."

But Hitler had learnt his lesson too late. The German Fleet was quite incapable of withstanding the Allied armada of more than four thousand ships, while in the air they were also hopelessly outnumbered. Doenitz conceived the only possible solution to the problem to be cutting off of Allied supplies. He informed Hitler that he intended to remove the few U-boats that he had been able to send into the Channel, and instead that he would muster a strong U-boat force to send back into the North Atlantic where he expected Allied defences would be less alert. But this, too, was of little use. Allied supremacy at sea had enabled such a large stock of supplies to be built up in England that the little damage the U-boats could do would have small effect upon the situation.

It was not only in the west that Germany was being attacked; in the east, too, Russian troops were pressing relentlessly against the retreating German armies. The fact was slowly being driven home to the German High Command that defeat was becoming inevitable. With this realization came a change in the mentality of Germany's war leaders. Previously they had been sure and comprehensive in their grasp of the big issues of the war; now they concentrated instead on smaller tactical problems. At the following conferences, held between 11 and 13 July, the change is clearly shown:

" *July* 11, 1944.   1300 *Situation conference.*

The situation in the East is as follows:

The position of the Central and Northern army groups, which was so optimistically described by the Commander of these two army groups, is not developing quite as expected. . . . The possibility that events may take a turn for the worse must be considered. It is therefore necessary to make plans in advance in case there should be a successful Russian penetration into East Prussia. . . .

July 12, 1944. 1300 *Situation conference.*

During the discussion of further enemy invasion possibilities, *the Commander-in-Chief, Navy,* points out the necessity for air reconnaissance in the Thames area so that enemy operations starting from there may be discovered in time. The transfer of a large part of American troops from the area south of the Thames to between the Thames and the Humber suggests a possible enemy surprise attack in the direction of Holland–Belgium, the German Bight, or even Jutland–Skagerrak. On the other hand the transfer might be the result of V.1 bombardments. . . .

The Fuehrer asks whether the Navy could spare 10,000 men to occupy part of the Narva position (Eastern Front) so that one division may be released for duty on the front of the Central Army Group. It is a well-fortified position and all the soldiers would need would be high morale in order to carry out their task there. They would be relieved by 1 September at the latest because the last divisions are to be brought up to strength and will be ready for action by then.

The Commander-in-Chief, Navy, replies that he believes that he can provide 10,000 good soldiers, but that the Navy is absolutely deficient in weapons and is particularly lacking in commanding officers and subordinate commanders who would be capable of handling such a situation which is not within the scope of the Navy. . . .

The Commander-in-Chief, Navy, asks that the motor vehicles needed by the Admiral in command of ' small battle units ' * be made available from the stocks of the Supreme Command. In return the Navy would forego claiming the equipment of the 2nd Naval Motor Transport Battalion from Army Group E. . . .

The Chief of Staff promises to deliver the required motor vehicles in time. . . .

The Commander-in-Chief, Navy, emphasizes that any naval personnel drafted for other types of duty will henceforth be at the expense of the U-boat Branch. . . .

* Midget submarines, etc.

July 13, 1944.   1300 *Situation conference.*

The Fuehrer decides that the 5000 men to be provided by the Navy for a special defence unit (Sperrverband) are not to be taken from men in training for U-boat duties. . . .

The Commander-in-Chief, Navy, again points out the possible danger to the Skagerrak. The main reason for this is the fact that the enemy, experienced on sea, chooses coasts protected from the prevailing west wind for his landings. This was the case in the Seine Bay.

The Fuehrer is more inclined to believe that further attacks will more likely be directed at the Holland–Belgium area or the Pas de Calais. . . ."

Such topics, with the possible exception of the last, might properly have been left to staff officers, but so great was the disaster confronting them that Germany's war leaders seemed to grasp eagerly at minor matters with which they could deal, rather than face the major problems which were rapidly getting beyond their control. Defence had changed into defeat, but under the Nazi philosophy surrender was impossible. It had to be victory or annihilation.

PART IV

DEFEAT

July 1944—May 1945

Chapter XXI

THE JULY TWENTIETH REVOLT

FIVE weeks after the Normandy landings, on 15 July, Rommel reported to Hitler:

> " The armies are fighting heroically everywhere, but the unequal combat is nearing its end. It is in my opinion necessary to draw the appropriate conclusions from this situation. I feel it is my duty as Commander-in-Chief of the Army Group to express this clearly."

If any proof of the superiority of the Allies or the inevitability of defeat was lacking in the Supreme Command, this report of Rommel's should have carried conviction. It described in detail the confusion and devastation in the battle area, and showed that surrender was the only sane solution. Moreover, Rommel was a general whose courage was beyond doubt and whose daring in Africa and Italy had been praised by Germans and British alike. It was improbable that he would lightly suggest defeat. The German Supreme Command, however, was not impressed, and Hitler's blind determination to go on fighting in spite of the possible extermination of the German race was the final spur to the group of men who had for years been silently plotting the downfall of the Third Reich.

The full history of the one genuine revolt against the Nazis by Germans themselves will probably never be told. The subsequent Nazi purge of the revolutionaries and the machinations of Goebbels have destroyed or polluted the evidence. What has not been tampered with by the Nazis is insufficient to give a full and accurate account. Goebbels sought to make what was a widespread revolt appear as a dangerous, but restricted act of treachery, and this propaganda distorts the documents in the German archives which refer to the attempted assassination of Hitler.

The brief history of the revolt given here is based partly on what was revealed at the Nuremberg Trials, partly on fragments pieced together by Allied intelligence officers, and partly on subsequent German accounts from those who had direct knowledge of the revolutionary movement.

The revolt had its origins in 1938 when General Ludwig Beck, who was then Chief of Staff to the German High Command, resigned as a protest against the intended invasion of Czechoslovakia. Until then Beck had paid little heed to Hitler's internal politics, but the invasion of Czechoslovakia, an unprovoked attack on a foreign country, could mean nothing but war. It is an indication of the hold which Hitler had over intelligent and responsible Germans that it needed the bloodshed in Czechoslovakia to open their eyes. As Ribbentrop had cynically remarked to Ciano: " It was not land that Hitler wanted, but war."

Having resigned, Beck set about gathering round him a group of soldiers and civilians with the intention of wresting power from the Nazis and overthrowing Hitler. Beck's difficulties were immense, and for the next few years his movement was driven deeper and deeper underground both by the Gestapo and by the popularity which Hitler gained from his early military successes. Nevertheless such men as Count von Moltke; Doctor Karl Goerdeler, the ex-Mayor of Leipzig; Count Friedrich von der Schulenberg, the former German Ambassador in Moscow; the Generals—Witzleben, Hoeppner and Olbricht; and Admiral Canaris, head of the Abwehr (Military Intelligence Service), joined Beck's circle in the early years.

The revolt was essentially a revolt from the top. It was impossible under the régime of Himmler's Gestapo for ordinary people to take part, but an indication of its extent is given by the fact that according to one source, based on names and places, 4980 Germans were exterminated by the Nazis in the purge which followed 20 July.

The circumstances in Germany were such that only the Army was in a position to seize power from the Nazis. To succeed, therefore, Beck had to have the sympathy of most of the Army commanders. But the one great obstacle to this was the personal oath of loyalty which all officers had taken to Hitler. In Western Europe or America it is difficult to understand how much this personal oath meant. Hitler's crimes alone would seem to have been sufficient reason for breaking the oath, but to the German officers nothing less than the death of Hitler could absolve them from their obligations. The success of Beck's movement, therefore, depended entirely on the assassination of Hitler.

The motives which inspired Beck's group were varied. They were obviously united by a common hatred of Hitler, but undoubtedly some of the other generals who joined the movement later were concerned principally for the salvation of the Wehrmacht. On the other hand such men as Goerdeler and Beck himself were genuinely determined not only to rescue Germany from the destruction of war, but also to rid themselves for ever of those elements within their nation' which had made Nazism possible. It was not until the defeat of Germany became certain, however, that sufficient numbers joined Beck to make the revolt feasible.

The realization of defeat divided Germany into two camps— those who wished to prevent further needless destruction, and those who still followed Hitler. This division gave Beck's movement the status of a full-scale revolt. Many more officers joined him, and success became possible. Among his new supporters was Count von Stauffenberg, whose vigorous and dashing personality gave an added impetus to the movement.

In the German Navy only a few naval officers joined Beck. They were neither sufficiently senior nor numerous enough to have any real effect on the Navy as a whole, and Doenitz, himself, remained staunch to Hitler. Most of the German Navy, imbued as they were with Nazi doctrine, followed Doenitz's lead.

This was the political background when on 20 July 1944 Count von Stauffenberg attempted to assassinate Hitler at Rastenberg. Briefly the plan was that as soon as Hitler's death had been established, General Witzleben was to assume command of the Wehrmacht, while Fromm, who was head of the Reserve Army in Germany, was to seize Berlin. All Gestapo and Sicherheitsdienst (Security Service—SD) headquarters were to be surrounded. In particular all communications with the Supreme Command were to be cut. As soon as order had been established, Goerdeler and Beck were to form a government and sue for peace with

the Allies.   They realized that the Allies would only accept
unconditional surrender, but they believed that however harsh
the terms were, they would still have saved many lives and
prevented the further destruction of Germany.

The plan failed.   Hitler was injured but escaped death.   There
was an additional failure to cut the communication to Hitler's
headquarters.   And Fromm, uncertain of Hitler's death, decided
to betray the plotters.   The failure of the assassination attempt
was rapidly broadcast throughout Germany—Hitler himself
spoke over the radio—and this, together with Fromm's treachery
lost Beck those supporters in the Army who needed Hitler's
death to absolve them from their oath and give them courage
to seize power from the Nazis.   The terror which followed was
one of the worst which Hitler ever organized against his own
people.   And of this terror Raeder, from his retirement in the
country, suddenly found that he was in danger of becoming a
victim.   In order to prove his innocence he flew to Hitler's
headquarters on 22 July.   He saw Hitler and had lunch with him,
hearing a first-hand account of what had happened:

" The Fuehrer's right forearm had been slightly bruised
and his hearing was affected.   He told me the details of the
attempt upon his life, and pointed out the spot where the deed
had taken place.   He had had a miraculous escape as the
others present had been more or less seriously injured.   The
would-be assassin, Count Stauffenberg, a brave soldier who
had lost an arm and an eye in previous campaigns and who
was greatly respected in the Army, had placed the dispatch
case containing the bomb under the end of the table where
the maps were spread.   Shortly before the beginning of the
conference, he had gone out again, supposedly to telephone.
He had asked for a number, but had not waited for it, and
had driven off immediately to the airfield, whence he flew to
Berlin, knowing nothing of the results of his plot.   The
Fuehrer had sat himself down at the plotting table about a
quarter or a third of its length from the spot where the
dispatch case lay, and he had placed his right forearm on the
thick table-top.

When the explosion took place (the Fuehrer and others
remember two distinct detonations) the shorter section of
the table-top on the right of the Fuehrer was shattered,

almost as far as the place where he was sitting. The only
effect, however, was the temporary paralysis of his right arm.
Even his legs escaped injury, while other people who were
present were severely hurt. A stenographer had both his
legs blown off, and the Chief of Staff, Luftwaffe, was mortally
wounded. . . . One officer was hurled out of the window on
to the window-sill and was injured. The effects would have
been even more serious had the building been more massive
with a strongly-built roof and a concrete floor. As it
possessed neither of these, the main blast went upwards and
downwards without meeting much resistance, and the
horizontal effects were less severe. The wreckage, however,
gave an impression of great desolation. The explosive was
of English manufacture: Count Stauffenberg's wife was an
Englishwoman. . . .

I declared to the Fuehrer before my departure that I was
still ready to throw my own life into the balance for the sake
of the German people, and he realized at once how concerned
I was at our present situation; but he expressed his conviction, as was usual with him in the face of difficulties, that
he would soon ' straighten out ' the position.

On leaving, I pointed out to the SS guard that I had lunched
alone with the Fuehrer, keeping a loaded revolver in my
pocket which would have made it an easy matter for me to
have assassinated him—even if only in a fit of madness. (At
that time I was obliged to carry a revolver for my own
protection and I had it ready for action in my pocket.) My
appearance at Headquarters had obviously so surprised my
enemies that from that time on they gave up all their attempts
to implicate me in the plot of July 20."

The plan failed. But how nearly it succeeded and what confusion it caused is shown in the official diary of Admiral Krancke,
who, as Admiral commanding Group West, was stationed in
Paris and experienced to the full the confusion which followed
Stauffenberg's attempt: [1]

" *July* 20, 1944.

After the report had been made over the radio in the
afternoon announcing the unsuccessful attempt on the

Fuehrer's life, a secret teleprint message comes in from 'Koralle' (Doenitz's headquarters):

To: Chief of Staff, Operations Division, Naval Staff.

Time: 1928.

'1. The Fuehrer, Adolf Hitler, is dead. An unscrupulous clique of non-combatant party leaders, utilizing this situation, has attempted to stab our fighting forces in the back and seize power for their own purposes.

2. In this hour of extreme danger the Government of the Reich, to maintain law and order, has decreed a military state of emergency and placed me in supreme command of the German Armed Forces.

3. I hereby decree:
The SS Branch is from now on to be included in the Army.

4. Officers with executive power are responsible for maintaining order and public security. In particular they are to:
(*a*) Safeguard communications;
(*b*) Eliminate SD resistance which is to be broken ruthlessly.

5. In this hour of extreme peril for the Fatherland, the unity of the Wehrmacht and the maintenance of discipline is of the utmost importance. I therefore make it the duty of all Commanding Officers of the Army, the Navy, and the Air Force to support all officers with executive power and so enable them to carry out their difficult tasks and to ensure that their orders are carried out by subordinate authorities. The German soldier has a momentous task and the safety of Germany depends on his energy and his demeanour.

WITZLEBEN,
C.-in-C. Armed Forces.'

This message, coming from a retired Field-Marshal and containing an order for the imprisonment of the Security Service must be false, although it is issued as an 'Officers only' teleprint message from Koralle.

I immediately 'phone the Grand-Admiral who assures me that the Fuehrer is alive, that this order is false, and that only orders from him or from Himmler are to be obeyed.

2135.

Proclamation from the Commander-in-Chief, Navy:

' Men of the Navy,

The treacherous attempt to assassinate the Fuehrer fills each and every one of us with holy wrath and bitter rage towards our criminal enemies and their hirelings. Divine providence spared the German people and its Armed Forces this inconceivable misfortune. In the miraculous escape of our Fuehrer we see additional proof of the righteousness of our cause.

Let us now more than ever rally round our Fuehrer and fight with all our strength until victory is ours.

Grand-Admiral DOENITZ.'

I try to contact Field-Marshal von Kluge by telephone in order to clarify any mistakes which might have arisen. The Field-Marshal answers that he is at present in conference and cannot speak to me. A short time afterwards I receive a 'phone call from General Blumentritt, his Chief of Staff. I inform him that after receiving the signal from Field-Marshal von Witzleben I had a conversation with the Grand-Admiral and that the declarations and orders contained in the signal are false. He had received a similar signal from Fromm. General Blumentritt has also received information of the real situation from General Warlimont of the Supreme Command and informs me that ' everything is in order '.

2300.

Message from the Grand-Admiral:

' (a) There has been a military conspiracy by a clique of generals—Fromm, Hoeppner.

(b) Reichsfuehrer SS Himmler has been made Commander of the Reserve Army.

(c) The Navy is ordered to be in a state of readiness.

(d) Orders issued by Army commands are not to be obeyed.

(e) Orders of the Reichsfuehrer SS must be obeyed by the Navy.

Long live the Fuehrer !

Commander-in-Chief, Navy.'

2315.

The Naval Liaison Officer with the C.-in-C., West, Commander Koenig, 'phones that all the rumours circulating

are false and that the Fuehrer has appointed Himmler in command of the Reserve Army. He is told that I am well-informed of the situation and that the Grand-Admiral has given clear orders.
2400.

Message from Communications Command:

'Increased watchfulness to-night. Beware of possible plot. Open fire immediately.

C.O., Paris.'

A telephone message comes in from the Naval Communications division:

'At 2210 to-night an Army establishment in the middle of Paris was attacked by disguised terrorists. The terrorists, wearing German uniform, drove up with four heavy lorries and disarmed the guards. All sentries are to be instructed immediately that no military personnel are to be allowed to enter military establishments or bases without first giving an explanation outside the gate. On the approach of every unknown Army vehicle the guard is to be warned. A sharp look-out is to be kept and everyone is to remain ready for immediate action.'

It later appears that the 'terrorists' incident was only an assumption by the Naval Communications division. In fact they were only German soldiers whose activity was so unusual that they were believed to be disguised terrorists.

July 21.
0030.

An army patrol stopped an armoured vehicle outside my Staff Quarters. The patrol explained to my sentry that they had an order to imprison the SD (Security Service). I immediately phoned Field-Marshal von Kluge who was at Army Group E's headquarters outside the city in order to inform him of this action taken by the usurpers. He thanked me for the information and assures me that he will have all the necessary steps taken in Paris.
0040.

In order to obtain reliable information I tried to speak to the General Commanding the Security Service, General Oberg. At his quarters, however, Lieutenant von Krewel answered instead and told my Chief of Staff, who is known to him personally, that General Oberg and all the SD have been arrested by Commander-in-Chief, France.

0045.

I order all Naval Commands in Paris to prepare their troops for immediate action.

0048.

I try unsuccessfully to reach Field-Marshal von Kluge by telephone to inform him of Oberg's arrest and to let him know that the order for this came from General Stuelpnagel. He sends me an answer that he is at present unable to speak to me—is there anything wrong?

0056.

Message is received that the Fuehrer, and after him the Grand-Admiral, will speak over the radio.

0111.

After the Grand-Admiral's speech my Chief of Staff informs General Blumentritt that I have been trying in vain to speak to von Kluge. General Blumentritt replies that he has been ordered to relieve Stuelpnagel of his command and to set General Oberg free again.

0136.

General Blumentritt informs my Chief of Staff that he is going to Paris and that everything will be settled in an hour.

0137.

I inform von Unger, Chief of Staff to the Commanding Officer, Paris, that General Oberg and the SD are to be released immediately or I shall take steps with my troops to set them free. I inform him that General Stuelpnagel has been relieved of his command. I demand to know what is happening. He reports that they can do nothing. Stuelpnagel has given orders.

0140.

I call up the Chief of Staff of the Military Officer Commanding in France, von Linstow. He informs me that Krewel, O.C., 1st Security Regiment, has received orders to free General Oberg and the SD. At his headquarters it was considered to be a Gestapo putsch.

0156.

I inform Naval Commands in Paris of developments and cancel the state of immediate readiness.

0206.

General Blumentritt 'phones my Chief of Staff: ' Where can I find General Oberg ? ' He answers: ' In the Hotel Continental which is being used as a place of detention.'

General Blumentritt asks: ' If I should be made prisoner there, can I depend on you to release me again ? ' My Chief of Staff answers: ' Yes '.

0215.

I try once more to reach General Oberg at his station, but I am informed that he has been held prisoner at the SD station in Avenue Foch; that he has, however, just been ~~se. ~ ~e~~ and is about to go to the SD station in the Boulevard Lannes.

0335.

Following delayed signal comes in:

' The Putsch attempted by irresponsible generals has been ruthlessly subdued. All the leaders have been shot. Orders issued by Witzleben, Hoeppner, Beck, or Olbricht are not to be obeyed.

I have again taken over command after my temporary arrest by force of arms.

FROMM.'

The signal causes astonishment. I again order that instructions issued by General Fromm are not to be carried out.

0655.

The following signal is received:

' The last sentence of the signal from General Fromm is invalid. In accordance with the order of the Fuehrer I have taken over the command of the Reserve Army. Only orders issued by me are to be obeyed.

HIMMLER.'

In the forenoon General Oberg phones me and expresses his appreciation of the Navy's energetic behaviour during the previous night."

The revolt officially ended on 7 and 8 August when, amidst the blare of Goebbels' propaganda, those leaders who had not yet been shot or tortured to death were brought before the People's court and tried for high treason. The verdict and sentence were previously ordered by Hitler, and Goerdeler,

Witzleben, Hoeppner, Schulenberg and von Moltke were either hanged or shot—von Moltke in spite of the fact that alone among the revolutionaries he had refused to countenance the death of Hitler because of his religious scruples against the taking of life. In the German Navy only three officers were caught and tried, one of them being Stauffenberg's brother.

For the rest, Beck committed suicide after twice wounding himself in the head in the attempt; Stauffenberg and Olbricht were shot by Fromm who was himself later court-martialled and shot by the Nazis; Admiral Canaris, after suffering some months at the hands of the Gestapo, was either murdered or forced to commit suicide; while the many other members of the movement were gradually hunted down and eliminated by Himmler. Terror raged for the next six months. Guilty and innocent alike were tortured and massacred in this the last and worst outburst of the Nazis against their own people.

Chapter XXII

THE BATTLE OF THE ATLANTIC (5)

By the autumn of 1944, it was quite obvious that Germany had lost the war. Against the enormous weight of British, American and Russian power they could not hope to win. Yet Germany continued to fight, like a punch-drunk boxer, blind and stupid with pain.

Three months after the end of the war, Doenitz was instructed by his British captors to write an account of what had happened. Describing this last phase, he said:

> "In the autumn of 1944, the situation was extremely grave. After losing the greatest part of the territories we had previously occupied in the west, south, and east, ' Fortress Europe ' had been reduced to ' Fortress Germany ', with the exception of Norway, Denmark and Holland which we still firmly held.
>
> In the east and west the opposing armies stood on the frontiers of the Reich or had in places actually crossed them. The ever-increasing air offensive of the Western Powers on

the German homeland had already seriously reduced the
industrial and economic resources both by direct destruction
and by cutting off our communications. . . . The German
Air Force had failed to bring the Allied bombing to a
standstill. Thus the prospect of success for Germany
appeared very slender. All thought of an early end to the
war was, however, destroyed by our enemies. Leading
figures of the opposing side repeatedly declared that only
unconditional surrender was acceptable. Enemy propaganda
painted a gloomy picture of the intended treatment of
Germany after defeat. For this reason our leaders had no
alternative but to continue resistance as long as possible in
order to exploit every opportunity of saving the German
people from the fate painted in such fearful colours by the
enemy press. The German people themselves, through the
continual air attacks and the numerous restrictions on their
daily life, had become here and there somewhat weary, but
for the most part they stuck to their task faithfully and with
admirable determination. The terror raids on open towns
which had no military or even industrial significance brought
horror and misery to all, but they only stiffened the will to
resist of the defenceless population of women, children and
old folk. Men and women carried on grimly and obstinately
with their work, bringing unbelievable energy to the maintenance of production."

But Doenitz giving his opinion as a prisoner-of-war after the
event, and Doenitz issuing his orders as Commander-in-Chief
of the Navy at the time, were two very different people. The
situation then did not appear nearly so hopeless to him as he
described, and his remarks about the effect of Allied propaganda
are at best but half-truths. In fact, the Supreme Command was
buoyed up by hopeful expectations from at least four different
sources. First, Hitler was planning a major military attack which
was intended to drive the Allies back to the sea (the Ardennes
offensive); second, the Luftwaffe, which had been deliberately
kept out of the war in the air, was building up a huge reserve
of the new jet-propelled fighters which was intended to drive
the Allies from the skies; third, Doenitz had promised spectacular
successes with the new Walther U-boats (types XVIII, XXIV and
XXVI) which were to strangle the Allies' supplies; and fourth,

there were hopes and rumours that the Western Powers were about to break off relations with Russia.*

These four factors, apart from Hitler's determination to follow his policy of victory or annihilation through to the end, were quite enough to keep the Supreme Command going. They were by this time incapable of clear thinking, and the prospect of working on comparatively straightforward tactics appealed far more than trying to deal with the complexities of the situation as a whole. Few dared to look beyond the fighting in Europe to the vast arsenals of the United States and the British Empire with all that they meant to the future of the war in Germany. The nearest that any came to seeing further than the immediate tactical problems was Doenitz, who, faithful as ever to his U-boats, was planning to cut the pipe-line between these arsenals and the front. But Doenitz, too, had shut his mind to the realities of Allied power and resources. His U-boats, in the second half of 1944, sank 60 ships in the invasion areas and in the waters round Britain. As there were more than 4000 Allied ships taking part in the invasion these losses were insignificant, but Doenitz refused to consider them against such a background, and instead put the sinkings down as an important contribution towards German success. He talked of the possibility of forcing the Allies to accept a stalemate.

The hope of a split between the Allies was a comfort which had worn rather thin with the years. Hitler had come to see in it a source of peril rather than of hope, and a conference with Doenitz in October 1944 revealed the dilemma of the Supreme Command:

" *The Commander-in-Chief, Navy*, is of the opinion that no large-scale landing attempts will be made by the British in northern Norway. Since Churchill and Stalin could reach no agreement concerning this region at the Moscow Conference (as is clearly revealed in Churchill's last speech) and since on the other hand Churchill will avoid everything which might cause friction between him and Stalin, he (Doenitz) does not expect British action in northern Norway as this would obviously be directed against Russia.

* There might have been a fifth hope—the V-2; but belief in the V-weapons appears to have evaporated somewhat by this time and there is very little mention of them at the Fuehrer Conferences.

The Fuehrer does not consider this sound reasoning. Relations between Churchill and Stalin are strained in any case, and England can only prevent Russia's advance into Norway, *e.g.*, in the region of Narvik, by occupying that territory herself. The Fuehrer fears that the British might establish themselves in certain places in order to cut off our land and sea communications by penetrating inland."

The new U-boat campaign and the Ardennes offensive, however, were Hitler's real hopes, and the preparations for both were pursued vigorously. Doenitz later commented on the U-boat campaign:

" We were entitled to assume that the U-boat war would enter a new phase. Considerable successes had already been achieved by the old types of boats fitted with the ' Schnorkel ' on operations of long duration without needing to surface at all. The strain on crews who remained submerged up to 70 days was surprisingly small. Thanks to the ' Schnorkel ' the air remained fresh during underwater cruising and considerably better than in former circumstances. But the most important reduction in strain came from the removal of the continual nervous tension in U-boat crews caused by the earlier danger of surprise air attacks. The type XXI, with its range of 22,000 miles, was capable of scouring all waters of importance to the U-boat war without once having to surface. It was obvious that this would bring about a change in the naval war. Hitherto control of the sea by the great sea Powers had been exercised through surface craft supported by aircraft; a warship whose primary operational sphere lies beneath the surface renders such control of the sea largely impossible. If, in addition, such a warship has a high underwater speed, making it easier to approach the enemy, it would obviously be a very valuable instrument of war."

But the chief obstacle in the way of the new U-boat campaign was the destruction caused by Allied air attacks on the shipbuilding yards. Prefabrication in widely scattered areas was adopted, but even so out of 290 boats promised by the constructors only 65 were delivered by the end of 1944, while the number of U-boats actually in commission fell from 181 in

June to 140 in December 1944. Nevertheless Doenitz decided
to continue with his plans. He was so optimistic that in a conference with Hitler on 3 December he discussed as well the
future training of German naval officers for major surface
operations:

" *The Commander-in-Chief, Navy*, announces his intention
of sending ten to fifteen German naval officers to Japan,
giving them the opportunity of becoming acquainted with
naval warfare on a large scale by taking part in fleet operations there. Their experience could later be used to build up
a German Fleet. Since German naval warfare, with the
exception of U-boat warfare, has developed into a purely
coastal war, there is no opportunity at all of gaining experience of this nature in the European theatre.

The Fuehrer agrees.

The Commander-in-Chief, Navy, submits to the Fuehrer
the report of Lt.-Commander Nollmann who was in
command of a U-boat fitted with Schnorkel for operations
off the east coast of Scotland. Nollmann speaks in the most
positive manner about the great possibilities of this boat and
states his conviction and that of his crew that with the
introduction of Schnorkel the old effectiveness of the U-boat
had been re-established. In view of this very favourable
report, corroborated in other instances, the Commander-in-
Chief has no misgivings about the new U-boat models which
will be even better fitted for underwater warfare. He believes
that the revival of U-boat warfare will chiefly be a home and
shipyard problem since the enemy will concentrate all his
efforts on the outward-bound routes of the submarines, on
their construction and repair yards, and on their bases as
soon as the first successes of the U-boats get known. . . .
As for the propaganda angle of U-boat warfare, the
Commander-in-Chief proposes to lull the enemy into a state
of security and not to inform the public at first of our
successes, in order not to provoke the enemy prematurely
into taking counter-measures.

The Fuehrer agrees."

Accordingly, in the last days of December, U-boats slipped out
of German harbours (most of the French ports had by then
been liberated) and made their way to the Bristol Channel, the

Irish Sea, the Minches, and the north-east coast of England, areas where they had not ventured since 1940. In these shallow waters, aided by the ' schnorkel ', the U-boats hoped to evade patrol vessels and convoy escorts and to deliver their final blow against Allied shipping.

The new U-boat offensive disturbed the Allies more by its novelty than by its actual success. By the end of January only nine merchant ships had been sunk for the loss of seven U-boats. In the following month Doenitz extended the operating area to the Arctic, once again attacking Russian convoys. The result was fifteen merchant ships sunk for the loss of fourteen U-boats. Eight more U-boats were destroyed by air attack in harbour.

Meanwhile U-boat production made a spectacular recovery, and raised Doenitz's hopes. On 15 February Doenitz reported to Hitler:

> " U-boat success per U-boat amounted to 9000 tons in December 1944 and 11,000 tons in January 1945. These figures are as high as they ever were during the most successful period of U-boat warfare, but the total is considerably affected by the small number of U-boats in the operational areas and by the long periods of time required for the U-boats to get to and from the operational areas. The number of U-boats will increase considerably during the next few months. At present 237 U-boats are being prepared: 111 of the old types, 84 of type XXI and 42 of type XXIII. Apart from these about 60 additional U-boats will be commissioned each month. The present total of 450 U-boats in commission is the largest number Germany has ever possessed."

Besides the development of more or less orthodox U-boat warfare, Doenitz had also managed to put into practice his twenty-year-old scheme for midget submarines. During most of 1944 various types had been tried out, and by the beginning of 1945 it had been decided to concentrate on two particular types—the ' Seehund ', a two-man midget submarine carrying two torpedoes, and the ' Biber ', a one-man midget submarine also carrying two torpedoes. Doenitz persuaded Hitler to accept his scheme with an argument which resembled that of a novice about to take up chicken-farming:

> " Assuming that out of the eighty ' Seehund ' midget

submarines scheduled to operate per month, only fifty are able to attack, then one hundred torpedoes will be fired at the enemy. If 20 per cent. of the torpedoes hit their targets, then about 100,000 tons will be sunk." *

These optimistic calculations were somewhat damped by results, and in a later report to Hitler, Doenitz explained:

" Of the ten ' Seehund ' submarines which left Ijmuiden on 21 January, nine have so far returned. Partly because of technical defects and partly because of bad weather, their mission was unsuccessful. They underwent a severe test during their first operation, but despite negligible successes the operations were of the greatest value. All the defects which might never have been discovered in the Baltic Sea showed up under the severe conditions in the Hoofden and can thus be corrected. . . . They have been found to be relatively immune to depth charges because due to their shape they offer so little resistance. They are tossed aside like a cork instead of being damaged. Thus the ' Seehund ' has proved relatively immune from enemy defences. . . . The crews have gained considerable confidence in their equipment, and future mass operations of the ' Seehund ' submarines under favourable weather conditions are expected to score considerable successes."

That was the last recorded report Doenitz made on midget submarines to Hitler. Thereafter he returned to the new U-boats which really did offer better possibilities. The results in February showed a slight improvement, and Hitler stressed the importance he attached to maintaining the U-boat campaign.

In March the first of the new Walther U-boats went into action. It was not as successful as had been hoped, but there was no reason yet to abandon it. In all, during March, twelve Allied ships were sunk for the loss of eighteen U-boats. Sixteen U-boats were also destroyed by air attacks in harbour. The losses were becoming more than Germany could stand, and on 8 April Doenitz once more explained the situation to Hitler:

" Because we have concentrated our U-boats in the coastal waters round the British Isles, as has been the case for several months now, the enemy has also concentrated his

* Doenitz; speaking to Hitler at a conference on 3 January 1945.

defences in these areas. Although enemy defence forces can no longer find our U-boats by radar or other locating devices, as soon as a U-boat discloses its presence by attacking, such a concentrated attack develops that the vessel is often lost. At the moment four boats which were expected to return in the last few days are missing. Because of their low underwater speed, the old types of U-boat cannot escape once they have been discovered, but the new types will be able to leave the danger area at high speed and thus escape the concentrated enemy defence. To counter the above situation, I intend to take the U-boats out of coastal areas for the present and to send the old type VII to the open ocean just west of the British Isles and the old type IX in a rake formation along the Great Circle in the direction of America. My purpose is two-fold: on the one hand I hope that the U-boats will be able to make successful surprise attacks in new regions where there should be only slight opposition; on the other hand I want to force the enemy to disperse his defences and thus to improve the U-boat warfare conditions in British coastal waters. Our chances for successful U-boat warfare would be great now if we still had the Biscay ports."

Doenitz's two-pronged attack was cut short by the capitulation. The Battle for Berlin was developing and this was the last general report on U-boat warfare which Doenitz made to Hitler.

The new campaign failed. As Doenitz had woefully stated, the loss of the Bay of Biscay ports greatly increased the difficulties which beset the U-boats. It added at least a thousand miles to the voyage to and from the operational areas, as the bases had to be transferred to Norway. Apart from the reduced time on actual operations which the move entailed, the longer voyages made the U-boats more vulnerable to attack, and during the last campaign in April, 57 U-boats were destroyed—33 at sea and 24 in harbour. It was the highest monthly total of U-boats sunk during the war. The U-boats themselves sank only 13 merchant ships.

Although, in view of the military situation in Germany, Doenitz's last campaign was both stupid and suicidal, one cannot but admire the gallantry of the U-boat crews, who, in

spite of the overpowering weight of Allied naval forces, continued
to fight in remote areas with undiminished spirit. In the last
month of the war, U-boats penetrated as far north as the Kola
Inlet off Murmansk and as far west as the St. Lawrence River
in their hopeless battle against Allied supplies. The damage
they did was negligible; the losses they suffered were enormous;
and yet, alone of all Germany's armed forces, they fought on
to the very last day of the war. Their record at sea during the
whole war, too, was not as bad as it has been painted. Whatever
they might have condoned or even applauded on shore, in all
the evidence assembled at Nuremberg, there were only five cases
of criminal conduct by U-boats at sea.

Chapter XXIII

'FORTRESS GERMANY'

DURING the last few months of the war, Doenitz was in constant
touch with Hitler, and the records of these meetings provide
what is almost a day-by-day account of the closing stages of
Germany's defeat. A comparison of these last few months with
the period immediately preceding the Italian collapse shows how
much the ability of the German Supreme Command had declined.
Then, in the summer of 1943, Hitler had been able to appreciate
the situation as a whole. He had drawn up both military and
political plans to avert disaster—Mussolini had been rescued,
Fascism had been restored, defence zones had been adequately
prepared—with the result that he had succeeded in delaying the
Allies for more than a year.

By the beginning of 1945, however, Hitler had become incapable
of large-scale planning. Where one would expect to find an
acceptance of military defeat leading to schemes for guerilla
warfare and for continuing the fight underground, one finds
instead nothing but a series of tactical plans for bolstering
individual sectors of the three fronts—neither related to nor
co-ordinated with any general strategy. The records of the
'Fuehrer Conferences' give in fact a clear picture of Hitler and
his staff, desperate in the face of a situation they could no longer

control, and so harassed that they could not think beyond the immediate requirements of battle.

The shortage of manpower became acute, and both the Navy and the Luftwaffe were combed for extra troops. Doenitz was in the forefront in finding extra men for the battle, and after the war he wrote:

" All new construction, reconstruction, repairs and developments which could not be made ready for front-line operations in the shortest time were abandoned. The authorities and staffs concerned were then reduced or dissolved, and the personnel were turned over to operational duties. The manpower of the Navy was continually and carefully supervised so that personnel rendered superfluous by the shrinking theatres of war could be transferred immediately to the Army. To maintain naval tradition, to which there was great devotion, naval infantry divisions were created which were purely and simply for land warfare. . . . As a result of the short training period, losses were relatively high. Only the U-boat and small craft building programme was maintained. But here too the increasing destruction of industry and communications, together with the loss of building yards and factories, compelled a gradual decrease until finally, shortly before the capitulation, new construction was stopped altogether, and only boats which were working up were made available."

Indeed, Doenitz alone of Hitler's staff appeared to keep his head. He continued to give Hitler encouraging reports and practical assistance until two weeks of the end. Besides the success he promised for his U-boat campaign and his offer of Naval Brigades to assist the Army, he undertook the distribution of coal ; organized the movement of troops from remote theatres to the German home front; planned the evacuation of refugees from East Prussia; and in general took upon himself the position of Hitler's principal military adviser and comforter. He was spurred on partly by his blindness to the realities of the situation and partly by his overweening ambition to become Hitler's second-in-command. But whatever his motives, he alone remained cool and efficient. He drew closer and closer to Hitler until finally he was rewarded with the dubious goal of his ambition and became the second Fuehrer of the Third Reich.

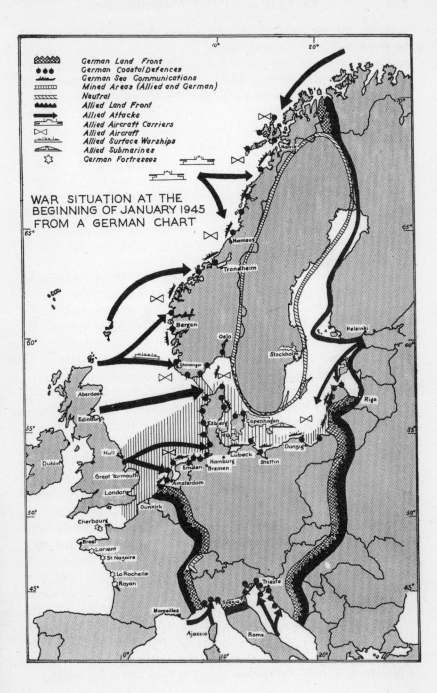

Legend

German Land Front
German Coastal Defences
German Sea Communications
Mined Areas (Allied and German)
Neutral
Allied Land Front
Allied Attacks
Allied Aircraft Carriers
Allied Aircraft
Allied Surface Warships
Allied Submarines
German Fortresses

WAR SITUATION AT THE BEGINNING OF JANUARY 1945 FROM A GERMAN CHART

Narvik
Namsos
Trondheim
Bergen
Oslo
Stavanger
Stockholm
Helsinki
Riga
Aberdeen
Edinburgh
Esbjerg
Copenhagen
Danzig
Dublin
Hull
Lübeck
Stettin
Great Yarmouth
Emden
Hamburg
Bremen
London
Amsterdam
Dunkirk
Cherbourg
Brest
Lorient
St Nazaire
La Rochelle
Royan
Trieste
Marseilles
Ajaccio
Rome

By the beginning of 1945 the German armies in the west had been pushed back to just within the German frontier; in the east the line was more or less straight from East Prussia to Jugoslavia with a western bulge in Austria; and in the south the front stretched across Italy from Spezia to a point south of Venice. There were German outposts in the Channel Isles, in Lithuania (Kurland), and in five French ports. Norway and Denmark were still in German hands.

The old year saw the culmination of Hitler's long-prepared plans for an assault on the Western Front—the Ardennes offensive. At the same time the Luftwaffe struck with a force of 800 aircraft, but were quickly defeated by Allied air power, and by 16 January the land offensive had also failed. After their temporary set-back the Allied armies from west and east closed in on Germany with irresistible force.

On 18 January Doenitz went to Hitler and stayed by his side until 23 January. During the six days every aspect of the situation—except the inevitability of defeat—was discussed. Doenitz offered first a naval brigade of 3000 ratings. On 20 January he increased their numbers:

" In view of the threatening developments in the East, *the Commander-in-Chief, Navy*, puts 20,000 naval troops at the disposal of the land forces.

The Fuehrer accepts this offer, and after a discussion of the type of troops to be used he decides that the above-mentioned number of men from training units of the Navy are to be transferred to the Danish area, where they are to join the land defences. This would free twenty-two Army replacement battalions from the Danish area for service on the Eastern Front."

With the destruction of land communications the distribution of coal had become extremely difficult. Doenitz stated the situation and offered advice:

" After the situation conference *Field-Marshal Keitel* informs the Fuehrer of the difficult coal situation and of the necessity for organizing coal distribution very strictly.

The Commander-in-Chief, Navy, declares that the present situation is untenable, because everyone is confiscating coal for his own purpose, and the most important tasks of the Armed Forces are therefore being endangered. Coal must be secured for sea transports and defence forces; otherwise divisions can no longer be sent to the front, and the Army Group, Kurland, which can be supplied only by sea, will be cut off entirely from supplies. The distribution of coal is a military task, and it can be accomplished only by a determined member of the Armed Forces with the necessary authority. The agencies concerned must keep in constant contact with one another and get the facts on the coal situation; on these findings the coal czar must base his decisions as to the proper distribution according to military needs.

The Fuehrer approves the proposal that a member of the Armed Forces be appointed coal czar.

The Commander-in-Chief, Navy, also reports that Rear-Admiral Engelhardt is organizing seventy to ninety tugs and a corresponding number of barges on the Rhine to ship coal to the Netherlands. The Navy is supplying the required number of officers and 1000 men for this task. Light anti-aircraft guns are needed.

The Fuehrer welcomes this initiative and decides that the anti-aircraft weapons are to be provided.

(*The Commander-in-Chief, Navy*, offers his services as coal czar to Field-Marshal Keitel who had declared that there was no one with sufficient authority available for this position. Keitel will see to it that the matter is regulated in this way.)"

Meanwhile, on 20 January, the Russians had broken through on a 50-mile front in East Prussia, and the problem of evacuating German refugees was added to the other problems. Again Doenitz took the initiative:

" *The Commander-in-Chief, Navy*, reports to the Fuehrer with regard to the evacuation of refugees from East Prussia that . . . as there is only a three weeks' supply of coal available for military sea transport tasks, *e.g.*, supplying Army Group, Kurland, and only ten days' supply for rail transport to take the troops to the front, the evacuation of the refugees will have to be abandoned. The Navy will do everything possible to evacuate refugees in oil-burning vessels which can temporarily be spared from other operations.

The Fuehrer agrees with the view of the Commander-in-Chief, Navy, and decides that coal supplies which are still available must be reserved for military operations alone and must not be used for evacuating refugees.

Afterwards *the Commander-in-Chief, Navy,* informs Reichsleiter Bormann of this situation and of the Fuehrer's decision, and asks him to instruct the Gauleiter concerned accordingly.

(*The Commander-in-Chief, Navy,* issues orders to use cruiser *Emden* for the evacuation of refugees as soon as she is ready for temporary duty; also other naval vessels which are being transferred to the region west of the Gulf of Danzig are to be used for this purpose. Under no circumstances, however, is this to interfere with vital strategic operations of the Navy involving the transport of troops and supplies, and the escort services.) "

In spite of the seriousness of the land situation, Hitler still clung to Doenitz's belief in the efficacy of U-boat warfare. When Doenitz himself suggested using the U-boat training division to help the Army, Hitler refused:

" *The Commander-in-Chief, Navy,* proposes to the Fuehrer that the submarine training division in Gdynia . . . be used on the land front in the defence of Danzig.

The Fuehrer rejects this proposal, pointing out that these 1500 valuable specialists would be unable to change the situation on land, while every single U-boat operating against the enemy is of more value to the war effort than this entire division if used for fighting on land."

But these minor measures which were all that the Supreme Command were capable of taking were of little use. Before the end of January Memel had been captured and the whole of Lithuania occupied by the Russians. Even in the Baltic, where the German Navy had had no real opposition throughout the first four years of the war, British and Russian submarines struck effectively at the German transports. In spite of Doenitz's own extensive use of submarines, he had not worked out any adequate form of anti-submarine defence, but he found a scapegoat in the Luftwaffe:

" *January* 31, 1945.

In connection with the sinking of the passenger ship *Wilhelm Gustloff* by torpedoes off the Stolpe Bank, *the*

Commander-in-Chief, Navy, declares that, with the extensive use of transports in the Baltic Sea, it was realized from the start that there would be losses. Painful as any loss may be, it is very fortunate that more have not occurred. However, he must point out that Russian submarines are able to operate undisturbed in the Baltic Sea only because there are no German aircraft there to attack them. . . . The only practical defence against submarines is the radar-equipped aircraft, the same weapon which enabled the enemy to paralyse our own submarine warfare.

The Chief of the Air Force, Operations Staff, reports that the Air Force lacks both fuel and effective equipment for such operations.

The Fuehrer underscores the arguments of the Commander-in-Chief, Navy, and orders the Air Force to investigate how the matter can be remedied."

At the same conference the refugee situation was again discussed:

" *The Fuehrer* orders that the ships evacuating refugees should carry food for the refugees on their return trip to the east. . . .

The Commander-in-Chief, Navy, reports that there is a congestion of more than 20,000 refugees in Swinemuende. These endanger troop transports from Kurland. Though it is a strategic necessity to evacuate these steadily increasing hordes of refugees, only one hospital train left Swinemuende yesterday, and not even one train of refugees.

The Fuehrer orders that the refugees be dispersed at once among the surrounding villages, and that facilities are to be provided to speed up evacuation. Reichsleiter Bormann is to be responsible for the execution of this order."

During February and March the steady pressure of the Allied armies continued unceasingly. The Rhine was crossed in the west and the Oder in the east; refugees began streaming back into Germany from all sides; the shortage of manpower became so acute that youths of 16 were conscripted; air attacks crippled factories and towns with ruthless efficiency; and, as the end drew near, neutral after neutral declared war on the crumbling German state.

Doenitz continued in favour as the only cool head at Hitler's headquarters. His advice was sought on everything from military tactics to international law, and somehow he managed to give an optimistic twist to all his statements. Although he could not conceal the disasters that were now happening daily, he contrived to shield his Fuehrer from their full significance.

The following conference, held on 10 March in Berlin, is typical of Doenitz's tactics and the attitude of the Supreme Command:

" ITALY.

1. The possibility of a British landing in the northern Adriatic is again discussed. *The Commander-in-Chief, Navy,* believes that the British seem to be trying to spare their strength in view of the overall political situation. For this reason, large, independent British landing operations are not likely to be undertaken either in the Adriatic or in the German Bight. Holland is a different matter; the British must have great interest in occupying it because of the danger to the Channel traffic.

The Fuehrer agrees with the opinion of the Commander-in-Chief, Navy. He thinks, too, that the British inaction in Yugoslavia, where even a few troops could have caused us great difficulties, can be explained only by the fact that the British are intentionally trying to save their forces.

NORWAY.

2. General Jodl reports to the Fuehrer a request from the Commanding-General, Norway, asking for permission to withdraw from the northern Norwegian area to the region south of Narvik because of lack of supplies, especially coal and fuel.

The Fuehrer believes that if we vacated Narvik we might be providing Sweden with an opportunity to enter the war against us, since she would then have excellent connections with the Anglo-Americans. The Lofotens are also one of the most valuable Norwegian fishing areas and they are important for our food supply. The Fuehrer therefore does not permit an evacuation of this area. However, he asks for suggestions how more troops might be withdrawn from there so as to release troops for the home theatre of war. The supply difficulties, especially in regard to coal, caused by the many troop transports in particular must be overcome. Of prime consideration in the Fuehrer's decision is the fact that if northern Norway were occupied by the enemy, southern Norway, which is an indispensable submarine base, would also be endangered.

COAL.

3. As for the coal situation, *the Commander-in-Chief, Navy*, states that it is entirely a matter of inadequate transport within Germany. If sufficient quantities of coal are brought to the German ports, he can assure their transport by sea. According to the reports so far, 28,000 tons of coal are still to be shipped to Norway in March. The efforts of the Commander-in-Chief, Navy, to get additional quantities of coal to the coast via canals, by-passing the dangerous stretch near Ladbergen by means of narrow-gauge field railways, promise to be successful, and they are being continued energetically.

REFUGEES.

4. Concerning the transport of refugees, *the Commander-in-Chief, Navy*, reports that he has requested the Fuehrer to give orders that the refugees be disembarked in Copenhagen, so that their evacuation will not be interrupted in spite of the loss of Sassnitz and in spite of the minefields in the western Baltic Sea. Besides the immediate evacuation of about 50,000 refugees from Kolberg, the area Danzig–Gdynia remains the main point of refugee evacuation.

CHANNEL ISLANDS.

5. During the report on the successful raid on the port of Granville by the forces stationed on the Channel Islands, *the Commander-in-Chief, Navy*, states that the newly-appointed commander of the Channel Islands, Vice-Admiral Hueffmeier, is the heart and soul of this vigorous action.

6. The representative of the Air Force, *Major Buchs*, reports that a gap 80 metres long was torn in the Lippe Canal near the place where it crosses the Dortmund-Ems Canal near Datteln, and the water has run out at that place.

Concerning the repair of such damage, the *Commander-in-Chief, Navy,* says that the population must be called on to do this work just as it has been the custom for centuries, even in peace-time, to repair breaks in dykes on the coast.

The Fuehrer agrees absolutely with this, and he states that he has already ordered similar measures for damages along the railways. (About 800,000 workers are in readiness.)

7. The 2nd Army in West Prussia reports shortage of ammunition. *The Commander-in-Chief, Navy,* states that in such a situation, if necessary, even ships already at sea and carrying ammunition must be diverted and sent to the places where the need is greatest.

8. *The Chief, General Staff, Army,* reports that the Norwegian tanker *Gerdmor,* which was intended for the eastern area, has been lying in Swinemuende for several days because of sabotage by the Norwegian crew, and it still has not left port. (It was discovered later that it was not a case of sabotage, but that the tanker was rammed twice and that in addition the Norwegian captain had to be replaced because of drunkenness.)

9. *The Fuehrer* decides that the Naval Divisions will henceforth be known as Naval Infantry Divisions."

The end was coming nearer. By the end of March Allied armies were well within the German frontiers. The Ruhr was surrounded and the province of Brandenburg was captured by the Russians; the British were nearing the Kiel Canal; and the Americans had practically completed the conquest of southern Germany.

On 18 April Doenitz had his last conference with Hitler. There was still no apparent appreciation of how serious Germany's position was. The conference consisted of a slight quarrel between Doenitz and the Luftwaffe's Chief of Staff about anti-submarine warfare in the Baltic; of naval transport tasks; and of detailed reports of the damage done to the pocket battleship *Luetzow* (the ex-*Deutschland*) by special R.A.F. units. The only indication of what was happening in Germany was contained in a short discussion about the defence of Berlin.

On 23 April the Russians broke through the northern and eastern defences of Berlin; on the following day Himmler offered to surrender to Great Britain and America only. 'Fortress Germany' had virtually collapsed, but its troops struggled on for a few days more.

Chapter XXIV

' UNCONDITIONAL SURRENDER '

THE events of the last few days of the Nazi régime in Germany form a patchwork of desperate moves and jealous intrigues. Hitler crossed the borderline of sanity, and in his bunker underneath the Reich Chancellery in Berlin he deluded himself that he once more controlled vast armies moving freely over the continent of Europe. Goering and Himmler vied with each other to seize power from their mad Fuehrer [2]: Himmler so little appreciated the abhorrence with which he was regarded by the world that he sought to curry favour with the Western powers by privately seeking a separate peace. He apparently believed that he would be allowed to remain in power. Doenitz and Bormann alone remained loyal, although they too each had an eye on the power and authority that might fall into their hands.

Hitler's last military plan was to stake everything on the defence of Berlin, hoping that some last-minute change would turn defeat into a stalemate. To begin with, his orders and tactics bore some relation to reality, but as the disorganization in Germany increased and the Russians began to penetrate the outskirts of Berlin, the armies and air forces that Hitler so diligently moved into action were nothing more than coloured pins on a map.

On 26 April Goering, as second-in-command, tried to take over the leadership of the Reich from his retreat in Bavaria. Hitler was informed, and, screaming with anger, ordered the immediate capture and execution of Goering. The command of the Luftwaffe was given to a favourite general, Ritter von Greim.

Two days later Hitler received even worse news when he learnt for the first time, from a press report, that Himmler six days previously had sued for peace with Great Britain and the United States. To Hitler it seemed as if he was surrounded by traitors, and early on the morning of 29 April he ordered Bormann to send the following signal to Doenitz:

" To: C.-in-C., Navy.   Time: 0325/29.

Foreign press reports a new treason. The Fuehrer expects you to take immediate and decisive action against all traitors in North Germany without discrimination. Schoerner, Wenck, and others must prove their loyalty to the Fuehrer by coming to the Fuehrer's aid as soon as possible.

BORMANN."

On the afternoon of the same day (29 April) the Russian encirclement of Berlin cut all the communications with the Reich Chancellery except the radio link with the German naval headquarters. When Hitler rose—he used to sleep from 5 or 6 a.m. until noon—there was no information available for the usual afternoon situation conference. The following signal was sent:

" To: C.-in-C., Navy.   Time: 1602/29.

All outside contacts with army positions cut. Urgently request information concerning the battle outside Berlin over Naval W/T * wave.
                    Admiral at Fuehrer Headquarters."

There is no record of the reply, if any was sent, but by then the Russians were drawing steadily closer to the centre of Berlin. Three hours later Hitler sent this hysterical signal via the Naval radio link:

" To: General Jodl.   Time: 1952/29.

Inform me immediately:
    1. Where are Wenck's spearheads ?
    2. When are they going to attack ?
    3. Where is the 9th Army ?
    4. In which direction is the 9th Army breaking through ?
    5. Where are Holste's spearheads ?
                            ADOLF HITLER."

* W/T—wireless telegraphy.

Nothing more was heard direct from Hitler. On the following day, 30 April, he committed suicide with Eva Braun. Goebbels and his family followed suit.

Doenitz at first did not know what had happened, but late that evening he received a signal from the Admiral on duty at the Reich Chancellery:

" To: C.-in-C., Navy.   Received at 2310/30.

1. Reichsleiter Bormann has sent the following message:

In the place of the former Reichsmarschall, Goering, the Fuehrer appointed you, Grand-Admiral Doenitz, to be his successor. Written authority is on the way. From now on you are to order all measures necessary to deal with the present situation. . . .
                                         Admiral on Special Duty."

Doenitz assumed office as Chancellor of the German Reich on 1 May, and decided to make peace as quickly as possible. He wanted to prevent as many Germans as he could from falling into the hands of the Russians, but Himmler's abortive efforts had shown clearly that a unilateral armistice with the Western Powers was out of the question. Doenitz still hoped, however, to be able to bargain with the Allies, and he disposed his forces accordingly.

" To: Naval Staff, Luftwaffe and C.-in-C., North-West.

Date: 2/5/45.

The Grand-Admiral has ordered:

1. Hamburg is not to be defended. The troops are to be moved out of the city into the area north of Hamburg, and, to avoid the threatened bombardment of the city, this fact is to be reported to the enemy by an officer with a flag of truce.

2. In order to gain time, the battle is to be continued throughout the whole area of C.-in-C., North-West. A surprise break-through on and over the Kaiser Wilhelm Canal must be prevented, so as to give the German Government sufficient time to negotiate with Montgomery over North-West Germany. . . .
                                                     JODL."

This scheme was not successful. On 4 May negotiations were begun in earnest, while efforts were made at the same time to extricate the forces on the Eastern front:

To: Kesselring and Winter.   Date: 4/5/45.

Field-Marshal Kesselring and Lt.-General Winter:

You are authorized to conclude an armistice with the 6th American Army for the troops on the Western front between Boehmerwald and the upper Inn. In this it must be made clear how far eastwards the Anglo-American forces intend to advance. We must thereby create the conditions for the escape of Army Groups Loer, Redulic and Schoerner. Negotiations concerning latter remain in the hands of the Supreme Commander of the Wehrmacht.

The 7th Army is to be placed under Schoerner.

Winter's staff must escape into that area not affected by the armistice.

DOENITZ."

The Allies, however, would accept nothing except unconditional surrender, and on 7 May arrangements were made for complete capitulation:

" To: All.   Date: 7/5/45.

Situation at 2000 : 7/5/45.

May 7. Provisional signing of capitulation at Rheims.

May 8. General Keitel, General Stumpff and Admiral Friedeburg sign the complete unconditional surrender. Thereafter, peace on all fronts as from 0000. 9/5/45.

C.-in-C., Navy."

Two days before the surrender Doenitz, through his newly-appointed Foreign Minister, Count Schwerin von Krosigk, had begun negotiations with Japan, but, as the following exchange of telegrams shows, neither country would accept responsibility for ending the Three-Power Pact and the situation was left in mid-air:

Coded W/T message to Naval Attaché Tokio for Ambassador Stahmer.

" Date: 5/5/45.

Please convey my heartiest greetings to the Japanese Foreign Minister and give him this message:

Up to the last minute, the Fuehrer believed that through a military success in the decisive battle for Berlin, he could bring about the turning-point in this war. For these beliefs he gave his life and died a hero's death in battle. After the adverse outcome of the battle for Berlin, the war must be considered militarily lost. Considering the complete exhaustion of the German power of resistance, it has become impossible to carry on the war and thereby continue to fulfil the obligations of our alliance with Japan.

To avoid further useless sacrifice and to maintain the substance of the German people, the German High Command considers itself compelled to enter into discussions—not yet concluded—with the Western Allies with a view to an armistice.

I ask you to inform the Foreign Minister that I deeply regret that one of my first duties as German Foreign Minister should be to have to send this communication to the Government of allied and friendly Japan. Without prejudice to the tragic outcome of this war, the German people and its Government will follow Japan's future with great interest and in the spirit of that indestructible German-Japanese friendship which is sealed by blood spilt in a common cause. We shall not give up hope that, in the interests of world peace and the welfare of all peoples, the just claim of the German and Japanese peoples to an honourable and secure future will eventually meet with success.

As far as is possible we shall keep the Japanese Government informed of the further developments in our affairs.

GRAF SCHWERIN VON KROSIGK."

2. Coded telegram from Tokio to German Foreign Minister.

"Date: 10/5/45.

In accordance with instructions I contacted the Japanese Foreign Minister and gave him your message. Foreign Minister Togo took cognizance of my statement and the compliments of the German Foreign Minister. He said that the Japanese people had followed with great admiration the German fight to the last and the death of the Fuehrer. The Japanese Government, however, must consider that the German Government, in commencing capitulation proceedings with the British and Americans without notifying the Japanese Government, desires to withdraw from the Military Alliance of 11th December 1941. He asked me for written confirmation of this view. I replied that I could not

do this because, from the telegram, I only understood that
we were no longer in a position to carry on the war, but
that the Three-Power Pact and Military Alliance also provided for political and economical co-operation. I also
pointed out that the German Foreign Minister particularly
stressed the desire of the German Government to cease
hostilities with the Soviet Union. I got the impression that
the Japanese Foreign Minister wishes to release Japan from
her alliance with Germany but wants to push the responsibility and initiative for this on to Germany. The Japanese
Press confirms this impression. In the last few days it has
become very unfriendly towards Germany and has been
drawing comparisons with the Badoglio régime. In my
opinion we must word our communications to Japan in such
a way that we merely stress the impossibility of continuing
the fight, but we must leave the Japanese to make the
decision with regard to dissolution of the Three-Power
Pact and Military Alliance, and possibly the breaking off of
diplomatic relations.

In conclusion, it is significant that the attitude of the
Japanese Army towards Germany is, so far, unaltered.
Request instructions by return.

                                STAHMER."

The German Government, in fact, made no attempt to continue the fight from Japan or elsewhere. The much-vaunted
' Werewolf' organization of Goebbels was only a bubble of
opposition easily pricked by the occupying armies, and no
belligerent Nazi régime appeared in any other corner of the
world.

Of the German Navy, 156 U-boats surrendered to the Allies,
and a further 221 were either scuttled or destroyed by their
crews. The *Tirpitz*, which had been repeatedly attacked in its
anchorage in northern Norway by the Fleet Air Arm, was finally
sunk by the R.A.F. on its way south on 12 November 1944. Of
the only two modern ships of the surface fleet which were left
unsunk, the *Prinz Eugen* was destroyed during the atom bomb
tests at Bikini, while the *Nueremberg* was given to Soviet Russia.
The auxiliaries—minesweepers, etc.—were manned by German
crews, and, under the orders of the British Admiralty, cleared up
minefields and harbours, sweeping up the litter of war.

Germany suffered total military defeat and there was no
possibility of ascribing that defeat to anything except military
subjugation. The German Army, the Luftwaffe and the German

Navy were severally and jointly beaten by the Allies. The revolt of 20 July was squashed long before the end, and there were no revolutions and no mutinies to make possible any future sophistry about the ' unconquerable ' Wehrmacht. Hitler's policy of world conquest or national suicide ensured that defeat, when it came, would be complete. Germany paid in full the price of dictatorship.

This book may fittingly end, as it began, with Raeder. According to his own story, Raeder had also come to realize the full guilt of Hitler and his Nazis, but, as a retired Commander-in-Chief, he still kept up his intense interest in military affairs. He described the last few days in his evidence at the Nuremberg Trials :

" When I realized the madness of carrying on with the struggle and, above all, with the defence of Berlin, I repeatedly tried to interview the Fuehrer at headquarters. . . . I was not successful in my request, but I can imagine that it would have been embarrassing for him (Hitler) to have to acknowledge to me the complete military collapse. Early on 24 April I heard from Admiral Voss (the Admiral at Fuehrer H.Q.) that women personnel (typists, etc.) and relatives of the H.Q. staff in Berlin had been removed to the south, but that the Fuehrer was remaining in Berlin. After that the blowing up of the bridge at Wannsee resulted in the complete breakdown of telephone communications so that I was obliged to depend on the radio. According to the radio, the Fuehrer lost his life either in battle, as announced by the High Command, or by committing suicide. I am convinced that no other way lay open to him as he had always criticized and disparaged the conduct of Kaiser Wilhelm II, who had fled into neutral territory instead of meeting death at the head of his troops. Hitler, through his own personal guilt, brought the German people into an incomparably more calamitous position than Wilhelm II.

I consider the report of Hitler's marriage to a certain Eva Braun and his flight with her to the Argentine to be totally unfounded. I do not believe that the Fuehrer would have shown such disregard for the fitness of things at such a moment.　More in keeping with the Fuehrer's mentality of never giving in and always seeking a loop-hole for escape was the rumour of his having flown to Manchukuo in a Kondor aircraft, although it is difficult to see how he could have hoped to influence Japan at this stage of the war, especially as he had broken the German people and plunged them into untold misery, drawing upon himself their boundless hatred.　I therefore still prefer to believe the radio version of his death.　It would have corresponded with his nature to have had a concrete tomb prepared for himself in his air-raid shelter where his remains would be secretly hidden.　This is only conjecture, however, in an attempt to deduce what the Fuehrer would have done from my knowledge of his idiosyncrasies."

THE FOLLOWING DOCUMENTS FROM THE GERMAN NAVAL ARCHIVES HAVE BEEN GIVEN AS APPENDICES TO AVOID SPOILING THE CONTINUITY OF THE HISTORY:

Appendix I

GERMAN NAVAL RELATIONS WITH FRANCE

NAVAL relations with France during the critical years of 1941 and 1942 are best shown by the series of conferences with Admiral Darlan which took place in December 1941 and January 1942.

Contact with Darlan was first established by the German Admiral Commanding in France, Otto Schultze, who reported to Raeder:

" From the Commanding Admiral, France.   Paris,
To: Grand-Admiral Raeder.   4 *December* 1941.

SIR,

Attached I am forwarding you a report on my meeting with Admiral Darlan. It includes only the most important points.

I am checking once more the question of going into the locks at St. Nazaire. Admiral Darlan, however, insisted emphatically on his point of view. The most important item for the Naval War Staff is his proposal to forward French information of British fleet movements. I told Admiral Darlan immediately that I would forward this proposal to you as quickly as possible.

In case you should require further details of my conversation, I request a date when I and my adjutant, who sat next to Admiral Darlan at the table, can come to Berlin to make our reports.

                    I am, Sir,

                    Your obedient servant,

                    (Signed) OTTO SCHULTZE.

Enclosure.

Report on dinner, 3 *December* 1941:

Guests: Admiral Schultze,
         Lt.-Commander Fischer,
         Lieut. Fudikar,

         Admiral Darlan,
         M. Monneraye (Commissaire General de la Marine),
         Capt. Fontaine,
         His Excellency Ambassador de Brinon,
         Madame Darlan,
         Comtesse La Rochefoucauld,
         Madame Mittre.

Coming from Vichy, Darlan had arrived in Paris on the evening of 3 December. At the table he very quickly lost his initial reserve and related a number of personal experiences from the China War and the World War. He also described the coronation ceremonies in London. He mentioned several times the fact that, generally speaking, he was not treated very politely in London. When the British Admiralty had had to look after him, he had been received cordially, but when he had been the guest of the British Government, as one of the three representatives of the French Government, the reception had not been in accordance with his position.

At the beginning of the war he had laid special stress to the proposal that the French Admiralty should leave Paris and its political atmosphere, although, after war had broken out, he was no longer subordinate to the Minister. He therefore made his headquarters at Chateau Maintenon and had moved his whole staff there and had been very comfortable.

He commented very unfavourably on the co-operation with the British Admiralty. He said that the organization of the whole of British naval warfare was suffering from a lack of personalities and a lack of responsibility among the leading officers. He mentioned that while preparing the Norway operation he had tried to get in touch with the British Commander responsible. He had not succeeded in this, but had finally been referred to a committee. He had fared similarly on numerous other occasions. The British Admiralty lacked all offensive spirit. He had proposed in

December 1938 to occupy Narvik and Trondheim which at that time would have been possible with weak forces. This proposal, however, had been refused.

After dinner the conversation was continued among the gentlemen. Admiral Darlan as well as his companions were very open, nearly comradely. Moreover, he proposed to me that a direct teleprinter line should be installed between the French naval command in Vichy and the German naval authority in Paris. Based on his co-operation with the British Admiralty he had a very well-informed intelligence service and was in a position to supply Germany with valuable information about British ships' movements and intentions. For example, in the case of the *Bismarck* he had had knowledge of the positions and intentions of the British forces at the time when it would have been possible for the *Bismarck* to have avoided destruction by escaping to the North East.* A few similar cases had occurred in the Mediterranean.

Admiral Darlan warned us not to take the 35,000 ton battleships into the dock at St. Nazaire. If it was at all possible to get these ships in when fully equipped—slack water, a quarter hour before and a quarter hour after high water—it would not be possible to get them out again in time, because, in spite of dredging, the depth of water and local conditions were exceedingly unfavourable. He was one of the most experienced French seamen and probably one of the greatest experts on the French Atlantic coast, and he described the attempt to take a battleship into St. Nazaire as the certain loss of this ship for at least a year.

To the question of further training and a possible active participation of the French Fleet, Admiral Darlan mentioned that this was mainly a question of oil as well as a question of manufacturing ammunition. In case of action he had sufficient oil stocks to supply the French Fleet for one month. In an action like the one off Dakar his ships had fired off all their ammunition. He said about the battleship *Dunquerque* that she was ready to go to sea, but as she had only been provisionally repaired she could only make good 9 or 10 knots. Owing to the good English intelligence service he could not risk moving her to Toulon as he would have to reckon with attacks from the British forces.

* This is correct. (Author.)

He spoke further of the difficulties of victualling the Fleet and obviously was anxious to obtain French sailors from the occupied areas and to extend recruiting there too, especially in Brittany. He also mentioned that apart from the French naval liaison officer in Paris, he intended to appoint liaison officers at Cherbourg and Bordeaux as well.

Admiral Darlan criticized violently Italian Naval warfare in the Mediterranean. He described the Italian attitude with contempt. He mentioned again in this connection his knowledge of English ships' movements in the Mediterranean which he thought would be exceedingly valuable to German-Italian warfare. He particularly pointed out that it was impossible to forward such information to the German Armistice Commission in Wiesbaden as the time delay of several days would make it impossible in many cases to evaluate this information. . . . Darlan also mentioned the five merchant ships which the British had seized at the Cape of Good Hope, and he related that as a reprisal he had ordered two French submarines to sink British merchant ships in the area round Madagascar. One of these submarines had put into Madagascar the day before yesterday and reported the sinking of one merchant ship. This had been confirmed by British reports.

He spoke then of the success of the French Fleet off Dakar. He obviously wished that the British Fleet should be driven out of the Mediterranean as soon as possible. On the possibility of the participation of France to attain this end, he said that the French Fleet was united in its dislike of England. There was, however, not the necessary response among the people and that it was impossible to act alone in such questions. Added to this was Italy's suspicion of France. Italy seemed to fear that he, Darlan, would one day attack them in the rear with this Fleet. He said that nothing was further from his mind and he intended no such action.

Finally, Admiral Darlan repeatedly expressed his pleasure at meeting for the first time in this war German Naval officers at a private dinner party. He expressed a hope to meet the Commander-in-Chief of the German Navy at a future date.

(Signed) OTTO SCHULTZE."

To this report, Raeder replied as follows:

" From: C.-in-C., Navy.   18 *December* 1941.

To: Commanding Admiral, France,
      Admiral Schultze,
      Paris.

DEAR SCHULTZE,

Many thanks for your letter and report of 4/12.

I have informed the Fuehrer about the remarks made by Admiral Darlan concerning information he could supply on the movements of the British Fleet as well as his wish to meet me.

The Fuehrer has agreed to both proposals.

I would therefore be grateful if you would inform Admiral Darlan in a suitable manner that the Navy would gladly accept his proposal. For this purpose a direct teleprint connection would be installed between him and the Commanding Admiral, France.

At the same time I would ask you to inform Admiral Darlan that I gladly accept his offer for a meeting and that I hope to be able to name a date very shortly.

I have instructed the Chief of Naval Communications to make the necessary arrangements for the teleprint line between Vichy and Paris, and I expect that he will get in touch with your authorities.

With the best greetings and Heil Hitler !

             Yours,

                  (Signed) RAEDER,
                      Grand-Admiral."

Raeder met Darlan at Evry-le-Bourg on 28 January 1942. Darlan repeated what he had told Admiral Schultze. Co-operation was arranged in most naval matters except the operational use of the French Fleet. On this question, though Darlan was willing and indeed anxious to use his ships, Hitler had apparently instructed Raeder not to accept. He evidently distrusted Darlan, whose readiness to turn against his former Allies probably made Hitler fear that if circumstances altered Darlan would as readily turn against Germany.

Appendix II

THE QUESTION OF INVADING IRELAND

THE question of whether to occupy Ireland cropped up towards the end of 1940, after the virtual cancellation of Operation ' Sea Lion '.

(*Extract from Fuehrer Conference*, 3 *December* 1940.)

" *The Fuehrer* . . . makes the following statement regarding Ireland: a landing in Ireland can be attempted only if Ireland requests help. For the present our envoy must ascertain whether De Valera desires support and whether he wishes to have his military equipment supplemented by captured British war material (guns and ammunition), which could be sent to him in independent ships. Ireland is important to the Commander-in-Chief, Air, as a base for attacks on the north-west ports of Britain, although weather conditions must be investigated. The occupation of Ireland might lead to the end of the war. Investigations are to be made."

The Naval Staff duly carried out a survey of the possibilities of invading Ireland and reported as follows:

" 1. The first condition necessary for the transfer of troops (to Ireland) is naval supremacy along the routes to be used. This naval supremacy could never be attained by us in view of the vastly superior British Home Fleet, not even for the duration of one transport operation. . . . The possibility of surprise is ruled out due to the necessity of starting from the French coast.

2. The geographical position is extremely unfavourable, since the coast of Wales and Cornwall extends like a wedge to our line of approach; the distance from enemy bases to Ireland is less than that from the ports of embarkation in north-west France. In contrast to the Norway operation, it would not be possible by surprise attack to establish a supply

line which could be defended. Such a supply line is of decisive importance for the success of the operation.

3. The island has no defended bases or anchorages at all. Although the Irish might willingly open their ports to us, they would also be open to the enemy pursuing us. There would be no time for planned harbour and coastal fortifications and undisturbed disembarkation of the expeditionary force is unlikely. It would not be possible to send supplies in view of the superior sea power of the enemy and the limited area through which the approach would have to be made.

4. To a defending force, cut off and left to its own devices, the topography of the country does not afford us much protection. . . . Without supplies and reinforcements they would soon feel the increasing pressure of a British expeditionary force brought over under the protection of British naval power; sooner or later our own troops would face a situation similar to Namsos or Dunkirk.

5. Support by the Air Force would depend upon the weather. Ireland, the westernmost island of any size in the Atlantic, is known to have a heavy rainfall and consequently low clouds and very frequent damp and foggy weather. Air support would have to come primarily from the mainland since the airfields in Ireland would not meet our requirements —it would scarcely be possible to expand them because we could not supply equipment. Every attempt at transporting troops by Ju 52's would be in great danger from British fighters which are again increasing in numbers.

6. It is therefore concluded that it would be impossible to follow up an Irish request for help . . . in view of the enemy's superior naval force, the unfavourable geographical conditions and the impossibility of forwarding supplies. Troops landed in Ireland without supplies of foodstuffs, weapons, and ammunition would sooner or later be wiped out by an enemy whose supply routes are difficult to attack.

7. It will be possible in the winter months to bring occasional blockade runners with weapons and ammunition into Irish harbours and bays as long as there is still no state of war between Britain and Ireland and as long as the Irish co-operate."

Appendix III

RELATIONS BETWEEN RAEDER AND GOERING

SOMETIME in June 1940 Goering sent a telegram—unfortunately destroyed—to Raeder commenting rudely on the part of the German Navy in the Norwegian campaign. The telegram infuriated Raeder who at once reported the matter to Hitler. Goering was ordered to apologize and the following exchange of letters took place:

" From:　The Reichsmarschall　　　　　　　　Berlin,
　　　　　of the Greater German Reich.　　8 *August* 1940.

MOST ESTEEMED GRAND-ADMIRAL,

Due to special circumstances it was only a few days ago that I read the actual contents of the telegram sent to you some time ago containing my opinion with regard to your part in matters concerning Norway. I can assure you that I was extremely shocked when I realized that, due to a chain of misunderstandings in my staff, this telegram was delivered to you in this form and with this wording. I alone am of course responsible, for I was in a state of excitement because your proposition was presented to me as so categorical that I saw therein an interference in my own sphere of command. Not for a moment, however, could I assume that my attitude would be so interpreted that such a telegram would be sent to you personally. You can rest assured, my dear Grand-Admiral, that I too share the point of view that such a tone in communications between the Commanders-in-Chief, and especially between two men whom nothing separates but much more unites, is absolutely unthinkable. I regret most deeply that such a thing has happened and I wish to apologize personally and in all due form for having, though quite by mistake, been responsible for such a grave offence.

Although the matter in question has been clarified and settled I beg of you, nevertheless, to destroy this telegram. The thought of having telegraphed you in such an impossible tone is absolutely unbearable to me. The high esteem which

I hold for you would at all times make such a tone toward you seem impossible to me. The only explanation which I can offer you is that the matter was presented to me at a time when other important things were passing through my mind, so that I did not read the telegram myself afterwards. Had I done so, the telegram would of course never have been sent. I would like to assure you once more that really no one ever drew my attention to this telegram up to the moment a few days ago when I myself saw it for the first time in the files. It was clear to me immediately that only a comprehensive apology to you could make amends for it. I would greatly appreciate it if you would not hold the matter against me in the future although you would certainly be entitled to do so. May I also beg that this letter be considered as a purely personal matter ?

With comradely greetings and Heil Hitler !

Yours,

(Signed) GOERING."

Raeder replied :

" From : The Commander-in-Chief, Navy.   Berlin,
13 *August* 1940.

MOST ESTEEMED REICHSMARSCHALL,

It was with great satisfaction that I read your letter. I thank you most sincerely. In view of our mutual efforts to co-operate most closely and most effectively, it had depressed me very much of late that it could have appeared as though differences had arisen between us which in turn seemed to have affected the co-operation of the lower echelons.

The very comradely form in which you stated your point of view in this matter touched me deeply. The telegram is destroyed.

You may rest assured that my personal esteem and respect for you, my dear Reichsmarschall, has at no time undergone a change.

Heil Hitler !

Yours very respectfully,

(Signed) RAEDER."

Appendix IV

THE following is a full transcription of a normal conference between Raeder and Hitler. It shows the variety of subjects discussed and the form of a " Fuehrer Conference." A fortnight before this conference, British forces had raided St. Nazaire. The raid was the biggest yet carried out on the European coast-line, and had as its object the destruction of the large lock which was capable of being used as a dry dock, the only one outside Germany big enough to take the *Tirpitz*.

The raid was led by Commander R. E. D. Ryder, V.C., R.N., in the ex-American over-age destroyer, H.M.S. *Campbeltown*. The *Campbeltown* was disguised as a German destroyer, and by using German recognition signals managed to lead the force to within 1½ miles of St. Nazaire before meeting serious opposition. The operation was entirely successful. The *Campbeltown*, loaded with high explosive, rammed the lock gates and later blew up exactly according to plan.

The attack disturbed the confidence of the German High Command. An inquiry was held and Raeder reported to Hitler:

" Naval Staff. Berlin,

16 *April* 1942.

Report by the Commander-in-Chief, Navy, to the Fuehrer at Wolfsschanze,* 13 April 1942, in the evening.

In the presence of the Chief of Staff, Armed Forces High Command; during the discussion of points IX and X, Lt.-General Jodl, Vice-Admiral Krancke and Captain von Puttkamer were also present.

I. *Attack on St. Nazaire.*

The Situation in the Western Area since Summer 1941:

Enemy strength is increasing. Army and Air Force are weaker due to the situation in the East. Nearly all naval forces have been transferred to Norway. We have no means of repulsing an enemy landing attempt.

* Hitler's headquarters at Rastenberg.

The situation provokes enemy operations like the one of 28 March 1942.

The following statements are taken from a British operations order:

Mission: 1. Destroy the floodgates of the large dock that can accomodate the *Tirpitz*.

2. Destroy small locks and all submarines and other craft in the vicinity.

The enemy knew exactly the strength of our naval forces (5 torpedo boats) and could adjust his own strength accordingly. The attack was timed according to moon and tide (28 March to 31 March). The route from Falmouth to the objective took 35 hours at a speed of 12 knots. They flew the German flag and used German recognition signals. (Comment in longhand: ' Air Force recognition signals.')

One submarine was used as marker boat. The air attack was co-ordinated with the naval attack.

Mission of the Destroyer *Campbeltown* :

Force a lane through the torpedo net and ram the outer floodgate so that the forecastle extends over the floodgate. Land the troops, then sink the *Campbeltown*. Remove the crew in motor boats. *Campbeltown* was loaded with a demolition charge with a two-hour time fuse.

Advantages for the Enemy :

A. Poor, changing visibility, 200–4000m.

B. At high water the sand bars are flooded, making it possible for the enemy to evade mines and other obstacles.

C. Good reconnaissance through air attacks, which probably had the additional purpose of distracting our attention and drowning out engine noises of the E-boats. Nevertheless, shore batteries and anti-aircraft batteries observed the enemy boats as soon as they came into view. A short delay was due to exchange of recognition signals. The artillery fire was very effective.

The Fuehrer criticizes the exchange of recognition signals *under such circumstances* and also the delay ($6\frac{1}{2}$ minutes) before the alarm order was given.

(Comment added in longhand: New regulation: shore station demands recognition signal. If naval forces do not answer immediately with naval recognition signal, open fire. New, uniform alarm signal for the Navy has been ordered.)

The Commander-in-Chief, Navy, states that, considering the available means, the defence had been handled correctly in all essentials. However, it should be impossible for a destroyer to reach the floodgate; besides, due to inexperience, the search for the demolition charge and its subsequent removal were not carried out correctly. In other cases demolition charges in locks, etc., were expertly located and removed at great risk. —

Possible Counter-measures Necessary to Prevent Similar Raids :

A. Aerial reconnaissance is a prime requisite for prompt recognition. The British were at sea for 35 *hours*; they approached during daylight. Even during the World War evening reconnaissance was carried out to protect the coast whenever the weather permitted. It is possible that some airfields at high altitudes (as in Norway) have different visibility conditions than prevail at sea. In such cases *sea planes* operating from the harbours must do the reconnoitring, since they can see as long as visibility allows enemy naval forces to enter coastal waters.

Fuehrer : Sea planes are too greatly endangered.

Commander-in-Chief, Navy : No more than patrol boats without proper rear protection. All ship-based planes are sea planes. Furthermore, to assure the necessary protection, some bombers will have to be used for reconnaissance along the entire West Coast. The Naval Air Force is of great importance.

B. Flotillas for patrolling and for protecting the harbours have been established as far as possible and additional ones are being built. There are not nearly enough of them to protect the bases and the long coast.

The Commander-in-Chief, Navy, using a chart prepared by the War Economy Section of the Naval Ordnance Division, demonstrates on the one hand the repeated efforts of the High Command, Navy, to obtain the workers and raw materials necessary for reinforcing escort and patrol flotillas;

on the other hand he shows how naval requirements continually had to yield to those of the Air Force and of the Army. If the Reichsmarschall is perhaps able to build more aircraft it proves that he has manpower and raw materials at his disposal which, by rights, should belong to the Navy. It is certainly not the fault of the High Command, Navy, that there are so few vessels. The cause lies in the distribution of men and raw materials no doubt always made in view of the particular war situation—in spite of continual requests made by the High Command, Navy, to the Fuehrer, to Dr. Todt, and to the Armed Forces High Command.

The Commander-in-Chief, Navy, also points out that patrol boats in coastal areas which do not have a rear protection of light naval forces are gravely endangered. It is not difficult for a few destroyers to sink them, once they have been located by enemy reconnaissance.

Even then one or another of the boats would be able to report.

C. Minefields:

1. Heavy ground mines are to be buried in the sand bars to prevent passage at such places.

2. A field of ground mines is to be laid which will be electrically detonated from the shore. Their success depends largely on a foolproof detonator cable.

D. Harbour booms have been placed wherever harbour and current conditions permit, for example Boulogne, Brest, Dunkirk. They have not been approved for St. Nazaire, since neither buoys nor dolphins can be used there. The former cannot hold the booms in place due to the swift current, and the latter cannot be driven into the rocky bottom near the mouth of the harbour. Trellis masts on concrete blocks will be tried out if they prove workable. Experiments will be made with a new type of obstacle consisting of a series of barges connected by iron chains.

E. Location finding devices: The number on the West Coast will be increased as more devices become available (two, possibly up to four a month).

F. Alarm signal in case of invasion: The Navy has such a signal, but all parts of the Armed Forces should know it and use it. All posts which see the signal must repeat it continuously until certain that it has been received everywhere.

The Fuehrer asks whether it would be possible to illuminate the coastal area with parachute flares.

Commander-in-Chief, Navy : The coastal artillery has star shells which illuminate the coastal area widely. The searchlights used in conjunction with artillery fire have the advantage of blinding the enemy.

Summary by the Commander-in-Chief, Navy :

Experiences gained as the result of this attack are being utilized to the utmost. Nevertheless, we have to consider the possibility of similar raids whenever the enemy is favoured by good visibility. The danger is particularly great as long as there is neither an effective naval defence nor an adequate air reconnaissance. In the absence of almost all naval forces as well as the Air Force from the home waters, due to the changed war situation, even islands in the German Bight, like Borkum and Wangeroog, greatly exposed by removal of guns to the occupied territories, must be better fortified again (*e.g.* by placing the *Gneisenau's* 15-cm. battery on Wangeroog).

The Fuehrer stresses the fact that he must demand that at least the most important naval bases, like submarine bases, be so well protected that successful raids would be impossible. In his opinion this was *not* the case at St. Nazaire.

The Commander-in-Chief, Navy, mentions experiences with British explosives which should not only be brought to the attention of the entire Armed Forces, but also of the civilian population in order to prevent sabotage. He hands a large number of photographs to the Chief of Staff, Armed Forces High Command.

The Commander-in-Chief, Navy, reports that the population of St. Nazaire and its vicinity strongly favours De Gaulle. Two days *before* the attacks a successful police raid was staged.

II. *Naval Situation in March* 1942.

Home Waters and the German Sphere of Influence :

A. Norway. The cruiser *Admiral Hipper* was transferred to Trondheim as planned. *Luetzow* will presumably follow in mid-May. *Prinz Eugen* will probably return for repairs at the end of April. Since there are very few destroyers in the Arctic Sea future operations of surface forces must depend on the possibility of effective air reconnaissance, so far as fuel permits.

The twenty submarines assigned to the protection of the northern area have the following missions:

1. To paralyse enemy convoy traffic in the Arctic Sea and near the ports.
2. To recognize and thwart promptly any enemy plans to land in the Norwegian area.

B. The attempt made by Norwegian merchant ships to break out of Swedish harbours, which we have been expecting since the beginning of January, was completely unsuccessful. Reports have furnished us with the details.

C. Traffic of merchant ships during March: Traffic between German and German-occupied harbours consisted of 1274 merchant vessels of 2,566,017 tons. Of these, 1011 ships of 2,177,136 tons were convoyed. They were distributed as follows:

Norway	. .	405 ships totalling 1,062,666 tons.
North Sea	. .	519 ships totalling 1,145,351 tons.
Western Area	.	330 ships totalling 358,000 tons.

No traffic in the Baltic due to ice.

Foreign Waters :

A. Cruiser warfare. Ship ' 10 ' operated without success in the Antarctic. However, in the South Atlantic five enemy steamers were captured without firing a shot. These were *Pagasitikos, Wellpark, Wellesden, Aust,* and one other. Ship ' 10 ' will be supplied by *Regensburg* and proceed to the western part of the Indian Ocean as planned.

An agreement was reached with the Japanese Navy reserving the area west of 80° East longitude and south of 10° South latitude for ship ' 10,' and possibly permitting Japanese submarines to operate in an area 300 miles wide along the eastern coast of Africa. *We recommended to the Japanese the use of submarines near the entrance to the Persian Gulf.*

Ship ' 28 ' is en route in the South Atlantic. *Doggerbank successfully fulfilled* her minelaying mission off Capetown. She received new orders to lay mines near Cape Agulhas with the coming new moon. Meanwhile she is waiting in the South Atlantic.

B. Blockade runners. Supply ship *Regensburg* in the Indian Ocean and *Tannenfels* in the South Atlantic are both en route to Japan. The tanker *Charlotte Schliemann* is in the waiting zone in the south-west part of the South Atlantic.

Of the five blockade runners returning home, two have already arrived in Bordeaux: the *Osorno* and the *Rio Grande*, the latter with 3700 tons of rubber and 3800 tons of whale oil. The *Fusiyama* is in the South Atlantic, and the *Portland* and the *Muenster* are still West of Cape Horn.

The Mediterranean and the Black Sea. The *Valiant* left Alexandria after three and a half months of repairs. The *Queen Elizabeth* docked there. Since no sign of the *Valiant* has been found in the Mediterranean for several days, it is assumed that she left by way of the Red Sea. It is not known whether she is ready for action. The *Malaya* sailed westward from Gibraltar. Attacks made by German and Italian submarines and planes have seriously weakened light enemy forces. In short, *the situation in the Mediterranean* is extremely favourable right now.

Therefore the 5th and 6th Transport Squadrons were sent to Tripoli as planned.

The 3rd E-boat Flotilla is to be used to lay mines off Malta in connection with the current major operation against that island.

The 6th Motor Minesweeping Flotilla is to be transferred to Tripoli for escort duty.

Four more E-boats, now at Cologne, are being assigned to the Mediterranean. These could ultimately be sent to the Black Sea through the Dardanelles.

The Fuehrer permits them to attempt passage through the Dardanelles camouflaged as merchant vessels *without* previous political negotiations.

In the Black Sea new minefields are being laid off the Roumanian and Bulgarian coasts.

The plan to mine the Crimean coast had to be dropped

temporarily because the necessary Roumanian naval forces were refused.

The Fuehrer orders that none of the German batteries be given to either Bulgaria or Roumania.

C. Submarine warfare. We had 288 submarines on 1 April 1942, of which 122 are operational units. Location of the 125 boats in operation areas on 9 April is as follows:

(*a*) Arctic Ocean: Total 19; 5 are at Kirkenes, Narvik and Trondheim, and 14 at sea.
(*b*) Atlantic: Total 81; 45 in North Atlantic and U.S. coast; 2 in South Atlantic; 34 in bases on the western coast of France.
(*c*) Mediterranean: Total 20; 7 at sea.
(*d*) Home ports: Total 5; 3 overdue.

Submarines sank these vessels in March (confirmed):

German submarines: 89 vessels totalling 524,286 tons.
Italian submarines: 19 vessels totalling 82,000 tons.
Japanese submarines: 19 vessels totalling 101,098 tons.

Total enemy losses for March 1942 in ships sunk or captured (Great Britain, U.S.A., Russia, and the Netherlands): 362 vessels of 1,095,393 tons.

The Fuehrer agrees with the Commander-in-Chief, Navy, that victory depends on destroying the greatest amount of Allied tonnage possible. Thus all offensive operations of the enemy can be slowed down or even stopped entirely. The Fuehrer believes that attacks on the Murmansk convoys are most important at the moment.

The Commander-in-Chief, Navy, states that construction of submarines should be stepped up to the very limit. He requests permission to get copper on the black market in France and Belgium.

The Fuehrer wants confirmation whether this is still actually possible.

III. *Support of the German offensive in the East by Japanese naval warfare in the Indian Ocean.*

It is of decisive importance that Japanese forces attack British supply lines to the Red Sea and Persia in the northern part of the Indian Ocean. The purpose would be to disrupt Russian supplies and thus aid our eastern offensive. The Armed Forces High Command must therefore point out to the Japanese Liaison Staff that a strong Japanese attack on British supply lines would support German operations most effectively.

The Fuehrer has already given Ambassador Oshima some general indications of the spring offensive.

IV. *Germany's relations with France.*

The Fuehrer is asked for his opinion in regard to further developments.

The Fuehrer believes that Marshal Petain plays a very insignificant role, being very old and easily influenced. He thinks it likely that Laval will replace Petain, but he does not consider the French capable of energetic action of any kind at present. Their whole attitude is weak (witness the Rion trial). According to Ambassador Abetz 5 per cent. of the population is for collaboration and 5 per cent. for De Gaulle; the rest are watching and waiting. The Fuehrer believes that the French will try to repulse attacks on West Africa.

V. *The fuel oil situation in* 1942.

The Commander-in-Chief, Navy, refers to the report made to the Fuehrer.

(This report stated that the supply of fuel oil which had become critical in the last quarter of 1941 was even more serious by April 1942. The Italian Navy was in continual need of supplies and German stocks were running low. The passage of the Brest Group through the Channel and on to Norway had consumed 20,000 tons of fuel oil alone, and by April 1 the reserve stocks of the German Navy were down to 150,000 tons.

Roumanian deliveries fell from 46,000 tons per month to 8000 tons, and as this had been promised to the Italians, who urgently required it for the Mediterranean campaigns, further withdrawals had to be made from the German reserve stocks.

The total allocation to both the German and Italian navies for April 1942 was cut from 97,000 to 61,000 tons.

The shortage of fuel oil did not affect submarines and pocket battleships, however, as they operated on diesel oil which was still in plentiful supply.—Author.)

VI. *Completion of the aircraft carrier* Graf Zeppelin.

A. It will take at least until the summer of 1943 to complete the hull and instal the engines.

B. The total time necessary to complete the carrier does not depend on completing the hull and engines but on changing the flight installations for the use of aircraft adapted from the Ju 87D and ME 109F.

About two years are required to develop, construct and test the catapults necessary for these planes. If it is possible to convert the existing catapults the time limit will be reduced by six months. New winches for the arresting gear are needed. The company producing these winches has not yet announced when they can be delivered.

The carrier cannot therefore be completed before the winter of 1943.

The Fuehrer points out that in general the Armed Forces set their requirements too high.

C. Aircraft. Only ten converted fighters and twenty-two converted bombers (including reconnaissance planes) will be available. There are *no* torpedo planes. If a new type of special carrier aircraft is developed, mass production cannot be attained until 1946 !

The Naval Staff maintains that the results of our efforts so far do not justify continuing work on the carrier. While the technical problems concerning ship construction and plane conversion can evidently be solved, the disadvantages which still remain reduce the carrier's tactical value to a critical point.

The Commander-in-Chief, Navy, will approach the Fuehrer again, if the discussions with the Commander-in-Chief, Air, in regard to carrier aircraft do not have satisfactory results.

The Fuehrer believes that torpedo planes are necessary in any case; it is furthermore important that our own types of aircraft are a match for those of the enemy.

VII. *Miscellaneous.*

A. The steamer *Scharnhorst* is in Japan and can be sold to the Japanese.

B. Distribution of the *Gneisenau's* guns: Three guns, 280 mm., from turret A were installed on coast defence gun mounts near the Hook of Holland. Turrets B and C were mounted whole in Norway (by blasting into solid rock).

VIII. *Admiral Krancke reports on manpower of the Navy :*

Upon information about the composition of the First Naval Brigade, *the Fuehrer* admits that the Navy is very short of officers (only 15,000 officers for 500,000 men). On the other hand it is not advisable to use Army divisions which can be employed in combat for occupation of the French islands, for if they should be needed in the East they would then not be available. The division on the Channel Islands, for instance, is practically lost to the Army. The protection of the coastal islands is a part of the Navy's coastal defence assignment, and as such is particularly a naval responsibility. Since the Army is in urgent need of additional forces, he must give this task to the Navy in spite of the shortage of naval officers. The Army has had tremendous losses among its officers; it can transfer officers temporarily, but cannot dispense with them permanently. The Naval Staff, Quartermaster Division, proposes that the Navy be given until October to complete this task. *The Fuehrer* considered October too late.

Additional remarks.

On 14 April 1942 the following telegram was sent confirming the results of the above conference:

To the Fuehrer and Supreme Commander personal; copy to the Armed Forces High Command, Operations Staff.

' Request confirmation of yesterday's conference on naval brigades: Navy entirely responsible for defence of islands in Western Area to be designated by Armed Forces High Command. Necessary personnel and *matériel* to be determined in collaboration with Commanding General, West, and to be installed as soon as possible. Troops to be trained on the islands. Army ordered to furnish necessary officers temporarily until Navy can train its own. Army and Air Force to provide arms and equipment which Navy lacks. This method of taking over naval defence of the islands seems quicker and more economical than adhering rigidly to previous orders.'

GRAND-ADMIRAL RAEDER.

IX. *Definition of authority in the Netherlands* among the Commanding General, West; the Commanding General, Armed Forces, Netherlands; and the Commanding Admiral, North Sea Station.

Vice-Admiral Krancke reports on organization:

According to the Fuehrer's order No. 40, the Commanding General, West, is responsible for the conduct of the war along the coast in the French, Belgian and entire Dutch area, without referring to the Commanding General, Armed Forces, Netherlands. In Holland, therefore, he is responsible not only for the area of the Commanding Admiral, Netherlands, but also for that part of the Dutch area commanded by the Admiral, Coastal Defences, German Bight. The Commanding General, West, is responsible not only for coastal warfare, but also for its preparation as regards tactics, organization, personnel and *matériel*.

The Netherlands belongs to the North Sea area as far as *naval* organization is concerned (ship traffic, coastal and anti-aircraft defence, widespread dock and supply systems and replacement units). The Commanding Admiral, Netherlands, is subordinate to the Admiral, North Sea Station.

This means that both the Commanding Admiral, North Sea Station *and* the Commanding General, West, are in charge of the *same* coastal defence. Their orders overlap. The authority of the Commanding General, West, has to deal continuously with matters coming under the jurisdiction of the Commanding Admiral, North Sea Station. The organization must therefore be changed. The Armed Forces High Command, Operations Staff, is asked to investigate this question and to define clearly the respective spheres of command.

The Fuehrer will decide.

X. *The question of a naval representative at the Fuehrer Headquarters.*

In a private conference *the Commander-in-Chief, Navy*, explains why it is necessary to have a permanent representative of the Commander-in-Chief, Navy, at the Fuehrer Headquarters. He compares the Navy with other branches of the Armed Forces.

The Fuehrer approves a permanent representative of the Commander-in-Chief, Navy, at the Fuehrer Headquarters. He will be a flag officer authorized to move freely between the Naval Staff and the Headquarters; he has the right to report to the Fuehrer on all matters pertaining to the Navy, and to be present at all conferences dealing with the general conduct of the war.

(Signed) RAEDER.
(Countersigned) ASSMANN."

INDEX

THE LIBRARY
ST. M........ ...... OF MARYLAND
ST. MARY'S CITY, MARYLAND 20686